Have you ever wondered why everything in the Universe fits together the way it does? Or why we're the fortunate inheritors of a very rare planetary oasis that has the amazing ability to create, evolve and support lifeforms such as ours? Given that human life on the planet only started 200,000 years ago, how have we been able to make such giant strides in our knowledge of actions throughout the Universe from the largest to the smallest scale? Knowledge that has enabled us to put people on the Moon, look inside atoms and given us all the technological goodies that today we take for granted.

18 Holes is the amazing story of how we've built this knowledge over the last 2,800 years starting with Thales in the Greek City-State of Miletus right up to our current understanding by way of Aristotle, Galileo, Newton, Einstein and many other deep thinkers. Unlike most normal popular science books, the story's told in a chatty, humorous way during a round of golf by two senior citizens who've been best pals since their first day at primary school. If you're looking for a simple insight of how far science has taken us and why 90% of the physicists who have ever lived are alive today, then this is the book for you.

18 Holes of Quantum Golf

or

A Duffers Guide to the Universe

W. J. Hendry

For Christine with love (1941 – 2021)

Contents

Friday Afternoon

Bob stood on the first tee and marvelled at the changes the last few sunny spring days had wrought to what he had always considered to be 'his' golf course. The last time he stood here the course had its winter face on and looked dull and lifeless whereas today it was all so different. The fairway had its first cut of the year and was positively inviting his perfect opening drive. The trees which gave the course its character were busily bursting forth into their forty different shades of green. The protective mats that he'd played off all winter had been stored away and the tee looked immaculate with its trimmed grass and freshly painted tee box. He looked around savouring the scenery and thought, all this and the chance to renew the old challenge with my best mate must be as near to heaven on earth as it gets when his musings were broken by a sudden cry of, "Gotcha, ya wee bugger, Have you noticed that as you get older the damn thing you're looking for always manages to hide itself away in the last place you look?" Bob smiled and, as this was the first part of a ritual they'd been observing for over fifty years, took the small purple jewellery bag handed to him by Alec his lifelong friend. Loosening the drawstrings he slid out a once clear piece of plastic that years of rattling about in their golf bags had reduced to the appearance of a tatty old beer mat. He could just about make out the two folded squares of paper encased in it. One showed the Queen's head and the other 'Pay the Bearer Ten Shillings Sterling'. He fingered it thinking that it was about time that this insignificant trinket, worth more to him than its weight in gold, was returned to its rightful owner's possession. They'd been playing this perpetual game of golf for most of their lives.

though neither could remember exactly when it started. Similarly neither could remember a time when they hadn't been the best of pals and both were quite adamant that 'they' remembered meeting each other on their first day at primary school. However both agreed that it was more likely that what they remembered were snippets of their mother's later conversations. What they could never agree on was which one of their mothers had said while looking at the boys sitting side by side in an old wooden two-seater desk and chair "Look at them, they're already chatting away like a pair of old men." The other mum had replied, "They look like two peas in a pod." It took the boys some time to understand why their mothers always blew their noses and wiped the tears from their eyes after making comments like this. Bob, however, was quite certain that he could clearly recall one thing about their first hectic day (morning only, as they didn't start full time till after Christmas). While he was walking home with his mother he said, "Alec's great mummy, he can write a Spitfire." After she explained that Alec was drawing a Spitfire he said, "He's going to teach me how to do it and he says it's dead easy so then I'll be able to write a Spitfire of my own." He later realised that drawing was not his forte and although he laboured long and hard trying to match Alec's quick freehand drawing skill his aeroplanes looked dumpy and out of proportion, whereas Alec's sleek drawings looked ready to fly off the page. He consoled himself that when it came to headers against a wall or keepy-uppy he was a match for anyone in the class. Both were only children and had been competitive from an early age. Although they delighted in getting one over the other, neither let it bother them too much when they didn't. They developed a healthy respect for each other and after a couple of short fall-outs agreed that although winning was great, their friendship mattered more. This youthful rivalry found the perfect outlet when they reached the age of twelve and were able to join the local golf club as juniors. Both their fathers were longstanding members and from an early age had encouraged them to chip golf balls around the garden with some old clubs cut down to fit them. However two years before they were old enough to join the club this privilege was abruptly withdrawn when their parents found out that they'd been taking their clubs to a nearby field and hitting balls to each other from a distance apart.

One afternoon the inevitable happened. Alec hit one out of the middle and 'conked' Bob on the forehead. Seeing him lying there apparently lifeless Alec ran to the nearest house and told a man working in the garden that he'd just killed his best pal. After querying Alec about what had happened the man, one of the few in the neighbourhood who owned a motor car, ran back with Alec and carried the still inert Bob onto the back seat. The nearest hospital was over five miles away and, turning the first corner without looking, they narrowly missed colliding with a police car. The police officers agreed that getting Bob to the hospital was more important than booking a wee lad for riding his bike on the pavement. Saying, "Switch your lights to full beam and follow us" the police car drove, sirens blaring, through red traffic lights and across junctions without stopping. Screeching to a halt outside the hospital they were surprised to see Bob sitting up and wide-eyed. A trolley was brought and as they wheeled it into the A & E Department Bob told everyone within earshot how much he'd enjoyed his madcap ride. Much to Alec's relief Bob was given the all clear after a thorough examination and when his parents arrived fearing the worst they were told that he was very lucky as he had only slight concussion. He spent the taxi ride home extracting from his pal the bits of the cops and robbers ride he'd missed. To their mutual disgust the golf clubs were confiscated and hitting golf balls at each other was banned. For the next couple of years their golf was confined to visits at a nearby range and a few rounds of putting when they were on holiday. When Bob returned to school as a death defying hero he told everyone that when they examined him in the hospital the doctor could clearly see the ball maker's name and number imprinted on his forehead. Unfortunately the week he'd spent in bed had faded his mark of honour into a large bruise and his status went from hero to zero before the morning interval.

Both matured into reasonably competent, safety conscious golfers. Bob served for some years as Junior Convenor and was forever stressing to his charges their duty of safety to others on the golf course. He told every new batch of juniors how he'd nearly been killed after being hit on the head by a golf ball, conveniently missing out the circumstances. He always got a laugh when he warned them "Your mothers will never forgive me if I take you home dead!"

Their daily routine changed at the end of their fourth year at senior school when Bob left to take up an apprenticeship with the national telephone company while Alec, the more dedicated scholar, remained. Two years later he left school as dux and went on to the local university to study mathematics for four years. Although they were no longer in each other's company on a daily basis, their friendship continued and they met regularly as well as at the golf club. As they grew older they found that when they did golf together it was usually in a four-ball, so one day Bob put on his Victor Meldrew voice and complained, "When are we going to get a game with just the two of us like it used to be?" Alec replied, "I've been thinking about that, how about we book a tee time just for us and have a few holes together?" "Great idea, said Bob, are you on for a match?" "What else, replied Alec and I've got ten bob here that says I'll beat you." "You're on" Bob happily agreed and the following week they met, shook hands on the first tee and set out on their odyssey. The first game was halved and they agreed that this shouldn't be a one-off but should continue till the end of the season with whoever was 'up' pocketing the spoils. The season-end came and as Bob was lining up a ten foot putt on the last hole to half the overall match, Alec walked over and picked up his ball then handed it to him saying "Let's call it all square so we have to continue next year."

A few years later, sterling was decimalised and fifty pence coins replaced their ten shilling notes, but neither made any suggestion that they be cashed in for the new-fangled coins. Their ten-bobs were kept folded in an old sweetie tin and were getting the worse for wear when Alec mentioned that his daughter Sandra had been given a paperweight making kit as a birthday present and was looking for things to do with it. Bob said, "You could get her to preserve our ten-bob notes as a paperweight. "Great idea said Alec, but wouldn't a beer mat be more appropriate?" Beer mat was agreed and the Ten-Bob Trophy became their badge of honour. The holder kept the beer mat in his golf bag and handed it over for safekeeping to the challenger at the start of the next match. This small piece of resin with two worthless bits of paper encased in it quickly became a totem and was keenly missed when either went a few games without winning it back. One early rule they made was that the holder always bought the first beers whenever they met and a few years later added a 'joker' allowing a player who was two or more holes down to replay a shot during the round. Then one day disaster struck!

After a match where he'd regained the trophy by winning the last hole, Alec was late collecting his wife from a theatre where a long-time friend was acting in the matinee performance of a play. He left his car in the nearest parking space he could find but in his haste he forgot to move his clubs from the back seat into the safety of the boot. There was a brief pause while his wife Brenda hugged, kissed cheeks and planned next meetings. She asked him if they could drop off two of her friends at a nearby railway station and as they rounded a corner with them Alec sensed that something was wrong. A group of theatregoers were standing beside his car where a shattered window and a brick lying where his golf clubs had been confirmed his worst fear. The theatregoers told him that they'd heard a bang and saw a plain white van speeding away but they were sorry that they hadn't noted the van's regy number. Alec thanked them and set about reporting the theft. The local police arrived quickly and, although sympathetic, they could only offer to take down a description of the bag and clubs. After giving him the details that he'd need for insurance purposes they told Alec that they were unable to give him any direct help, but would keep his details on file should the bag and clubs turn up. As he closed his notebook one of the officers advised him "As you're well insured you'll get your clubs replaced. However, if there's anything important that your insurance company can't replace your best bet is to give it a week or so and check out the local second-hand shops." Alec phoned his pal in despair to tell him he'd lost their trophy and after a few expletives questioning the parentage of the thieves, Bob consoled him with, "The clubs will soon be replaced and after all it's only two worthless wee bits of paper we're talking about so it's no great loss." Deep down however, both knew better.

Without telling his pal Bob regularly stopped and enquired at any likely looking shop if they had any golf clubs for sale. Many enquiries later he was getting out of the car when his wife Alice asked, "How much longer are you going to keep this up. I know how much the pair of you treasured that wee trophy, but you'll have to accept that it's long gone by now." Bob grimaced and said, "As we're here anyway I may as well try this last one." After he asked his usual question, the owner went through to the back shop and returned with a golf bag resembling Alec's. He volunteered that a chap had brought it in that morning saying that his wife had just had a baby and he has to sell his clubs to buy a pram, but Bob wasn't listening. He was busy searching through each of the bag's pockets when his fingers closed on a small cloth bag and, consoling himself against disappointment, he loosened the strings and took out their trophy. Speechless, Bob turned and walked out of the shop quickly followed by the owner shouting that his CCTV system had recorded full details of him stealing something from the golf bag. He backed it up with, "And I've got your car registration number to corroborate it." Bob showed him the wee beer mat with two bits of brown paper in it and agreed that he was guilty of a theft and it was the owners duty as an honest citizen to report it to the police. "However, he added, the most likely outcome would be that the police would charge you with resetting stolen property of which this little thing I'm holding would be cast-iron proof." By this time Alice had come out of the car and, glancing down at Bob's hand said, "Oh my god, you've found it." Back in the car with the stolen clubs in the boot Bob considered putting off telling his pal about it until their next match. He imagined standing on the first tee and nonchalantly handing the recovered trophy to Alec with something like, 'Look what's just dropped out of the sky. Alice said that she knew what he was thinking and that wouldn't be fair to Alec. So, with nothing better to do, they drove the fifty miles to Alec's house and re-united him with their trophy.

Another event which turned out to have important consequences for them both occurred during the last of their teenage years when Frank, a friend from early schooldays, asked if they would join him the following evening for a couple of beers. After having a short catch up chat Frank dropped his bombshell. He started it simply enough with "I'm getting married." After a short pause and a look at each other to check whether this wasn't the start of a hoary story they offered him their congratulations.

There was no need to ask who the lucky lady was as Frank and Christine had been an item since their first year at secondary school. Alec was the first to start the practicalities with, "And when's the wedding date." Frank dropped his second bombshell with, "Well, it's not that easy." When they both looked at him for a further explanation he nervously said, "Me and Christine, or should I say Christine and I, had a meeting with her parents, oh and mine also." When he stopped and searched for a 'how will I put this' phrase Alec, chipped in with, "It's best to get both families involved right from the beginning when you're planning a big event like a wedding." Bob added, "It was only a matter of time till the pair of you got hitched." "No, Frank blurted out, Christine's pregnant and our parents are insisting that we get married as soon as possible, as in eight weeks on Saturday!" "That's still great news." said Bob. "It's probably not quite the way you wanted it, but the pair of you were always intending to tie the knot." "Aye", nodded Frank, "But not this way." We've disappointed both our parents, but if we co-operate they're willing to help us out. Christine's mum and dad said we could stay rent-free at their house for a couple of years and mine are going to double up our savings for a house of our own. However, both lots of our parents are adamant that it's only on the condition that we agree to having a full-on wedding. It's not the way we imagined it would be, but neither of us fancied quietly slipping off to Gretna Green and that's where you two come in, I need a best man."

"Wow." said Alec. "I never imagined this when you asked us to join you for a quiet pint But why the two of us, is Christine having two bridesmaids and you've got to supply joint best men?" Now that he'd hooked his prey Frank relaxed and continued "Although she's having both her sisters as bridesmaids, it's just one of you I need." "Do you want us to toss it?" said Bob. "That would be the fairest way, replied Frank, but Christine's mum, who as you know is a bit stuck-up, said that the nice boy who's at university would best fit the bill." Bob shook Alec's hand and with a smile said "This is one match I'm happy to concede, we wouldn't want to upset Christine's mum, would we?" He felt a bit miffed at coming second in Mrs. P's estimation, but was immediately cheered up when Frank added "Well, she thought that the university boy would be better at the Best Man's speech." While they digested this, he added "There's a wee bit more where you both come in. Alec, as the Best Man, you'll have to do the first waltz with the main Bridesmaid, and you." looking at Bob who was still smiling, "You're second on the floor with the other one and Christine's mum's adamant. She said that she wants a dance out of the pair of you, not a shuffle!"

Three days later saw the lads standing in a circle while husband and wife instructors at the Victor Silvester School Ballroom Dancing demonstrated the various steps that makeup a graceful waltz. Starting with half an hour of learning the basic box step or as Alec called it, learning the art of not stepping on your partner's toes, a short break was called. As they sat down at a table two young ladies came over and asked if the other chairs were taken. When the lesson resumed twenty minutes later they paired off and learned how to do a basic waltz without constantly repeating 'sorry'. A few years later when they were dissecting that night, Alice admitted that she'd said to Brenda "Look, there's a couple of nice looking chaps sitting over there, let's join them." Brenda, whose romantic thoughts were elsewhere, had replied "If we really have to." Her attitude slowly changed as they got into conversation with the two shy boys. She said that it was the quiet, unthreatening feeling that she got from Alec that impressed her most and when they parted after the class it was she who said that they were looking forward to meeting up next week.

They became regular partners on the training dance floor for the first couple of weeks and, when Alec hesitantly said that their wedding invitations were for two, partnered them to Frank and Christine's wedding. Bob later admitted to Alice that she was his type of girl when, after their third class, she invited them to come and meet some friends the following Wednesday at the Magic Stick. Bob and Alec looked puzzled so she explained "The Majestic dummy, the dance hall." When they still looked puzzled she laughed and said, "We all know it as the Magic Stick", then added, "That thing you boys have and we girls don't." Bob came back with "Oh, you mean brains," to which Alice replied "Aye, dream on sonny boy." Two years later Bob and Alice were married, followed a year later by Alec and Brenda after Alec completed his degree. During his final year he'd been head-hunted by a major bank and after honeymooning they set up home fifty miles away.

Today's game had been mooted several months before. Jean, a classmate from schooldays and a very dear friend of the girls had, by her own admission, an insane love of the theatre. She'd never married and had been Auntie Jean to all their children and grandchildren. She'd encouraged every one of them in school plays, taken them to innumerable performances, introduced them to some major acting names but still hadn't been able to infect any of them with her all-consuming love of things theatrical. Over the last few years she'd become badly affected by arthritis, or as she usually called it, Arthuritis. Arthur, she would explain, had been her childhood sweetheart and he was coming back to haunt her as she'd never forgiven the sod for marrying someone else. "Not just anyone else, she would add, "a bimbo who's ten years his junior and a philistine who wouldn't know the difference between Shakespeare and The Follies Bergère." Some months previously she'd told Alice, Brenda and the gang that this was to be her last season with The Players who were the biggest amateur dramatic society in town. She explained that she was getting too old and stiff to be of any use and, as Brenda described it, "The theatrical light's shining as brightly as ever, it's just the wheels are starting to come off." One of their friends had been an early thespian with Jean and suggested to the director of the next production that something special might be arranged to mark her retirement as well as celebrating fifty years with the company. He came up with the idea of an extra afternoon performance for the second last day of their next play and he would cast Joan as the star's understudy so that she could step into the part should, just by chance, the star be indisposed. Audience arrangements for the performance were quietly made and the director agreed that he wouldn't tell Jean that she was 'on' 'til an hour before the start and would keep her rehearsing in the star's dressing room 'til the last minute. He knew that she was quite familiar with the understudy role as she'd been the fall-back on many occasions so he was confident that she'd relish this last chance. He'd also arrange for several interruptions so she wouldn't smell a rat or get time for a peek at the audience before curtain up. On the way through, Brenda told Alec that there would be at least a hundred friends, plus lots of others who'd heard of it and fancied an afternoon of fun. Even the indisposed star was determined not to miss out so she was coming in disguise. "Don't wait up for us, she told him, we'll probably be out partying all night. Though thinking about it, Jean's a stickler and she's still got her last two shows tomorrow, so it's more likely it'll be the last train for us. Don't worry, we'll save a wee bit of the fun for you and Bob at curtain down tomorrow night." After he dropped off his wife at the restaurant where the gang had arranged to meet, Alec started to realise that he was a bit envious of his wife and maybe he should be going to the theatre with her. When he told his pal on the short drive to the course Bob's snorted response was, "Away with you ye old daftie." "Imaging putting the theatre before golf and here's me feeling really good about my game while all you want to do is go and play wi' the lassies."

They checked in with the starter, dropped off their bags in the locker room and headed for the lounge where Alec, as was the custom, ordered two beers. While they were being poured Bob was tapped on the shoulder and when he turned round saw that it was Frank. Or as Alice had named him many years before, that randy laddie who's responsible for us meeting you pair. Giving Alec a nudge Bob said, "Hello Frank, how are you? I haven't seen you since your sad funeral last year." Alec put out his hand and shook Frank's saying "How's it going old mate, long time no see." Frank told them that the last year had been painful and he'd gone off golf a bit. "In fact, he added, not just golf. After Christine passed away I found that our house contained too many painful memories, so I've downsized to a nearby flat and I'm slowly getting back to having an occasional game. It's sad, but I've got to accept that life moves on regardless." Bob replied "Time's the great healer" and Frank nodded a sad agreement. "I know it's payback time for all our happy years together, but that's not the reason that I came over." He turned to Alec and asked "It was maths you took at the Uni, wasn't it?" Alec looked baffled and said, "Yes maths, why?" Frank apologised for his bluntness, telling them that he was with a four-ball waiting for a call to go in for lunch and the fourth member of the group was his new next-door neighbour who was a Professor at the university. Alec looked a bit baffled so Frank explained. "When the pair of you walked in I remembered that you were the only one of our class who went on to university and thought that maybe you and the Prof's paths might have crossed. I mentioned your name to him but it didn't seem to ring a bell. Prof, he prefers you call him that because he dislikes his real name, said that he's always delighted to meet an old student. So would you come over and join us for a few minutes?" Bob couldn't resist it and, looking at Frank, replied in a flat monotone "Why, are you coming apart?" Frank, like most of their friends, knew all Bob's witticisms by heart so he grimaced and asked Bob if he was still getting his jokes from the old 1950's Comic Cuts magazines. Bob was pleased tho' when he saw a faint smile as the pair turned away. After introductions Alec sat down next to the Professor and they started passing names and dates back and forward with shakes or nods of their heads.

When Bob came over with the beers, Frank introduced him to his colleagues and they chatted about the course and the good condition it was in considering the long, wet winter they'd had. A few minutes later, the group were called for lunch came and, after handshakes all round, Alec sat down with a faraway look in his eyes. After a few sips of beer Bob was about to ask if it was an interesting conversation when his pal looked at his watch and said that they'd better get a move on as they were due on the tee in twenty minutes. And, he added, you know me, I need a couple of practise putts to smooth out my stroke." Then, "Yes, it was an interesting conversation, I'll tell you about it on the way round." Bob turned and could see about a dozen golfers milling around the first tee and said, "It looks like three more games before us, around twenty-five minutes or so. Did I tell you that we're following a works outing of six four balls and I don't think many of them have played the course before?" Alec said that he'd mentioned it earlier and it was OK with him. "We've all afternoon to play eighteen holes, down a few beers, have dinner and a pleasant walk back to your house on a lovely evening for a nightcap." Bob added "and, knowing our ladies, that could be well into the small hours." They drank up and with Bob humming the theme from The Magnificent Seven headed for their duel in the afternoon sun.

First Hole 378 yards par 4 - Clober Bridge..

Alec - Heads or tails.
Bob – Tails.
Alec – Sorry old mate its heads, I'll bat first.

Bob groaned inwardly. It had been quite a while since he'd taken their trophy home with him and he'd the feeling that today could well be his day. Earlier while waiting for Alec he'd pictured winning the toss and getting in the first blow, long and with a slight hook. While the ball was still in the air he'd nonchalantly bend down, pick up his tee and turn to Alec with a gentle smirk that said 'go on Steady Eddie, follow that!'

The opening hole's been described in several course reviews as the best opening hole in the area. It's a 45 degree dogleg to the left with banks of high trees deterring anyone foolish enough to think of taking the direct route. It's been done tho' and Bob's still awestruck every time he recalls watching a visiting sixteen year old junior take it on with a three wood and land his ball in the middle of the fairway less than a hundred yards from the green. "Mind you" he always added, "that young lad went on to have a successful career as a professional."

After a handshake, Alec hit a nice straight drive. "Not great, he conceded, but it's down the middle and it's in play." Bob followed with a longer shot, but it had a gentle slice rather than his hoped for hook and the ball ended up in the first cut of rough a couple of yards off the fairway.

Bob - Should be OK, the grass hasn't had time to put on much growth.

Alec picked up Bob's tee and handed it to him before they both headed for the golf cart that was their sole concession to old age. Being a moorland course, it's very scenic, but as the soil is mainly peat rather than sand based, there's not much run at this time of year. This puts the emphasis on good ball placement and the ideal drive has a slight hook to help the ball swing round the corner leaving a you straightforward six or seven iron to the green. As they drove down to where Alec's drive had finished, they could see that the foursome in front we're searching for a ball behind the green so they sat in the buggy and waited for them to play out the hole.

Alec – That conversation I had with the Professor took me back to when we were wee boys.

Bob – As I get older I often think back to when we were kids. Most of my memories are pleasant except for the time you tried to kill me! And when that didn't work, you tried to finish me off with a crazy car chase.

Alec - No, I'm being serious. After Frank introduced me, Prof asked if Frank was correct and I'd studied maths at the University. I told him the dates when I was there and he gave it a bit of thought then said it was round about then that he'd started as a Junior Lecturer so I'd probably be in my third year. He asked me if I might have attended any of his lectures and I enquired what his subjects were. He told me and I could place him as a much younger man. I said that he'd been a breath of fresh air after some of the stuffy sessions I'd sat through. He asked me my name again but it didn't jog his memory, so he asked if I could remember any people who'd been in my year.

When I mentioned Dan Bartholomew his eyes lit up. "Dan, he said, Dan Bartholomew, my first superstar, I can place your lot now. Dan was a bit of a practical joker, wasn't he?" He gave me a quizzical look and asked "I don't suppose you'd have been in on any of his escapades." I tried to give him my 'who me' look, but when he raised his eyebrows and smiled I had to admit that I'd taken part in a few. He said that Dan had proved to be a star and went on to do some outstanding work in the early days when they were setting up the European Atom Smasher project. He ended up going over to The States and helped develop those integrated electronic chips that are everywhere nowadays. "Though, from what I can remember, some of Dan's stunts would get him asked to stand down nowadays." Then he said, "And it's equally likely so would some of his cronies." He gave me his quizzical look again and said, "A few lives might've have gone down quite different paths, mightn't they?"

Bob chuckled – One of the sights that I'll never forget was watching you and half a dozen others togged up in flimsy dresses and veils as Ladies of the Harem. You were chained in single file and walking behind a very regal-looking Arab Prince carrying a notice proclaiming him to be Sheik Mahand.

Alec nodded – Aye, Dan had us walking down the middle of the road stopping cars and jumping on and off buses. But hey, we were far and away the top rag week collectors that year and we even got our photo on the front page of the evening newspapers. Dad saw it and thought it was hilarious, but when he showed it to my mother she was wasn't best pleased in case some of her friends

19

might have recognised me. Another of Dan's wheezes was to find an unused room and give a lecture in it. Not just any lecture tho', he would do a brilliant take-off of a prominent member of staff who we'd recently suffered in silence. Dan was a top class mimic and could easily have had a career in showbiz. Two or three times a term the word would go round. 'Dan, room such and such,' and he'd have us laughing 'til our sides ached. Sometimes a member of staff would poke their head round the door and enquire "What's going on here?" Dan always replied "It's these dunderheads, they've asked me to explain this subject to them and as you can see I'm not having much success." The funniest bit was when the interloper left Dan would give a great impersonation of them walking away sniffing and saying "Damned tomfoolery, it wouldn't have been tolerated in my day". Dan always tried to hide it, but he was very bright and much quicker on the uptake than us mere mortals. I think his wheezes came from being bored with the slow pace us dunderheads learned at.

Bob – You've mentioned him several times before. It must've been a hoot to be in lectures with him.

Alec – No, he took them very seriously and at lectures he was a totally different person. Then Prof asked me how I got interested in maths and I said that I'd always felt at home with numbers as they seemed to make more sense to me than words. He asked me what age would I be when I started calling numbers my friends and I realised that I'd never thought of it that way before but the answer came to me in a flash. I looked over at you, but you weren't looking, so I told him it was when I was at Primary School and that it's all your fathers' fault. That's when they were called in for lunch so he wished me an enjoyable round and hoped that we might meet up again.

Bob – My father was responsible for you taking up maths, you've never told me that before. How come he was able to do it for you, but not for me?

Alec – Do you remember when we were kids how your dad used to enjoy teasing us with his silly magic tricks and riddles?

Bob grinned remembering his father.

Alec – Do you remember the time he asked a bunch of us, "Which one of you is the best at counting" and we all shouted me, me, me. Your dad looked at me and said, "OK clever clogs, tell me how many fingers you've got?" "Ten." I told him. "I've counted them." He asked me if I was sure of that and when I nodded he said, "I think you're wrong and I can prove that you've got eleven fingers." When I shook my head, he said, "OK then, let's count them and see who's right." He took my left hand, held up my little finger and said that if I had ten fingers then this finger would be finger number ten. I nodded and he folded it down and then the others counting nine, eight, seven, then my thumb, six. He held up my right hand and asked "How many fingers have you got on this one?" I said five. He looked around to check that we were all in agreement and said "So you've got six fingers on this hand and five on the other one, what's six add on five?" We all chorused 'eleven' and your dad said, "There you are, you've actually got eleven fingers." Then he gave us his innocent little grin and added "Now, isn't that magic!"

21

Bob – Dad loved an audience, especially kids. Up to their fifteenth birthdays ours and then the grandkids always got a puzzle of some sort as part of their Christmas and birthday presents.

Alec – It's wonderful the way our mind stores images we haven't thought about for years. When Prof asked me where I got my liking for maths I had a flashback to the minute's silence at your dad's funeral when we were asked to recall our memories of him. When I closed my eyes, I could see him standing in front of me with that grin on his face saying "Now, isn't that magic," and I realised that it was his magic trick that got me into maths.

Bob – I remember him bamboozling lots of kids with that one. He'd several similar tricks so why that particular one?

Alec – At the time it bugged me and I was certain that he must be wrong, and the more I thought about it the angrier I got with myself that I was unable to see thru' it. I was convinced that there's no way you can make ten fingers equal eleven fingers so somewhere in the trick there had to be a different way of counting.

Bob – What age would we be then?

Alec –I'm pretty sure we were in Miss Currie's class, so I'd be eight, maybe nine. It was a few days after he showed us the trick and I was copying down my homework sums when the answer came to me. My fingers were getting sore so I tried to hold my pencil with two fingers instead of three when I had a thought, how would a person who's unlucky enough to be born with no fingers manage to hold their pencil? I realised that if I'd been that unfortunate person and your dad asked me how many fingers I had I'd reply none and he'd have to accept that as a valid answer.

Counting them that way no fingers is answer number one and when I added on my ten fingers I got his answer of eleven fingers, even though we've only got ten actual ones. At the time I felt that I'd joined a secret society and I was able to read their code.

Bob - All that when you were eight or maybe nine, that's quite a bit of reasoning. I'm glad you never confronted dad with that, it would've spoiled his fun. Even late on in life he was still bamboozling his grandchildren and friends with silly tricks like that.

Alec – Someone in our class who'd a big brother told us that they called Miss Currie 'spare the homework and spoil the child Currie'. What about the time she told us that the Suspectors were coming next day to check up on us and if we acted normally everything will be all right.

Bob – When I went home from school I told my mum that we were having Suspectors in the morning and after a bit of digging she said, "Ahh, you mean that the Inspectors are coming to check up if you're being taught properly. Suspectors is Miss Currie's little joke so that you won't get worked up and decide to catch a cold for the day.

Alec – My mum said much the same and I told her that I thought that having Suspectors in sounded like a bit of fun.

Bob - After Miss Currie introduced him the Suspector sat at the back while she took a sums class. He asked us a few questions and when he was leaving he congratulated us for being the best sums class he'd the pleasure of assessing for a long time and said that we were a credit to our teacher.

Alec – Yes, and we were all disappointed that he didn't say that we were the best sums class he'd the pleasure of suspecting for a long time. Miss Currie was hard on us, but she always had time for a bit of fun in the classroom.

Bob – You can say that again. Do you remember the time she was explaining the big red moon that'd recently been in the night sky. I think she called it a blood moon, and asked us "Does anyone know where Mars is?" I'm sure it was Archie Lindsay who put up his hand and said, "Please Miss, you're sitting on it."

Alec – I was surprised when she burst out laughing as I was thinking that Archie was talking about the planet. I asked you why everyone was laughing, but you couldn't tell me for giggling along with her.

Bob – Remember the time she introduced us to gizinties? I still think of division tables that way.

Alec – That's right. She has us chanting two gizinty four two times, two gizinty six three times and so on. It's a good job she didn't do division tables when the Suspector was there, I don't think he'd be overjoyed at us being taught like that, but her gizinties worked for me. Tho' going back to your dad, starting to count from zero wasn't an option until relatively recently. Starting at one would've been the natural thing to do when we used our fingers to count with and you can imagine early humans holding up a number of fingers then pointing at something. Along with the ancient forms of writing, there's evidence that for many years people used upright strokes for their four fingers and a sideways one thru' them for their thumb. Once they'd settled into villages they developed ideas to help them measure fields and construct buildings and in the process discovered that there were several magic numbers such as Pi and three, four and five!

Bob looked blankly at Alec – Three, four and five? Twelve.

Alec – Euclid dummy, as in how to line up square walls and buildings. Tho' it was probably in use for many years before he came along and explained how it worked.

By this time the game in front had moved on so they got out and played their second shots. Alec under-clubbed and his ball just made it onto the front of the green. To Bob's delight he hit a smooth clean shot out of the semi-rough and watched as his ball came to rest a few feet past the hole. They motored down and a few minutes later Alec watched his long putt roll past the hole and finished further away than Bob's. Although his return putt grazed the hole it didn't drop and he conceded the hole. Bob elected to take a practice putt and stroked the ball right into the middle for his first birdie of the year. After smiling at Alec's backhanded compliment about him having spent the winter practising his putting on the carpet he took a club from his bag and said, "See you there." then walked up the short hill to the second tee.

Bob's game in recent years could be charitably described as inconsistent. Alec, along with many others, had been telling him that he should consult the club Pro as he was hitting at the ball and trying to punch it rather than following thru' with a smooth swing. Bob, however, had been aware for some time that when he attempted to follow thru' he got an electric jolt in his lower back and it seemed to be getting worse with each passing year. One evening the previous autumn, when was getting ready to go out for a few holes, a new member asked if he could join him.

Bob's drive off the first tee was a shocker and he excused it by his usual "I know, everyone tells me I'm not following thru." The new member, who turned out to be a recently qualified surgeon said "When you try to follow thru' do you get an electric shock in your back and a pain down your leg?" When Bob nodded he added "I'm not your doctor Bob, but if I was I'd send you for a scan. You're showing all the symptoms of nerve damage to your lower back." Bob nodded and told him that he had a scan for it some years previously but it hadn't shown anything. "Was the scanned image on a computer screen?" he was asked. "No", Bob replied. "It was on several sheets of negative film and I've still got them at home as I thought they might be needed someday." "In that case", the new member said, "I'd go down to your GP and get him to refer you for a new scan. I'd bin those old negatives, the digital scanners we have nowadays are very much sharper than those old photographic ones."

Bob plucked up courage and did as was advised. Not wanting to appear a coward he told no one that he was dreading revisiting the torture chamber he'd endured to get the first scan. He shuddered at the thought of once again being slid into a long narrow tube recessed into a wall and lying still with his nose almost touching the top of the tube. Before going in, he'd been asked if he wanted a blindfold mask or would he prefer a dim blue light. Within seconds he regretted not opting for the blindfold. One quick look up at the close proximity of the tube almost touching his nose gave him claustrophobia and he kept his eyes tightly shut throughout the whiz, bang, clang of the thirty minutes it took.

When he saw the new scanner, he got a pleasant surprise. Although it was still mainly enclosed it wasn't built into the wall and there was a small opening at the head end. When he was slid in his previous feeling of being very near to panic and having to fight against pressing the buzzer to get him out didn't recur. A few days later he sat in front of a large computer screen displaying the lower part of his spine while a doctor pointed out a bit of bone that'd sheared off one of his vertebrae and was lying close to a nerve. A couple of days in hospital, a short op, and he was pain free for the first time in years. He regretted the time he'd wasted thinking that getting another scan would be more pointless torture but kept telling himself that the past is past and all the regrets in the world wouldn't change it. Besides, it was great to be swinging a club freely again and, after a couple of visits to a local driving range and a session with the Pro, he felt some of his old confidence returning.

Second Hole   170 yards par 3 - Craigton.

Having driven the buggy by a roundabout route Alec joined Bob on the tee and broke into his reverie with "It looks like we're in for a bit of a wait." They stood back as two members from the game in front joined them on the tee. "That's some rough you've got there, said one. I could hardly see my feet never mind finding my ball." "Aye, agreed Bob, smiling and adding his usual joke. "Later in the summer when it really grows some visitors get lost in it and it takes the green's staff ages to find them!" They stood quietly while the pair, obviously playing the course for the first time, reloaded and hit their shots.

Alec – Could you hang on to this club for a minute, I'm getting hot and the damn zip on this jacket keeps jamming. It's probably trying to tell me it's time for a new one and I bet they've really shot up in price since I bought this one.

Bob – My recollection is that it was a birthday pressy from your dear wife. She asked me for my opinion after you told her "Buy the best, in the long run it's cheaper than the rest." And I remember you telling me, "This wetsuit's the very best quality and it'll see me out." Heavens my old mate, you've had over twenty years' wear out of it. Surely it's time you opened the piggy bank and treated yourself.

Alec – Yes and as usual you're right, but I bet that the cost of them has rocketed since Brenda bought it for me and that's inflation for you. It's all a trick to con us into thinking that we're better off without giving us any more real money. I doubt the ancients with their five finger bartering systems would've had any truck with inflation. They'd just take a few hens and go down to the marketplace where a smarmy guy with slicked back hair would stop them with 'Need a new jacket sir, we've got all the latest styles. After having a good look through his wares you point your finger at a natty sheepskin one with a matching cowhide studded belt and hold up three fingers then point at the hens. Seller scowls and holds up five fingers. You shrug, hold up four fingers and start walking away. Seller looks pained, but calls you back and nods his head. You knew where you were then and if you came back in twenty years' time it'll still be four hens for your new jacket.

Bob –That would be pretty pointless, you don't keep hens.

Alec – More's the pity. With some hens and your dad's eleven fingers trick I'd have got a real bargain. Mind you to get inflation going they'd probably need an agreed numbering system. Maybe inflation started with the Babylonians or Sumerians who were living over six thousand years ago in what's now Iraq.

Bob - I've heard of the Babylonians 'cos they counted in sixties and that's where we get our hours and minutes from. What did the Sumerians contribute?

Alec – They used the phases of the moon to count time and as that was a regular twenty eight day cycle they split it up into groups of four and that's where weeks come from.

Bob – We got our days of the week from the Vikings didn't we? Sunday was the Sun's day, Monday was Moon's, Tuesday was Thor's day, or was that Thursday?

Alec – Tuesday was Tiw's day and he was their God of war. Thor was the God of strength and Friday was ladies' day, named after Frigg their Goddess of Beauty.

29

Frigg was Odin's wife and he was the Raven God whose flag was flown on all their mastheads. Odin was also called Wodin and his day's Wednesday. Saturday's the odd one out as it came from the Greek God Saturn who was their Lord of the Universe.

Bob – So it was the Vikings who introduced the word 'frigging' into our language. Obviously meaning to make hay with Odin's wife!

Alec – 'Could be, our language is full of words borrowed from whoever and wherever we could find them.

Bob - Where did our ten fingered numbering system came from?

Alec – The Sumerians counted in fives, but for some obscure reason the Babylonians used twelve for their base. When they traded together, they used sixty so that both sides could understand and that's possibly when exchange rates came in.

Bob – Did they have their days divided up into sixty hours as well?

Alec – They must've been aware that the Sun splits the day into before noon then after noon and probably had the concept of morning, afternoon, evening and night, but it was the ancient Egyptians who were next to have a bash at it. They divided their days into ten segments and added one on at each end to allow for dawn and dusk.

Bob – Didn't that mean that their hours were longer in the summer and shorter in the winter?

Alec – It did, but that was balanced by having more work to do and this gave them more time to complete it.

Bob – That's ingenious, why didn't we follow them?

Alec – Sadly it only works for relatively small regions. But they didn't use daytime to calculate their twelve hours, they waited 'til the Sun went down to do that.

Bob – I know the Egyptians created lots of star maps, but wouldn't they only tell you the months and not the hours?

Alec – The Egyptian star maps are probably where we got our idea of horoscopes from, or horrorscopes as my old Auntie Sally used to call them.

Bob (smiling) – She did, didn't she? She used to enjoy reading us our stars from whatever magazine she was reading and putting her funny interpretations on them. I can remember her telling us our fortune by looking at the tea leaves we'd left in a cup. But what bit of magic did the Egyptians use to get their time from the stars?

Alec – By day they used sundials, but by night they were very ingenious. They picked out a group of thirty-six stars called decals where each star is spaced out evenly so that a new one popped over the horizon every forty minutes. This let them look up at the night sky and read off the time like a clock.

Bob – That would be alright for them as they had plenty of cloudless nights, but I don't see it working for us. Did they have a written counting system or did they count in five-barred gates?

Alec – No, they had a decimal system which had separate symbols for one, ten, a hundred, a thousand and so on which made it very long-winded.

Bob – Imagine being an Egyptian accountant, you'd spend all your time just writing down the numbers!

Alec - When The Greeks took over they used some of their letters with an apostrophe to show that it was a number. The Romans upgraded this to use combinations of I's, V's, X's and so on. Then they came over here and we were stuck with their system 'til a few hundred years ago.

Bob – I think the Roman numbers look classier than ours, but I wouldn't want to do any maths with them.

Alec – I think it's possible to do simple things like addition, subtraction and maybe some simple multiplication, but we certainly wouldn't have the really useful system we enjoy today. The numbers we have today aren't our numbers. They came from Hindu mathematicians working fourteen hundred years ago in the north of India and it was them who introduced one of the most important concepts of any useful numbering system. That's them cleared the green at last, time to move on.

The second hole's a short downhill par three from a high tee to a relatively small green. Bob hit a nice shot and his ball trickled onto the front of the green, but Steady Eddie, Bob's name for Alec when they were on the golf course, excelled himself by hitting one of his very rare slices into the deep rough that had gobbled up two previous balls. He hit a provisional ball which landed in the bunker to the left of the green, replaced his club and took out this sand iron telling Bob "I'll walk down and have a quick look in the rough and meet you down at the green." After a short look in the rough he walked down to the bunker and, failing narrowly to hole his fourth shot, conceded the hole. He picked up Bob's ball and handed it to him while grimacing and indicating the score by pointing two fingers downward. As they climbed into the buggy, Alec said, "The four in front are still waiting on the tee, and with five group's in front of them we're in for a long round." Bob, however, had only half his mind on the golf, the other half was remembering his father.

Bob – Could the important maths concept you mentioned be the number that my father kept banging on about?

Alec – Hole in one mate. It's the number he used in most of his magic tricks. Nothing, zero, nil, zilch, and although the concept had been 'sort of' used before, the first mention of zero appeared in a book called Arithmetic written around 630 AD by a mathematician called Brahamagupta. Over the next hundred and fifty years, this Indian maths with zero spread up and down the Silk Roads between China and The Middle East where it was adopted by the Muslim world. About eighty years later, an agreement was reached that the symbol 0 would be used to represent zero.

Bob – What's the advantage of having a zero?

Alec – It's easier asking what would happen if we didn't have zero.

Bob – OK, take away zero and what happens?

Alec - Without zero there'd be no algebra, arithmetic as we know it, no decimals, no accounts, some very convoluted ways of measuring physical quantities, no boundary between negative and positive numbers and, probably most important to kids today, no mobile phones or iPads. The beauty of zero is that it allows us to count as high or as low as we want with just ten numbers and it's the basis of the most powerful and precise set of tools we've ever had at our disposal.

Bob – Being a mathematician you would say that, but the

only time my dad talked to me about zero he made it sound as though it really was a magical number.

Alec – How come you've never told me about that?

Bob - Do you remember the time a boy in our class asked if we were interested in doing a wee job after school and hooked us in by saying that we'd get paid for doing it. I think his name was Tom.

Alex –That was Tom Wilson and we were in our last year at Primary School. He asked if we wanted to help him and his dad deliver leaflets for something called an election. Told us that it would only take a couple of hours after school and we'd get two shillings and sixpence a night.

Bob – Two and a tanner was a worthwhile sum of money to have in your pocket back then and we thought that we'd act grown-up and not tell our parents about it 'til we'd finished.

Alex – It was my first paid job and it was fun knocking on doors, handing in leaflets and asking if they wouldn't mind displaying this wee poster in their front window. We got away with it for four nights and I was hoping we'd get at least four more when you blew it by going home with a few of the leaflets sticking out your back pocket.

Bob – My mum's face went chalk white and I knew I'd committed a major sin when she used my Sunday name after I tried to gloss over what we'd been doing. She told me "Thank goodness Robert that you never got round to delivering those leaflets in our street. What would the neighbours have thought if they caught my son stuffing the Communist Manifesto through their letterboxes and asking them if they wouldn't mind doing him a favour by displaying this picture of Joseph Stalin in their front window!" She finished with the usual warning "Wait till I tell your father when he comes home," and stomped off to spill the beans to your mother. I wasn't too worried about what my dad would say, I was more concerned with losing the money that I'd planned to build up my stamp collection with.

Alec – My mum had a bit of a go at me for not telling her, but what did your dad say?

Bob – After she'd done her bit of ranting about our activities, he calmed her down by assuring her that I had no intention of starting the communist revolution in our street saying "Bobby's too young to be expected to understand politics so there's no real harm done." He agreed that I should've asked their permission before we started and, looking straight at me, said "We can be sure that nothing like this will ever happen again." I'd hoped for a wee while that we might be getting away with it so I tried to butter them up by telling them that I was just trying to behave more grown-up. Then I put the kybosh on it by saying that Tom's dad had told us we were doing a great job and were helping him and his friends to send twice as many members down to the Parliament. Dad came back with "You might think that you're doing the man a favour, but look at it this way. They currently have no Members of Parliament, so even without your help they'll have no trouble sending twice as many down to London. Two times no members is still no members. Even if he'd told you they wanted to send down ten times as many they still wouldn't have any members!"

Alec – Your dad was right and because zero isn't like any other number it had to be invented. It's a hard concept for us to get our head around because it actually means nothingness and that's impossible for us to experience. It's not a natural number because we never come across absolutely nothing in nature, and, even in the darkest depths of space, there's always something there.

Bob – But is zero an actual number?

Alec – It is as in being the number you experience when you check your bank account and find that you've no money in it. Zero's also a concept. It gives us a fixed reference point to start counting from, sits plum in middle between plus and minus infinity and gives us an almost unbounded numbering system. It's possible that there might be more to come on the logic side of maths, but I don't think there's any way we'll be able to improve on our numbering system.

Bob – You've got me there pal, run that one past me again.

Alec – What I meant was that we've got the simplest numbering system that it's possible to have as it uses only two numbers, zero signifying nothing and one meaning something. There's not much you can do mathematically with zero except insert it before or after a 'real' number to raise or lower its value by ten.

Bob – I'm with you there, but if you can't add, subtract, multiply or divide by zero how can you call it a number?

Alec – Maybe a better way to look at is to say that one's a real number and zero's a virtual number as it has no value. As I said, it's quite a hard concept to get your head around which is why it took so long for people to come up with it and Brahmagupta gave us a set of rules for working with it. Adding and subtracting zero doesn't change the answer

One plus or minus zero is still one, but it's the other two that are quite different. Take any number and times it with zero and you'll always get zero, but try to divide a number by zero and see what you get?

Bob – As you're only dealing with two numbers the answer must be zero or one.

Alec – When you divide anything what you're doing is cutting the whole into smaller parts then adding up the number of parts. As it's impossible to cut anything into no parts, cutting or dividing by zero is meaningless.

Bob – I've been using zero all my life but I've never looked at it that way.

Alec – Zero's defined as the number that sits between plus one and minus one and it's the only number that can't be positive or negative. As your dad said, it's one of our numbers, but it's special because it's the only one that can't have a quantity associated with it.

Bob – Using just zero and one relates directly to the numbering system that's used in computers.

Alec – That's called the binary system where you count with two numbers rather than ten. With binary you've only two symbols to work with and it can never be minus. It starts with zero, doesn't it?

Bob – Yes, zero's the first number and one's the other. To count beyond one you start the next set of numbers at two, and so on.

Alec – Didn't you find that difficult to work with?

Bob – Not really as we rarely had to do any actual work in binary. We passed it on to the computer and let the big expensive box get on with it.

Alec – You must've done some work with it even if it was just to understand how computers worked.

Bob – We did a bit on my first course when we attempted to write a simple program to add up long strings of ones and zeros. After half an hour's pointless toil the instructor came to our rescue by pointing out that computers don't work with long strings of ones and zeros, they split them up into groups of four. After that dealing with binary was quite easy.

Alec – Groups of four, in what way?

Bob – Inside a computer everything's carried out in multiples of four binary numbers. It sounds difficult, but when you write them down it becomes more obvious. A group of four numbers starts at 0000, the second number is 0001, the third one is 0010 and so on up to fifteen, which is 1111. It's normally assumed that computers work to base two, but they actually work to base sixteen.

Alec – What if I wanted seven in binary how would that look?

Bob – Binary numbers are like our normal numbers and count from right to left. Seven is three ones and a zero, or 0111 and that's as high as you can go with the first three numbers. Add on one at the left and it becomes 1000, or eight.

Alec – Do you stop counting when you get to nine?

Bob –That would be a waste of six useful numbers so we continue counting up to 1111 and build computers that work to base sixteen.

Alec – So we count in ten's and computers compute in sixteens. How does the computer recognise the numbers from ten to fifteen?

Bob – We use the old Greek way of numbering and replace them with a letter, and as they're mixed in with our normal numbers they don't need an apostrophe. Lower case letter 'a' represents ten and from there you count to fifteen which is 'f'. The only time we have to interact directly with a computer is to put in a binary password to validate a software program.

Alec – I've often wondered why passwords contain numbers and letters and I assumed it was for security reasons.

Bob – Going back to your maths, how do you treat infinity? Is it a number or another concept?

Alec – Infinity's neither odd nor even nor plus or minus so it can't be treated as a number. It's the symbol for something that's beyond our ability to measure.

Bob – I can understand plus infinity, but minus infinity's seems a bit weird.

Alec – Infinity at either end just means that you've reached an uncountable number. Unlike zero, infinity's the description of something that you can't normally do anything with.

Bob - I can see that maths would be in a different place without zero. But come to think of it, the old Roman numbers started at one and they didn't have any minuses.

Alec – Greek and Roman numbers went from 1 to 10,000 which they called a myriad. A myriad of myriads was sometimes mentioned but I don't think they ever found a practical use for it.

Bob - So there's a Hindu numbering system that had zero and arithmetic added to it. Where did the other bits come from?

Alec – They came about when Muslim scholars added 'al-jabr', or algebra, to the Hindu system and, strange as it seems, their Muslim religion strictly prohibited any use of al-jabr for science. They also developed trigonometry and the package became known as Hindu-Arabic mathematics. Six hundred years before Galileo a physicist and mathematician called Al-Biruni put forward the correct theory that the earth rotates around its own axis and he correctly measured its circumference.

Bob – Eventually modern maths comes to us. How?

Alec – We got wind of it when Spanish Muslim scholars visited universities like Oxford and Paris and for many years European Universities relied heavily on translations of their Moorish texts. What really got the ball rolling was the invention of the printing press by Gutenberg in 1450. This enabled the production of many copies of books which had previously been laboriously written by hand and led to the spread of all sorts of knowledge, including the Hindu-Arabic mathematics. Instruction books were published teaching people better ways to increase their business efficiency and mathematics gradually became a central part of many subjects.

Bob - Why wasn't countries in Europe involved in any of these developments of maths and science?

Alec – Probably because we were too busy fighting each other, but what's common to the three societies that developed maths and science?

Bob – You've got me there pal, let's see. Greek's, Hindu's, Muslim's and you want me to find a connection between them. Well Hindu and Muslim are religions, and although I think of Greece more as a civilisation, didn't they also have a multi-Gods religion. Is it religion you're looking for?

Alec – That's the one and it was their beliefs in different forms of Gods that gave these societies the strength and stability to make them long-lasting. The Greek Empire lasted from around 1,600 BC till 150BC when it merged with the Roman Empire. The Hindu religion grew out of ideas which had been prominent in India from 1750BC and it's still there today. Islam, the most recent, started in 610 AD at which time we were enjoying the pleasures of squabbling amongst ourselves in what's called The Dark Ages.

Bob – So for a thousand years after the fall of the Roman Empire its constant squabbling for us while the Hindus and Muslims get on with shaping the world.

Alec – There was another religion bubbling away under the surface, although it was more of an idea at the time rather than a fully formed religion.

Bob – You mean Christianity, but wasn't that born out of Judaism? And by the way clever clogs, how come you know so much about this? Don't tell me that you've been storing it up all this time in the hope that someone would question you about it? Maybe you fancy going on 'Who Want's to be a Millionaire,' or maybe you fancied yourself on Mastermind!

Alec – Wishful thinking laddie, if only my memory was still as good as that. Jimmy, our youngest grandson, asked me last year if I knew anything about the old religions. It turned out that his class had been given a project about ancient civilisations and his group's task for the term was to find out about their different religions. Like most kids nowadays he's a whiz at computing, well playing games on them, but sometimes an old dog like me can teach a pup a trick or two. He'd first asked his mother for help and, like a true daughter of Brenda, she pointed him at me. I showed Jimmy the best ways to search out the information he needed and helped him to put it together with a timeline. He seemed impressed that an old codger like me still had a wee bit of grey matter and I was really chuffed that he'd trusted me to help him out.

Bob – Our wee darlings only ever come to me when they've broken something and expect me to wave my fathers' magic wand and do the impossible. On the odd occasion, I'm able to solder a broken track or source a new part before they grab it off me and have another shot at its total destruction.

Alec – One thing that I did learn while helping Jimmy with his research was the debt of gratitude we owe to the Ancient Greeks.

Bob – Wasn't there a whole mass of Greek City States, but they seemed to be spread out in lands that I wouldn't associate with modern Greece.

Alec – To be a Greek back then meant that you were a citizen of a loose federation of over a thousand fiercely independent trading states that were scattered around the Med and Black Sea. The real hero we should be grateful to is Alexander the Great who settled in Egypt after running out of places to conquer and built a new city there called Alexandria

Bob – He was some boy wasn't he! I don't think he was King for very long but he created a vast empire that stretched from Gibraltar to India and he was responsible for Greek culture becoming widespread.

Alec – That he did, but his most important contribution was to knowledge. He set up the Great Library of Alexandria where scholars from all over the Greek world could come and work in safety. Up 'til then knowledge had been a state kept secret and was jealously guarded by Kings and their advisors. It's Alexander we have to thank for making all sorts of knowledge freely available to everyone.

Bob – I don't think that much of this ancient knowledge has survived to the present day. Didn't the library catch fire and almost everything in it was destroyed?

Alec – That's the popular myth, but when you dig into it that's all it is, a myth. The truth seems to be that after a few hundred years the King of Egypt put a lot of pressure on the Head Librarian who 'resigned' and the library went into a gradual decline which ended up with it being vandalised. Probably that's also when it was set on fire.

Bob – I'd imagine that passing information like that down the ages without books and manuscripts would have been a major problem. It reminds me of an old advert in a computer trade magazine about how easy it is to corrupt information as it's passed straight from mouth to mouth, never mind trying to pass it on down the ages.

Alec - I don't remember seeing that one, how did it go?

Bob - It started out with an officer in a First World War trench giving his runner a message to pass on to HQ. The message was pretty important. It was 'send reinforcements, we're going to advance' .After being passed on thru' three other runners, HQ received the message as 'Send three and four pence, we're going to a dance.'

Alec - As you said earlier, Christianity came out of Judaism which, according to the Bible started with God promising to make Abraham the father of a great nation even though they didn't have a patch of land of their own. During all their years of wandering they'd many prophets who foretold the coming of their Lord and one in particular made the biggest impact, Jesus of Nazareth. As the Roman Empire crumbled Christianity grew and Constantine, one of the last Emperors, converted to Christianity. With him the Roman Empire morphed into a Holy Roman Empire with its western HQ in Rome and the eastern one in Constantinople, named after you know who! It quickly became obvious that it's much more cost effective to staff an empire with a few thousand bishops and priests than trying to control it with huge costly armies.

Bob – I remember most of that from our years at Sunday school. Did knowledge of the Indo-Muslim maths spread slowly to the rest of Europe after the Moors conquered Spain?

Alec – No it didn't, and when the Christians re-conquered Spain they actually repressed the spread of Hindu-Arabic knowledge. That was the reason that The Renaissance, or Awakening, didn't start in Madrid but in the areas around Florence at the start of the thirteen hundreds. From there it slowly spread throughout the rest of Europe. The reason for Florence seems to be that when the Greek Empire was falling apart many of its scholars and philosophers relocated to Italy and settled in areas around Florence.

Bob – Did the Christian Church forbid the use of the new mathematics because they thought it might make the

Muslim religion appears to be more advanced that theirs?

Alec – The Church did a bit more than that. In their attempt to ensure that Christianity was the sole religion for the whole Roman Empire they classed everything else as pagan and burnt as many books and manuscripts as they could get their hands on. Including some that were priceless and nearly two thousand years old!

Bob – So the books and manuscripts that weren't destroyed along with the Library at Alexandria had to run the gauntlet a second time. How far back did these books and manuscripts go?

Alec – All the way back to a city state called Miletus and an erudite chap called Thales who set up a school of natural science there around 600BC. Miletus was a wealthy trading centre on the Mediterranean coast of what's now Turkey and it was one of the principal cities of the ancient Greek world. It had been set up 100 years earlier as a trading post with the Persian and Egyptian empires and grew to be the most important Greek city before the golden age of Athens and Sparta. Miletus was based on the Greek method of an open city with no hereditary rulers or priestly caste and it had the first parliament where people met to decide their own laws. It was there that Thales and his students came up with the revolutionary idea that the world might not be ruled by capricious gods and deities whose every whim must be catered for or they would extract a terrible revenge, but rather that it might be available to human reasoning. It was with this idea that our modern scientific world took its first baby steps. They also introduced an even more revolutionary idea, that the disciple or student should no longer be obliged to slavishly respect and share the ideas of his master but should be free to build on them without any fear of retribution and it was from this simple idea their knowledge grew at an ever increasing rate. Anaximander, their greatest thinker, came up with the revolutionary proposal that the Earth is floating in the sky which continues all round and below it. He understood that rainwater is water that's been evaporated up to the sky and the great variety of objects all around him must be built up from basic particles. It's also very likely that Pythagoras was one of his pupils. Another of his proposals was that plants and animals evolve to suit their environment and humans must have evolved from other animals

Bob – Amazing, he proposed all this 2,600 years ago and it's still valid today. Was society changing with these new ideas?

Alec – Yes, but there's a sting in the tale., Shortly after this the former rulers of the land returned with an army and the Miletans were badly defeated when they revolted against them. Miletus was razed to the ground.

Bob – That's a sad way to end a great idea, but was that the end of the story?

Alec – Twenty years later Athens returned with a larger fleet and defeated the Persians. They re-built and re-populated Miletus and it flourished again. It couldn't have been a land of milk and honey because fifty years later a Milesian called Leucippus moved to a safer haven called Abdera, a few hundred miles down the coast from what is now Istanbul and set up a new school there. Along with one of his pupils called Democritus they effectively founded the modern world. Democritus wrote dozens of books and manuscripts on every then known field of knowledge and proved that the world is available to reason. One of his books claimed that there are elementary substances that can be transformed into other substances by heating and therefore they couldn't be continuous. This was the start of atomic theory.

Bob – I've heard of Democritus, but I thought his work was in the political world.

Alec – You're probably confusing his name with democracy. Democritus and Leucippus proposed atoms and the space that they move around in. 'Space is boundless' they wrote, 'but importantly it has no centre'. They viewed atoms as the indivisible elementary grains of reality that everything apart from space is made up from. They wrote 'the only difference to an atom is its shape and how it combines with other atoms to produce the endless variety all around us'. 'Even all the lands, oceans and stars above us are made of the same atoms'. It's Democritus who spreads the word of all this and begins to clear away the myths and mysteries that had clouded people's thoughts up to then.

Bob – Did this knowledge spread quickly around the Greek world, and why did it take two thousand years before we were allowed a glimpse of it?

Alec – Leucippus and Democritus's ideas spread, but they weren't universally accepted and surprisingly it was Aristotle and Plato who were its main protagonists. They said that the Milesians' ideas were woolly and naturalistic and what's required is a world where everything has a direct purpose, rather that randomly combining where and when it wants. Plato didn't contradict Democritus directly, he wanted to know what the Earth gains from being round and central before he will believe it's true

Aristotle was an extraordinary scientist but in this case he was wrong and for centuries it was his and Plato's' mistaken views that prevailed over Leucippus and Democritus's more accurate knowledge. It took a lot of later effort to displace them and because of this we've been left with almost all of Aristotle's writings and mistaken beliefs and virtually nothing of Democritus. Our knowledge of the world might have started a lot earlier if it had been the other way around!

Bob – But wasn't this knowledge just speculation which they couldn't accept as it wasn't based on any hard facts?

Alec – That's true, but even this possible knowledge was denied to us for a long time and, when it did filter thru, the Roman Church put a ban on it. The Church's position throughout the ages has been that anything which doesn't agree with their creed that we are the sole children of God is a heresy. Even when the Hindu-Arabic maths was made available in 1299 the city fathers of Florence banned its use for all types of bookkeeping.

Bob – They probably had a point, but I take it that they eventually realised the advantages of the new system

Alec – They did and the new century marked the start of the Renaissance in Europe. As it grew, one of its main drivers was Johannes Gutenberg's development in 1450 of a more efficient method of printing using reusable metal type in a continuous press. This was the start of typeset once, print many and it was a real game changer. Gutenberg's innovation has every right to be regarded as one of the most important inventions of the second type in a continuous press. This was the start of typeset once, print many and it was a real game changer. Gutenberg's innovation has every right to be regarded as one of the most important inventions of the second millennium, but sadly he wasn't the one to profit from it. He owed money to his partner in the business and when he was unable to pay the printing press was snaffled as collateral and given to the backer's son-in-law.

Bob – Seems a bit unfair but I suppose that's life for you! Do you remember us watching a TV program called The Ascent of Man? I can still recall the amazing variety of life on Earth it showed us and the realisation of how ignorant we were about it. It got my attention right away by putting us in our place as johnnies-come-lately.

Alec – I remember it well. It was presented by Doctor Boronowski and the year would've been 1973 'cos that's when Brenda and I got hitched. Like you I can still remember the bit where he compared the four and a half billion years the Earth has been here to one of our Earthly years.

Bob – His take on it was that it took 'til the middle of March for our planet to form and cool down enough for life to begin but it wasn't 'til five minutes to midnight on the last day of the year before us humans put in an appearance. We watched it in our house and for about three months Saturday nights became a bit of a routine. Often some friends would drop in and we had some lively discussions over a few beers after the program.

Alec – Yes, 'til your Alice decided we were getting too noisy for the neighbours and chucked us out!

Third Hole   398 yards par 4 - Road Hole.

The third hole's a medium length slightly uphill par four with the road leading to the clubhouse crossing it about halfway to the green. The fairway dips down about a hundred yards before the green and rises quite sharply to just before it. Both hit reasonable drives which cleared the road then climbed into the golf cart and drove to where their golf balls lay almost side by side and waited for the green to clear.

Bob – I know that Gutenberg's printing press helped to spread the Renaissance, how did the scientific part of it start?

Alec – Mainly because early astronomers started questioning an Egyptian called Ptolemy whose fourteen hundred year old writings put our planet was at the centre of the Universe with everything else paying homage by rotating around us. In 1543 a Polish church worker called Nicolaus Copernicus proposed the idea that the Sun was central and all the planets circled around it at different distances. Long ago people had noticed that some planets occasionally stop moving forward and perform a backwards loop before returning to their original paths. Ptolemy created a model which attempted to explain this but it was very complicated as it had the Sun and other planets moving around us in two separate orbits. Copernicus updated Ptolemy's model and explained that the looping effect was simply caused by our faster moving Earth speeding past the slower moving outer planets.

Bob – I've heard of Ptolemy's universe, weren't they the clockwork models called Orrerys which had us at the centre with the Moon, Sun and the planets circling around us?

Alec - The earliest ones date from late BC and they continued to be refined until 1650 when the last one was made

Bob – I thought that the Church was very anti about ideas like Copernicus'. How did he avoid being burnt at the stake?

Alec - Copernicus came up with his main idea sometime around 1510 but didn't make it known 'til 1544 when he published it in a book called 'Concerning the Revolutions of the Heavenly Orbs'. He got away with it by conveniently dying before the Church had a chance to react against him.

Bob – Did it take a long time for Copernicus' ideas to spread to Western Europe.

Alec – Copernicus spent most of the thirty-four years between thinking about it and publishing by trying to prove his model mathematically, but in the end he'd to give up as his results were actually inferior to Ptolemy's. This idea that the Sun was central was taken up in Western Europe sixty-five years later by Johannes Kepler who published the three laws of interplanetary motion that we still use today. He showed that it was at last possible to calculate planetary orbits more accurately than the astronomers who lived in Alexandria 1,500 years earlier!

Bob – Did Galileo live at the same time as Kepler?

Alec – He did and was the person who proved that Copernicus was right by building the first astronomical telescope with around thirty times magnification. As well as observing the Heavens with it, Galileo promoted his telescope to Venice businessmen as a way for them to get early information about the cargoes their ships were bringing in.

Other amazing sights he saw was that there are many more stars in the sky than can be seen by the naked eye, the moon has mountains, Jupiter has four moons circling it and Venus waxes and wanes like our moon. He published his observations in a book called The Starry Messenger and it brought the wrath of The Roman Church down on his head. Claiming that our planet was only one of several circling the Sun was bad enough, but saying that our Sun was only one of many thousands was totally against the Church's creed that we're God's children and therefore central to everything. Possibly because he came from a prominent family they let him off lightly as long as he publicly recanted his heresies and remained under house arrest for the rest of his life

As the game in front had moved over to the next tee they lined up their second shots. Alec under-clubbed his and saw the ball spin back off the green and run down into the dip. Bob, feeling quite confident for the first time in several years, hit his ball past the hole and it spun back leaving him an almost level putt of about fifteen feet. After complimenting Bob on his shot, Alec took out another club and said, "I can't have you going three up after just three holes, I'll play my joker here.. Then, "Why didn't I do that the first time" as his ball stopped a foot short of the pin. Bob conceded Alec's putt after his attempt ran past the hole and their match was back to one hole. As they'd left the golf cart parked beside the next tee, they stood talking for a few minutes.

Bob – Does out modern knowledge start with Galileo?

Alec – Galileo's best remembered for having many brilliant insights, but by far his biggest contribution was to introduce the modern study of mechanics by observing actions, describing them mathematically and publishing the results so that everyone could check and confirm them for themselves. Like Alexander, he opened up science to everyone and I think there's general agreement that Galileo marks the point where the modern scientific method started.

Bob – Wasn't it Galileo who introduced the reasoning that you can't prove that a theory's correct, all that you can prove is that it's not wrong?

Alec – I don't think I've heard of that.

Bob – Recently I read somewhere that if you want the ultimate proof that your theory's correct you'll have to wait till the end of time as it's possible that future knowledge could prove it wrong. All you can safely say is, as far as we know it's not wrong. Now all scientific proofs come with the health warning – as far as we presently know.

Alec – Is that why if someone puts up a hypothesis it must be capable of being proved wrong before it can move on to be considered as a possibly proven theory?

Bob –My understanding is that if you want to get your theory to the starting gate it's got to make predictions that can be falsified.

Alec – OK, but in what way?

Bob – Suppose you put up a theory that there's an army of little green men massing on Mars while they prepare to attack Earth. That could be checked quite easily and would be proof that your theory's not correct. However, if you said that they're massing on a planet just outside the

Universe you'd have a theory that couldn't be falsified as we've no access to outside the Universe. If a theory doesn't pass that test it won't make it to first base. I remember when we were young you had a theory that the favourite horse seldom wins the Grand National so it's better to put your money on rank outsiders. Unfortunately most of the horses proved your theory wrong by falling at the first few fences.

Alec – That was apart from Foinavon who won the race for me at 100 to 1 when most of the others fell!

Bob – I'll give you that one, but didn't you draw it in the bank's sweepstake and you'd so much faith in it that you gave the horse for Brenda to cheer on. She naturally claimed the winnings and bought a lovely pair of curtains she'd been lusting after which left me with a problem. She took Alice with her and the crafty sod of a salesman also sold her a pair

Alec - Do you still get your tips for the Grand National from your cousin Billy? He's given you some crackers over the years, hasn't he?

Bob – Remember Anglo? I phoned Billy B on the morning of the race and he told me to put my shirt on it as it's a cert for at least a place!

Alec – So you got him to put a pound each way on it for you and found out just before the race that it was a fifty to one outsider.

Bob – I did, and if it hadn't won I'd have had endure weeks of earache. At the time we were saving like mad for a new house and I didn't dare tell Alice that I'd splashed out a couple of pounds 'cos cousin Billy said it was a cert. It gave our bank balance a nice boost and I nearly got Alice to agree that when we get the new house we'll name it Anglo instead of plain old number seventy eight.

Alec – I remember he tipped Red Rum to win and it obliged us on more than one occasion. And then there was another few horses with colours in their name that won on his say-so.

Bob – It was actually his sister Margaret who'd the 'colour in the horse's name' theory following Red Alligator's win, but between them we'd quite a run in the seventies and eighties and had some happy nights out on the winnings. Anyway going back to Galileo, didn't he invent relativity long before Einstein got there.

Alec – He did although he didn't call it relativity. He pictured a woman standing on a pier and tossing a ball in the air then catching it. While she's doing this a boat sails past in a straight line and at a constant speed with a man on its deck doing the same thing. Galileo asks them, "Which one of you is moving and which one is standing still?" The woman says "It's obviously me, I'm on dry land and my ball's going straight up and down." The man chips in with, "My ball's also going straight up and down so I think it must be me." Galileo tells them that they're both correct.as they're standing still with respect to themselves, but are moving relative to each other. The woman says, "That's nonsense, I'm on solid land and I can clearly see that it's the boat that's moving." The man counters with, "When I look I see the land moving past me." From this simple thought process Galileo deduced the amazing insight that everything in the Universe must be moving relative to everything else and, as the Miletans wrote two thousand years earlier, 'it's impossible for there to be a static central point that we can measure all our movements against' so everything in the Universe can only be measured relative to something else.

Bob – Galileo certainly opened our eyes to the wonders of the world.

Alec – The easiest way to make sense of the Universe not having a central point is for us to claim that we're at the centre of it because everything else is moving relative to us.

Bob – That must mean that every other point in the Universe can also say the same. How does that tie in with the theory that the Universe started out from a Big Bang?

Alec – There's several different theories about that, but the main one says that the Universe started out from a microscopic dot and created all of the space around us by expanding equally in every direction.

Bob – If space is expanding equally in all directions, surely that means that everything must be expanding from the microscopic dot!

Alec - The Big bang wasn't an explosion of matter moving outward to fill an empty universe. It was space itself expanding and increasing the physical distances between moving bits of matter. The Big Bang isn't an explosion in space, it was the expansion of space itself.

Bob – What happened to the microscopic dot?

Alec – Apparently the microscopic dot ceased to exist the instant The Big Bang started and the theory says that there's nothing that we can use to distinguish one point in space from any other point.

Bob – Going back to Galileo, he had his finger in lots of pies and was very observant as well as logical. Wasn't he sitting in church one day when he noticed that the candle-

Lantern's hanging on chains from the ceiling were swinging in a breeze?

Alec - What intrigued him was that they weren't all swinging to the same rhythm, so counting with his pulse he noted each one's swing duration. Back in his workshop he experimented and found that the timing of each lamp's swing depended solely on the length of the chain it was hanging on. This simple insight gave us the pendulum clocks which were our standard timekeepers 'til the 1930s. The story goes that one day he climbed to the top of the Leaning Tower of Pisa and dropped two unequal weights then worked out that if he allowed for the atmospheres resistance, both weights would've landed at the same time.

Bob - How did he manage to remove the air's resistance?

Alec - Like Newton's apple it's probably a hoary story that he used to illustrate a point. It's more likely that he worked this out when he was rolling balls of different weights down sloping channels and noticed that they took exactly the same roll time. He watched as the balls flew off the edge of a table and came up with a formula which exactly predicted the curve that each ball would take as it fell. He also recognized that light must travel in a straight line and even tried to measure its speed

Bob - Galileo Galilei, a man with so many insights in his life. I suppose it's only fair to say that the modern world started with him!

Alec – He gets most of the plaudits, but there were others who made telling contributions and we've already talked about the main one, Johannes Kepler. He worked as an assistant to a rich Danish nobleman called Tycho Brahe who was probably the last of the plain sight astronomers who worked without the aid of a telescope. Rather than astronomy Tycho was famous as the man with the gold and silver nose which he wore on ceremonial occasions to replace his own which had been sliced off in a drunken duel with a cousin to decide which of them was the better mathematician. Tycho developed a strange theory that the Sun and Moon were orbiting us and the rest of the planets were going round the Sun.

Bob – How on earth did he manage to keep the planets from crashing into each other?

Alec – I've no idea and his model universe was a backward step from Copernicus's earlier system. Maybe losing his nose made him careful with his life and keeping the Earth central so it wouldn't annoy the Church probably made excellent sense to him. When Tycho died in 1601 Kepler 'borrowed' his observations and used them to work out the three laws that are still in use today. He turned Copernicus' static solar system into a moving one with the central Sun pushing the planets around it in elliptical orbits. Fifty years later, Isaac Newton expanded Kepler's laws and explained that it wasn't the Sun that was pushing the planets around, it was the Sun's attractive force that was pulling them inward. All the planets remain in stable orbits because the Sun's attractive pull is being exactly balanced by each planets forward motion which is trying to make it leave its orbit and shoot off in a straight line.

Bob - Isaac Newton, now there's another thinker and a half. Didn't Albert Einstein reckon he was the cleverest man who ever lived?

Alec – Galileo might've disputed that, but we can't overstate Newton's contribution to science. Almost on his-own he established the basis of Classical Mechanics which ruled the roost for the next two hundred odd years. In 1665 he went home from his university to escape the Bubonic Plague and, as the story goes, while he was sitting in the orchard he asked himself, "Why do the apples from my apple tree always fall straight down?" Years later he said that this thought made him realise that because everything falls straight down, our planet must have an attractive force which, for mathematical purposes, could be concentrated down to a single point at its centre.

Bob – The Greeks had noticed this before, but they attributed it to everything wanting to find its natural place.

Alec – Newton's genius was to look at it from a different angle, mainly Kepler's.

Bob - Did he unite the three laws that Kepler had discovered.

Alec – At the time he may, or may not, have used an apple as a substitute for all earthly matter falling down toward the centre of our planet, but, however he got there, he had the earth shattering thought that if the 'apple' was falling straight down to a point located at the centre, then so must our Moon be falling down towards it. The only difference between the apple and the Moon was that the apple was stationary with respect to the Earth whereas the Moon was moving around with it. He used this idea to reason that our Moon must be located at the distance where its forward movement and Earth's downward pull are exactly matched and then applied Kepler's laws to it.

Bob – So Newton's great insight was to realise that because our force of gravity could be taken right down to a single point at the centre of the Earth it must also be the same for all the other planets, including the Sun. With this simple thought he reasoned that if he could calculate the mass of any object in our solar system, he could use a simple law to calculate the gravitational force there would be between it and any other object.

Alec – I know that he used this idea to calculate the amount of force that Jupiter's experiencing from the Sun's gravity and worked out that it's the same force that's keeping its four moons in orbit. From this he concluded that gravity must be the single force that's keeping everything in our solar system in place. He expanded this idea and showed that gravity's also the force which governs the entire universe and it's a revolution. It unites the Earth with the Heavens, and once again proves that the Universe can't have a centre around which everything is revolving.

Bob – I know that by using Newton's equations two new planets were discovered in our solar system, but didn't some jealous people at the time consider Newton to be lucky rather than brilliant as there's only one universal law and he was the lucky person to find it.

Alec – Pure green cheese, everyone else had the same opportunities as Newton. Another reason that Newton reigns supreme is altho' it was Galileo who developed the use of the telescope it was a long cumbersome tube. Newton used his laws of optics to reduce the tube down to one tenth of Galileo's length by using mirrors to reflect the light inside the tube and made it a much more efficient and easier to use telescope.

Bob – Tho' wasn't Newton a strange chap and his theory of gravity only came to light because one of the few people he regarded as almost his intellectual equal took on a challenge that he could get proof of why planets don't go round the Sun in circles?

Alec – That's how the story goes. After a Royal Society meeting in 1684 where the problem under discussion was the lack of a scientific proof of Kepler's assertion that planets move around the Sun in ellipses, three of the then giants of science, Christopher Wren, Edmund Halley and Robert Hooke, went round to a coffee house just off Fleet Street in London to mull over the problem. In an effort to solve it Wren offered a cash prize to whoever could provide a full proof that the shape of all the planetary orbits was elliptical rather than circular. Hooke said that he'd already worked out the proof, but was keeping his calculations secret so that others might have the pleasure of attempting them. Halley called him out by saying that someone he knew had already provided the proof of it!

Bob - You're kidding, or could it be that something stronger than coffee was being consumed?

Alec – History doesn't say, but Halley was serious enough to take a hot, dusty coach ride to Cambridge and ask Newton if Kepler was correct. Newton immediately told him that the planetary curves would be ellipses and he'd worked it out eighteen years previously. He started shuffling thru' a mass of papers on his desk, but couldn't find his calculations so he assured Halley that he would redo them and send him a copy. He was as good as his word and a few months later Halley received not one, but two proofs showing why all the planets move round the Sun in ellipses. The first was a full eighty page geometric proof and the other was on just three pages using Newton's new mathematical invention called Calculus. Halley read them and wrote back telling Newton that this proof was of such importance that it should be published immediately. Newton replied that although it was adequate, it wasn't quite complete. He promised that once it was he would send Halley a copy.

Bob – Typical example of Newton's obsession with secrecy. Who collected the prize money, Halley or Hooke?

Alec – History doesn't say, but eighteen months later Halley got a manuscript of the first of Newton's three great gifts to the world. All were written in Latin and are referred to as 'The Principia'. The complete set was published in 1687, but being very radical the scientific community was slow to accept them. The three volumes provided a complete proof of how every object in the Universe moves and they're still good enough to land an astronaut precisely on any spot on the moon. Halley then helped to prove that Newton was correct by calculating that several recently sighted comets were in fact the same one returning after a whirl around the solar system. He predicted the date of its next return but died before it came and the comet, which is due a re-visit to us in 2062, still bears his name. Within ten years of The Principia being published a completely new science called Classical Mechanics had been developed.

Bob – You mean that if Hooke hadn't boasted that he'd a proof, Halley wouldn't have visited Newton who might never have published his masterpiece?

Alec – It seems that way. Newton later explained that he'd worked out most of Kepler's theory, but for some reason he hadn't taken it to its final conclusion. Newton's remembered first and foremost as a mathematician, but he was a bit of a loner and, as you said, quite a strange chap.

Bob – We tend to think that he was born a genius, but I know that one of his early teachers described him as 'inattentive and idle'. When he was sixteen his mother decided that more learning was a waste of time and brought him home to learn how to manage the family farm.

Alec – How did that work out?

Bob – Newton wasn't a farmer and was so bad at it that his mother cut her losses by sending him back to school Maybe it was the thought of being a farmer for life, but when he returned to school he applied himself and in just one year gained enough qualifications for entry into Cambridge, his local University.

Alec – I know that he studied at Trinity College while at Cambridge which was strange given his religious beliefs and he was appointed as a Fellow of the College.

Bob – He kept working on his view of gravity, but was still obsessively secretive and told no one about it. While he was developing the maths that would prove his theory he invented a new way of calculating how things change with time and called it fluxations, but it quickly came to be known as calculus. Newton passionately hated the idea of being involved in any arguments, but his secrecy obsession backfired and he became embroiled in the biggest mathematical argument ever, the Europe wide dispute over who invented calculus! His papers show that he was calculating with it 1666, but he didn't tell the world about it 'til decades later and, even then, it was just as a minor description at the back of one of his Principia publications. Gottlieb Leibnitz, a German mathematician, started working on it independently eight years after Newton and published his paper on it before Newton. Priority on any invention is usually given to the first person to publish so this time Newton's secretiveness meant that he was left out in the cold.

Alec – Didn't Newton and Steven Hawking occupy the same chair at Cambridge University, but obviously not at the same time?

Bob – When Newton started at Cambridge the chair of Lucasian Professor of Mathematics was Isaac Barrow who was one of the few people at Cambridge he trusted.so he asked him for his opinion on his paper. Barrow read it and asked Newton for his permission to pass it on to a common friend of theirs, John Collins, a top rated mathematician. Newton gave his consent, but asked that no mention should be made of where the paper came from. Collins read it and commented very favourably so Barrow replied telling him of his pleasure that Collins had formed the same favourable opinion of the paper that he had. After getting the go ahead, he then told Collins that the author was Newton, a fellow of their college who was in his second year of a Master of Arts degree course and that he had an unparalleled genius for this branch of mathematics. Subsequently when Barrow resigned his chair he was instrumental in securing the twenty-six year old Newton's election as his successor which he held from 1669 'til 1702.

Alec – Hawking held it from 1979 'til 2008 and it's probably because it's linked to Newton that it's become the most prestigious maths chair in the world.

Bob – Being a professor wasn't something that Newton particularly enjoyed. Especially so was the requirement that he had to provide a two hour open lecture on a subject of his choosing every week. His lectures, like the courses he offered, weren't popular nor were they well attended. As a result he often ended up lecturing to an empty classroom.

Alec – We tend to think of him as a genius who worked day and night trying to resolve the deep scientific problems of the age. However, it turned out that he'd spent most of his time at Cambridge studying the Bible and doing dodgy alchemy experiments in his garden shed.

Bob – I never realised that. He's always pictured as a heroic figure sitting at his desk deep in thought!

Alec – Most people who came into contact with him must have thought the same, but he'd a vile temper when crossed and an unshakeable conviction that he was God's messenger on Earth. Despite this he became President of The Royal Society and for eighteen years was Warden of the Royal Mint where he completely revolutionised Britain's monetary system. After he died a bishop was sent to go thru' his private papers for posterity and was scandalised to find that Newton, who was supposedly a loyal adherent of the Church of England, had been a Unitarian all his life.

Bob – So Newton's a Unitarian, what's wrong with that? After all he's still a Christian isn't he?

Alec - Things were different in those days and for most people religion wasn't optional. Back in 1530 the Pope had refused to give King Henry the Eighth a divorce from his first wife, so he told him to go stuff himself and founded his own church. To make certain of his divorce he named it The Church of England and declared himself as its Head. Later, during a time of religious intolerance, King Charles the Second decreed that anyone who wasn't a full member of The Church of England and didn't fully subscribe to the Holy Trinity of Father, Son and Holy Ghost would be considered to be unfit to hold any government appointments.

Bob – Father, Son and Holy Ghost, now there's a blast from the past! It takes me back to our annual pilgrimage to Ireland for the Cork Jazz Festival and meeting up with Gerry Drew and his sidekick, Mad Mick from Mullingar!

Alec – That pair were something else weren't they? Gerry never told us why, but for some reason he was very anti the Church in Ireland and he'd a fund of hilarious stories about it.

Bob – I wish I could remember even half of them, but quite a few of them included the Holy Trinity which he always referred to as Dad, Lad and Smokey. And boy, could that pair sup their Guinness!

Alec – Mick usually played the trombone, or as he called it, his sludge pump. He told us that his true love was the banjo and he was quite good at it 'til one day someone told him that the mark of a true gentleman was someone who *can* play the banjo, but chooses not to! Like most things in his life, Newton deeply researched religion, but kept his beliefs to himself. He was an avid reader and interpreter of the Christian Bible and came up with a personal religion in which one God was supreme and as the Master Creator he didn't come in three separate parts. It appears that he didn't believe that anyone has an immortal soul or a personal devil, nor that the dead reside in Heaven and come back as good or malignant spirits.

Bob – It's amazing that all thru' his life he was able to

keep this secret. What happened after he died, did they hush the whole thing up? It certainly wouldn't have looked good if after he'd been given a Christian funeral they had to dig his coffin up and whisk him out of Westminster Abbey.

Alec – Newton had a long life and lived to be eighty-four. After his death I don't think Trinity College went out of its way to publicise his beliefs.

Bob – I read that at his funeral in Westminster Abbey his epitaph was read out by Alexander Pope who was the leading poet of the day and part of it's engraved on his tomb. I think it goes something like 'Nature and nature's laws lay hidden in night. God said let Newton be and all was light.

Alec – As you said it's very hard to overstate Newton's contributions to our modern world. Two hundred and fifty years ago he told us that you can take a pebble on the beach and, even when it's lying there minding its own business, it'll always have the properties of where it's located and how fast it's moving. But not only that, the pebble will always have these properties until a force is applied to change them.

Bob – Are you sure that's right?

Alec – Galileo's relativity tells us that nothing in the Universe is static and everything's moving relative to everything else and this applies to all the pebbles on all the beaches. Each pebble isn't moving relative to our planet, but it's moving relative to the Sun, Moon, the other planets and all the stars in the Universe. Newton's equations will tell you exactly where that pebble will land if you pick it up and supply his equations with the force and angle you throw it. If you turn that round and are a champion shot putter, it'll tell you what angle and force you'll have to give the shot if you want to set a new world record. It's an amazing insight because this applies not only pebbles and shots, but to everything anywhere in the Universe.

Bob – I think we've all enjoyed throwing pebbles on the beach but what in particular distinguishes him from all the other brilliant scientists?

Alec –Newton's greatness comes from being the person who created a whole new language called mathematical analysis which allows us to exactly describe almost everything that's within the reach of our human senses. Everyone knows that Newton didn't discover gravity as its effects must have been obvious to the earliest humans, but he was the first to explain what it was and give a 'sort-of' explanation of how it works.

Bob – Is his mathematical analysis what's now known as Classical Mechanics?

Alec – It is and it describes perfectly why the balls that Galileo dropped from the Tower of Pisa would fall at the same rate if we'd no atmosphere, why the moon goes round us in just under twenty-eight days and why our planet performs an ellipse round the Sun once a year. Apart from Mercury, it describes the orbits of the other planets and how all the objects in the Universe, from our pebble on the beach to superclusters of galaxies, are interlinked. A prediction of his Law was that there must be two undiscovered planets in our solar system and it told astronomers where to go and look for them. It was Newton who brought Uranus and Neptune into our planetary family.

Bob – Why didn't his law cover Mercury?

Alec – Mercury's a strange wee planet which is about the same size as our moon and it doesn't have a fixed orbit, it 'corkscrews' slowly up the face of the Sun. Newton's Law says that it should have a stable fixed orbit, but for once it didn't agree with our observations.

Bob – Surely that makes Newton's Law not a Law because it's been proved to be false?

Alec – In theory yes, but in practice no. We know precisely what the law describes and precisely why in some circumstances it fails. We now know that the reason it fails in this case is because Mercury's the nearest planet to the Sun and that allows all the other planets to heap their relatively small gravitational forces onto it. This is just sufficient to counter a tiny bit of the Sun's massive gravity and Mercury wobbles up its face.

Bob – I'm still confused. Newton used Galileo's theory which said that objects of different weights drop at the same speed in our gravity field. Wouldn't that mean that it doesn't matter whether we drop used toilet paper or cannon balls, gravity will attract them with the same force?

Alec – Common sense tells us that can't be true, but in this case common sense is wrong. All mass, or weight as we experience it, is equally affected by the force of gravity which is the one standard force. The only thing that affects gravity is distance as its force decreases the further you are away from it.

Bob – Is that the law that says if you double the distance, you only get a quarter of the force?

Alec – And if you triple the distance you only get one ninth of the force. The evenness of gravity's been proved on the moon by an astronaut dropping a hammer and a feather at the same time, and as the moon has no atmosphere to slow the feather down they both landed on the surface at the same time. I think the video of this is still available on You Tube.

Bob – So if everything throughout the Universe falls at the same speed, can we take this as early proof that gravity can't be the force which gives objects their heaviness? Are there any other ideas where cannon balls and feathers' weight might've come from?

Alec – Weight, or more strictly speaking mass, was a problem that stumped science for three hundred years and it's taken a lot of modern ideas and loads of money to resolve.

Bob - What was Newton's take on time?

Alec - Newton's view was that the Universe is composed of two separate things, matter and space. Matter's what we experience all around us and space is empty apart from invisible particles which he called corpuscles. Their sole purpose is to carry light throughout the Universe. His take on time was that its controlled by God and it ticks away endlessly in the background counting down the seconds from His creation 'til the end of time.

Bob – That reminds me of a birthday present you gave me last year and told me that it's a must read book called The End of Time.

Alec – That's the one written by Julian Barbour and it looked to be a good follow-up to Stephen Hawking's Brief History of Time, but I've a confession to make. I read it before I gave it to you. I skimmed thru' the first few pages in the bookshop then read another snippet or two on the way home and before I knew it I'd reached the end. Sorry, I should have told you at the time even though I knew it wouldn't bother you.

Bob – I really enjoyed reading the book and when you seemed to know so much about it I assumed that you'd bought a copy for yourself. Didn't Barbour depict Newton's idea of time as being similar to a cricket match where all the action's taking place on the pitch, but time's a totally separate entity that's being kept by a clock high up on the grandstand.

Alec - Barbour had a different take on time from Newton didn't he? His view was that time's simply a measure of change so if nothing changes, then neither does time. He compared Newton's cricket match time to a game of rugby, or American football, where time's part of the game and under the control of a referee who can stop and re-start it to allow decisions to be confirmed or injuries attended to. Newton's time by comparison is forever fixed and isn't a physical part of the Universe whereas Barbour's time isn't constant, but is linked to all the actions taking place throughout the Universe.

Bob – I remember Barbour recounting a conversation he'd had with an eminent physicist who he had asked for his definition of time. The reply he got was that time is what the super-accurate clock in the National Physical Laboratory tells us it is. My first thought was surely that's a cop-out, but he was probably very wise and didn't want to be drawn into a discussion as to what actually constitutes time.

Alec – Until I read Julian Barbour's book I'd assumed that time was like the eminent physicist's description and forever fixed like Newton's grandstand clock, but even now there's no general agreement on how we can describe time.

Fourth Hole   444 yards par 4 - Mount Zion.

This hole plays as the longest on the course as it's uphill all the way except for the last twenty five yards. The first half of the hole is a steep climb which switches to a moderate one before levelling off as you approach the green. It's the only hole on the course that doesn't have a bunker and the fairway's quite generous except when you reach the crest of the steep hill where it narrows down to a neck of around thirty yards.

During their chat they'd been watching the group in front searching among some trees on the right-hand side of the fairway. Eventually a ball was found and after a couple of swipes it was lifted. The group walked over to the other balls which were spread across the fairway with the fourth member going forward to check when it was safe to play. The hole plays much longer than its yardage as it takes two mighty swipes for the average golfer to get there in two shots. As there was no chance of any of them reaching the green from where they were they waited 'til the players in the group ahead approached the green before continuing. The rightmost golfer who'd obviously sliced his drive to the edge of the fairway sliced his second shot into a patch of deep rough and Alec's opinion was that they may as well wait in case he decides to come back and replay the shot.

Bob – Isaac Newton's picture of a static steady state universe was valid right up till 1905 when Einstein changed the world by having four revolutionary papers published in a respected German physics journal in just five months. His first paper delivered proof of an earlier theory that light comes in small chunks rather than in a continuous stream. The second one explained that the constant motion of pollen grains in water is caused by water atoms bumping into them. The third paper expanded Galileo's view of relativity and his last paper introduced the famous $E = mc^2$ equation.

Alec – That he did and his first paper showing that light's made up of waves and particles got him a Nobel Prize sixteen years later. The second paper provided conclusive proof that atoms exist and the last two completely changed our world view forever. There was over two hundred and forty years between the great leap of knowledge from Newton to Einstein, but in between them there was a steep learning curve that had to be negotiated before getting from one to the other.

Bob – Another reason Newton's regarded as very special is because he re-introduced the idea of invariance. Galileo started it by saying that no place or person is special and Newton extended this to include the Universe and everything in it. Invariance tells us that no matter where you are you'll always see the same laws and views around you. Newton's invariance had been gospel for two hundred years before it was challenged by a Scottish mathematician called James Clerk Maxwell who in four equations explained everything there is to know about electricity, magnetism and light. The equations were well received, but problems cropped up when it was realised that they didn't agree with Newton's invariance.

Alec – I know a bit about Maxwell. Back at the Uni. we'd to solve some of his electromagnetic equations and I found them very challenging. Although he hadn't explicitly set out to find it, didn't the exact speed of light fall out of them?

Bob – Richard Feynman, an American and one of the giants of physics commented, "Taking the long view of the history of the human race, in ten thousand years people looking back will judge that the most significant event of the 19th century will be Maxwell's discovery of the Laws of Electrodynamics." He said that their American Civil War which took place at the same time, "Will pale into provincial insignificance in comparison with this important event.

Alec – Didn't Michael Faraday have a big hand in it?

Bob – Without Faraday's experimental genius Maxwell wouldn't have had access to the crucial insights he needed. Stephen Hawking said that all knowledge comes as the result of scientists standing on previous giant's shoulders. Maxwell stood on Faraday's shoulders then Einstein stood on his and another man's shoulders to work out his relativity theories.

Alec – Didn't Faraday and Maxwell replace Newton's old idea that light is made up of corpuscles, whatever they were.

Bob – Whatever they were, they weren't the waves that we now know that lights made up of.

Alec - I've heard the name of Thomas Young as having something to do with a toy that changed how we think of light. Did he also provide a shoulder?

Bob – Young was an English doctor who took the first step that Faraday needed to explain light. In 1801 he set up a tank of water and watched how different waves in it interacted with each other, particularly when he dropped two stones into it at the same time. Next he took a piece of card with two small pinholes cut close together then shone a light and projected the image onto a screen. Over a hundred years earlier Newton had insisted that only particles and space existed and Young knew that if Newton was right the corpuscles of light would stream half thru' each slit and show up as two blobs on the screen. Instead what he saw was a series of light and dark stripes across the screen and he immediately realised that the only possible explanation for this was that the particles of light were going thru' both pinholes at the same time and interacting like the two stones he dropped at the same time into his water tank. The stones had created water waves and it seemed that that the two pin holes were similarly creating light waves. So light must travel as waves and not as corpuscle-like particles!

Alec – Was this the same Thomas Young who deciphered the stone tablet that had a translation of Egyptian hieroglyphs into Greek letters chiselled on it?

Bob – The very chap.

Alec – He was involved in all sorts of things wasn't he?

Bob - He excelled at almost every subject he took an interest in, tho' surprisingly he trained as a doctor but had to give it up as he was useless at comforting his patients. He was a brilliant linguist who joined the Royal Society as a lecturer and published discoveries in almost every field he studied. He's regarded as the last man who understood everything that science had a hand in at the time.

Alec – I've always had the impression that he was an archaeologist who worked out in the Middle East.

Bob - He played a key role in deciphering the Rosetta

Stone, but the work was carried out at the Royal Society, not where it was discovered at Heliopolis in Egypt. Among his many other discoveries he was the first person to propose that our vision's made up of only three colours and this wasn't finally confirmed 'til a hundred and fifty years later. It may have been that he wasn't the first person to do the double pinhole experiment, but he was the first to understand what it meant and give a rational explanation of it.

Alec – You'd think that in the hundred and twenty years between Newton and Young someone would have been playing about with what's essentially a kid's toy and noticed that it didn't agree with Newton's idea of light being some sort of particles flying thru' space.

Bob – Young based his insight on what happened when he dropped two stones into a water tank at the same time and watched the ripples spreading out. He saw that where they met crest to crest they doubled up and where they meet crest to trough they cancelled each other out. Newton's proposal was that light's a stream of particles moving thru' space and Young showed that if light's a particle it moves thru' space just like a wave travelling thru' water!

Alec – Young showed that light was waves travelling thru' space, but waves of what?

Bob – He assumed they must be waves of energy 'cos he also proposed that the different colours we see are due to light having different amounts of energy. That's them moved on at last so it's safe for us to go.

Alec hit first and smacked his ball straight up the middle to around 50 yards short of the hilltop marker post. Bob tried to match him, but he sliced his ball into the second cut of rough ten yards behind Alec's. They motored up to the top of the hill from where they could see the four ahead watching the players in front of them putting out. "May as well sit here and wait 'til they've cleared the green and next tee." said Alec. Bob took a club out of his bag and walked over to check how his ball was lying in the rough.

Bob - It's sitting up quite nicely over there so I think I'll have a go with my driver. I'd be less likely to sky it than with my three or five wood.

Alec – You said that Thomas Young lectured at The Royal Society in the early 1800s, would Michael Faraday be there at the same time as him?

Bob – Let's see. Young was elected to the Royal Society in 1794 and was its Secretary from 1804 'til his death in 1829. Faraday started as a Chemical Assistant in 1813 so I think it's safe to assume that their paths must've crossed at some point. Tho' talking of Faraday, a Danish physicist called Hans Christian Orsted could've stolen much of his thunder.

Alec - Orsted, the name doesn't ring a bell. What did he discover?

Bob – In 1820 he was looking for a better way to explain electricity to a class of students. He set up a battery, a length of resistance wire and a compass, but got called away and was unable to pre-test the setup. During the lecture he told his students that they should watch the compass needle closely as he wanted to demonstrate a new idea. The students noticed that the needle flicked towards the wire when he connected the battery but were totally unimpressed. Orsted was disappointed so he put the experiment to the back of his mind and moved on to other things. Eleven years later Michael Faraday performed the same experiment and discovered electromagnetic induction.

Alec – Wouldn't it be fairer to say that it was Orsted who discovered this induction?

Bob – No, I think it's only right that Faraday should get the kudos because he was the one who proved why the compass needle twitched. His explanation was that it was being momentarily attracted by a magnetic field created in the wire by the rapid change in the electric current as it builds up. The magnetic field disappears once the current is fully built and the compass needle swings back to point at north. To prove it he performed the experiment in reverse and showed that moving a magnet thru' a coil of wire produces a similar electric current in the wire which also disappears when you stop moving the magnet. Ten years later he showed that magnetism influences light and that electricity, magnetism and light are very closely related.

Alec – From what I've read of him Michael Faraday was the sort of guy that you'd be at ease with. He comes across as a very modest, self-assured chap who was happy in his job and worked hard all his life to spread scientific knowledge. He was the person who started the Royal Society's Friday and Children's Christmas Lectures and they're still running nearly two centuries later. He could have no greater accolade than to have his portrait, along with Newton and Maxwell, hanging on Albert Einstein's study wall to give him inspiration.

Bob – He'd an amazing life. He was born the son of a poor rural blacksmith and had only a very basic education. When he was sixteen he joined his brother in London and got a job as an apprentice bookbinder which was an ideal job for him as he was able self-educate by reading the books he was binding. One day a customer noticed this and asked if he would like a ticket to a lecture at the Royal Society. Faraday enjoyed the lecture and was very impressed with the lecturer, Sir Humphry Davy, inventor of the miner's safety lamp. Science fascinated him and he became a regular attendee. He wrote up some of Sir Humphrey's lectures, bound them and presented the book to the great man. Sir Humphrey was quick to size up Faraday as someone with a sharp incisive mind and when his chemical assistant at the Society blotted his copybook, Davy offered the position to Faraday.

Alec – That's quite a step from an uneducated son of a countryside blacksmith to become a chemical assistant at The Royal Society in how many years?

Bob – Let's see. He was sixteen when he moved to London in 1807 and six years later he was Humphry Davy's chemical assistant. I think meteoric would be the only way to describe it. He quickly found that Sir Humphrey wasn't a very pleasant man to work with, but he was in seventh heaven working in the Society's labs and quickly blossomed into the greatest experimental inventor who's ever lived. Among his many discoveries are the electro-magnetic force field, magnetic field lines and the electromagnetic properties of matter, along with electromagnetic induction. He invented the electric motor and generator, proved that electricity and magnetism are two parts the same force and demonstrated many important chemical reactions and processes. He was at the Royal Society for fifty-four years and was made a member. He was later promoted to be the society's Professor of Chemistry and was twice offered Newton's old position as President but on both occasions he declined. He was regularly called on by the Government and private industry as an expert witness and, all things considered, he didn't do too badly for an uneducated book-binder's apprentice.

Alec – Michael Faraday's an outstanding example of being the right person in the right place at the right time. But I think that he'd be a pretty unique exception because back then it must have been well neigh impossible to be a scientist without a formal education and the necessary moolah to ease your way thru' life.

Bob - He was offered a knighthood by Queen Victoria and turned that down as well. She and the Prime Minister attended one of his lectures on electricity and the answers he gave to them shows the worth of the man. On being presented to Her Majesty he was asked "Mr. Faraday, of what use is your invention." His reply was "Your Majesty, of what use is a baby?" William Gladstone, then Prime Minister, questioned him about possible uses for electricity saying "But after all Mr. Faraday, for what use is it." Faraday replied "Sir, there's every probability that you will soon be able to place a tax on it." Good fortune smiled on Michael Faraday not once, but twice. However the second time was because of the unfortunate circumstances suffered by another person.

Alec – I'd have enjoyed watching the Queen and Prime Ministers' faces as Faraday replied to their questions. It's a pity that TV reporting wasn't around back then to record their wee chat for posterity. But who was the unlucky guy?

Bob – He was the aforementioned James Clerk Maxwell and an example of how something that seemed at the time to be an unlucky decision can change the course of science. Maxwell was a clever and curious boy who published his first scientific paper when he was only fourteen. He studied at Edinburgh and Cambridge Universities and after graduating was recruited by Marischal College in Aberdeen as their Professor of Physics. While he was there he studied the rings around Saturn and wrote a very detailed paper on how they're able to stay in place. However shortly after this was published a decision was made that Aberdeen would be better served by merging its two colleges into a University and Maxwell, being the Junior Professor, got the heave-ho. Or as they put it more kindly nowadays, was made redundant.

Alec – Bit of a bummer. Once you're an established professor you'd expect to be there for life.

Bob – I imagine that's what Maxwell thought too, but fortunately he was quickly recruited by King's College and moved down to London. At Kings he took an interest in optics and joined The Royal Society where he became friendly with Michael Faraday. They had many detailed discussions from which Maxwell got the complete low-down on Faradays' electromagnetic experiments. He combined Faraday's work with existing electric laws by Gauss and Ampere and put it into mathematical terms. These equations became the Force Field Equations of

Electromagnetism which Albert Einstein used thirty years later to work out his 1905 blockbusters.

Alec – That's quite an amazing set of circumstances. Faraday moves to London, uses his bookbinding skills to impress Davy and ends up as the greatest experimentalist who has ever lived. Maxwell, forty years his junior, gets the bums-rush from Aberdeen and moves to London where he joins The Royal Society and they pal up. Because Maxwell believes that Faraday's electromagnetic experiments are kosher he writes them up and thirty years later a patent clerk in Switzerland uses them to turn the science world upside down. It would be quite difficult to make it up.

Bob – Just another example of the right people being in the right place at the right time!

Alec – The bit I don't understand is that Faraday must've explained his electromagnetic experiments many times before Maxwell arrived. Don't you think it's strange that none of the members of the Society seemed to come forward and help him put his work into mathematic form?

Bob – Perhaps some tried and failed or maybe it was snobbery that prevented them from kowtowing to a mere experimenter. Maxwell on the other hand was used to working with colleagues and students from different backgrounds. At that time Scotland had four Universities to England's two and they were based on the European system where a student's ability, rather than their wealth or social standing, was the only currency.

Alec – Interesting chap was Maxwell, didn't he also prove that light always travels at a fixed speed.

Bob – Our old friend Galileo made the first recorded attempt to measure light's speed, but as he'd only candles and water clocks at his disposal it's not surprising that he wasn't successful. He knew it was fast and suggested that light must be at least ten times faster than sound. A lot of attempts were made before Maxwell pinned it down with most early astronomers using telescopes to time when Saturn's moons appeared and disappeared at various times of the year.

Alec – Wasn't there some later attempts that got close to it by measuring the time it took for light to be reflected back from mirrors placed some distance away?

Bob – A few years before Maxwell nailed it a French scientist called Leon Foucault used rotating mirrors and got a result that was just fractionally faster than the actual figure. But as well as giving the exact speed, Maxwell's equations later became very important as they also proved that the speed of light is constant throughout the Universe.

Alec - That's the speed of light going thru' a vacuum isn't it, but it's slowed down when passing thru' water or glass.

Bob - I don't think Faraday and Maxwell had a long time together because Maxwell moved to London in 1860 and Faraday died seven years later. They could only have had three or four years together because in 1865 Maxwell published his eight equations. Six years later he moved to Cambridge and by 1873 he'd cut the eight equations down to four. I've seen them printed on t-shirts and the only reason I knew they're Maxwell's is because his name's printed underneath them. I couldn't make head 'nor tail of them, but I'm sure they're quite straightforward to a competent mathematician like you.

Alec – The important thing about them is that they describe not only electromagnetism, but optics and how electrical circuits work. As you said, Maxwell proved them by calculating the speed of light down to decimal places, but simple and straightforward they are not. The easiest way to describe them would be like that old video tennis game we once played in a posh pub in the city centre. The game that caused a bouncer to grab our pints and dump us out in the cold wet street because he said we were making too much noise.

Bob – Wasn't the pub called The Muscular Arms and we didn't argue with the bouncer as he certainly fitted the pub's name. How could he say that we were making too much noise when, apart from a couple smooching in the corner, we were its only customers. I'm sure they were hoping to close early and used us as an excuse, at least that's the story I tell Alice.

Alec – Aye, I've heard you try that one on her and she always replies that it's more likely any self-respecting pub would've thrown us two scruffs out for our lack of dress sense and not for playing a stupid game. Anyway, going back to Maxwell's equations and playing that game. We each had a control knob that moved our bat up and down to return the ball as it bounced back and forward on the screen. It took a bit of practice and co-ordination didn't it? Now imagine that instead of having one knob to control your bat you've got four and they're all interlinked. Every time you move one knob it affects the other three and you have to keep resetting them. That's what it's like working with Maxwell's equations because they're describing the effects of electricity and magnetism at the same time.

Bob – I'd enough trouble trying to play the game with one knob. Two might eventually be manageable, maybe I could control one with each hand, but four, even Mr. Spock on the Enterprise would struggle with that.

Alec - Another thing I remember about Maxwell is that when he went back to Cambridge he was largely responsible for setting up its world famous Cavendish Laboratory and was its first Cavendish Professor of Physics. He died when he was only forty-eight, but along with Faraday he'd proved that Thomas Young's description of light as a wave was correct. Here's a thought though, what if Maxwell had remained in Aberdeen and never met Faraday, would science have worked out differently?

Bob – Who knows, but Faraday had probably written up his experiments and someone would've picked up their importance.

Alec – In my early days at the Bank I attend a training course on what's now called time management and one of Michael Faraday's meticulous diaries was used as an example. He lectured all over the country and released detailed notes of many of his experiments, but I don't think that most of them were published 'til well after his death.

Bob – Near the end of his career Faraday proposed that the electromagnetic force must extend out from a conductor into the empty space around it. What's really surprising about that is that none of his fellow scientists followed up on the idea.

Alec – That seems odd to me. Surely they'd all watched compass needles twitching and noticed that they weren't in contact with the wire. How else did they explain why the needle moved without any physical contact!

Bob – Another thing I've noticed is that a number of books written by present-day scientists jump from Thomas Young to James Clerk Maxwell hardly mentioning Michael Faraday in the passing. They seem to imply that Maxwell thought up his equations without any experimental proof and some even give the final indignity by attributing Faraday's work to Sir Humphry Davy!

Alec – Are they saying that science is the providence of scientists alone! Without Faraday there wouldn't have been Maxwell's equations and Einstein's work could've been massively delayed.

Bob – It must've seemed obvious to early thinkers that light coming to us from the Sun must travel thru' some medium or other so they called it the 'aether'. In medieval times it was called quintessence and several theories were proposed that linked it to space and gravity.

Alec –What did Isaac Newton think that space was made of?

Bob –He thought of it as a rigid structure which was filled with miniscule invisible particles, something like tiny grains of sand in a glass jar.

Alec – Faraday knew that the compass needle twitched as a reaction to the magnetic field. Did he link this to light?

Bob – Not directly.

Alec – What's the difference between light and electromagnetism?

Bob – The main difference is that light is energy that's carried thru' space by photons and electromagnetisms caused by electrons flowing along an electrical conductor.

They're both forms of electromagnetic waves, but the fundamental difference is that photons are regarded as force carrying waves while electrons are considered more like particles.

Alec – And all this is contained in Maxwell's equations?

Bob – Yes, and because of them we know everything there is to know about light, electricity and magnetism. We know how they're created and the effects they cause when they interact with something. Since ancient times visible light had been considered as being a field of something, but it took a genius like Michael Faraday to recognise what that something was. I think any attempt to write him out of the story must be vigorously resisted!

Alec – I know that there's much more to light than just the visible bit we see by, but wouldn't the explanation of it come across more clearly if they'd used visible light to describe what our eyes detect and kept something like actual light for the rest!

Bob – The problem there is that both visible and actual light are part of the same experience and it has only one set of laws. It's not as tho' there's one set of laws for visible light and a different set for actual light.

Alec – I've no problem picturing atoms and molecules as particles. It's when things like photons and electrons are said to have both wave and particle properties which leaves me confused.

Bob – When they're describing the innards of atoms scientists routinely interchange waves and particles to describe the same actions. The important point to remember is that whatever they're describing can never have both wave and particle properties at the same time.

Light describes a whole range of energies from heat, radio waves, what our eyes see, x-rays and on up to gamma rays which carry so much energy that they can be lethal. This vast range of energy is carried by vibrating photons and the best picture I get of them is that they're like waves in the ocean or sound waves travelling thru' the air.

Alec – Like sound or ocean waves, in what way?

Bob – Waves are simply disturbances in a field of something. An ocean wave is an energy wave from a distant event passing thru' and making the water go up and down. Similarly, sound waves are compressions in the air around us. Electromagnetic waves are a bit more complicated as they're carried by waves moving thru' space and inside atoms. All waves whether they're water, sound or electromagnetic can be described in two ways, either by their wavelength or by their frequency. Wavelength is the distance from the crest of one wave to the crest of the next one and frequency is the number of waves that pass by in a set time. Photons, the carriers of the electromagnetic waves, differ from water and sound waves in that they have a truly enormous range of wavelengths from the highest energy ones which are so short that they can fit inside an atom down to the lowest energy ones where a single wave wraps around the Earth nearly twenty times. Most of the photons that the Sun radiates to us are in the low energy range which we feel as heat. but when the Sun goes down there's still masses of other photons whizzing about carrying radio and TV signals, mobile phone conversations, broadband information and many others. All vibrating at billions of different frequencies!

Alec – Are wavelength and frequency interlinked?

Bob – Yes, they're just two ways that can be used to describe the same wave.

Alec – Is it the wave's vibrations that give photons their energy?

Bob – It's vibrations which gives all the moving sub-atomic particles their energy.

Alec – OK, let's start with photons as they seem the simplest way to describe this dual personality thing.

Bob – A photon is a bundle of energy that's best described as a disturbance waving its way thru' the universal field of electricity and it's very easy to get confused when scientists talk about it having this dual personality thing. The most confusing thing is that altho' it's moving as a wave, it has some particle properties mixed in with it and it's said to be travelling thru' space as a wave/particle. When it 'hits' something, say a photon lands on your skin, it gives up all its wave properties and is localised as a particle at that particular spot. All waves have this dual personality property and the confusion comes when we try to visualise them both as waves and particles at the same time.

Alec – That's all very well, but where does the ocean or sound waves' dual personality come in?

Bob – Sound and water waves don't have a dual personality as they exist in the classical world which, as we know, is made up of 'real' particles. In the classical world we're allowed to measure an ocean wave's wavelength, frequency and height at the same time and this allows us to calculate where, when and how it'll behave when it reaches the shore. Photons and electrons exist in the sub-atomic quantum world and if we want to measure them we're not allowed access to all their information at the same time. While a photons moving it's possible to deduce the direction it's travelling and its speed, but not its energy. To measure that we have to interact with the photon and when we do all its direction and speed information that was available when it was travelling is lost. In other words while it's travelling a photons best described as a wave and when it interacts with something it's best described as a particle. While it's travelling a photon contains all the information on its direction, speed and energy within the wave and that's called its wave-function.

Alec – Does this wave-particle thing only apply to the actions inside an atom?

Bob – Trying to imagine all the goings-on inside atoms without describing them as either waves or particles is well neigh impossible. Some processes are best described as waves and others only make sense when they're considered to be particles. In Newton's classical mechanics waves and particles are quite distinct things and two very successful theories have been developed to describe how each of them behaves. Unfortunately this way of looking at them doesn't work in the sub-atomic world because when you ask the question, does light behave like a wave or a particle, the answer's always yes.

Alec – Thanks for clearing that up for me, I'm now more confused than ever!

Bob – Newton's view was that light's carried by particles and Young switched the particles to waves. Faraday and Maxwell confirmed light as waves of energy, but it was soon found out that even this insight couldn't be the complete explanation.

Alec – I can follow that, but is light waves or particles?

Bob – We tend to think of particles as being like tiny motes of dust floating in the air, but particles in physics refers to things that aren't simpler to be described as waves. A photon has the potential to be a wave or a particle and my simplistic way of looking at it is that it's a wave when it's travelling and a particle when it stops. The Sun constantly spits out photons, one of which has just travelled as a wave for eight and a bit minutes 'til it reached your skin and donated its energy to you. Job done, it then ceases to exist!

Alec – That seems way too simple, there must be more to it than that.

Bob – There's lots more depending on how deep you want to go into it, but that's them on next tee and it's probably safer that we wait here till they've cleared that as well.

Alec – My, we are feeling like a big boy today!

Bob – Better safe than sorry I always say, and in any case we're going nowhere fast.

Alec - You mentioned other energy waves and I've still got my dad's old radio set up in the loft. A couple of years ago I brought it down to show some of the grandkids what we called entertainment when we were young and when I plugged it in I was surprised that it still worked. The radio stations it received were marked on the tuning dial and there was a switch labelled long wave, medium wave and short wave which I assume refers to the wavelengths of the radio signals that carried the programs we used to listen to.

Bob – I remember that radio, but it's not the wavelengths that are marked on the dial which carried the programs we listened to. When we were teenagers we used to tune into Radio Luxembourg208 and get the latest music hits. As I found out later what we were doing was tuning the radio to detect a signal that has a wavelength of 208 metres and also had the Radio Luxembourg music signal 'piggy-backed' on top of it. The job of your dad's radio was to filter out the carrier wave and leave us with the audio wave containing the latest pop sounds all the way from Luxembourg. Essentially the 208 metre carrier wave was taking the place of a length of cable between us and Luxembourg!

Alec – So when we tuned in the radio it picked up those carrier waves which measured 208 meters from crest to crest just so that it could remove them and leave us with the music signal. Do modern radios still work this way?

Bob – All electromagnetic carrier systems work that way. Whether its voice, tv signals, computer data or anything else it's mixed, or modulated, with a carrier wave which is demodulated out at the receiving end leaving you with the signal that you want. That's why the bit of electronic kit that does this for us is called a modem which is short for modulator, demodulator.

Alec – Is it more efficient to transmit signals by wires than thru' the air?

Bob - They all have their uses. Cables should be the most secure, but sending thru' the air or outer space is now almost as reliable and very much cheaper. The lowest frequency waves are useful for talking down mines, powering heart rate monitors and communicating with submarines. Medium and slightly higher frequencies carry most of the information we use such as radio, TV, mobile phones, GPS location systems and a host of other things. The visible light waves that contain all the colours of the rainbow are slap bang in the middle of the range. Above our visible part are ultra-violet waves, x-ray's and at the very top, gamma rays. Never in their wildest dreams could Young, Faraday or Maxwell have guessed the amazing world they were opening the door to. But it's not all down to them as there were others who made essential contributions sometimes without even knowing it and Heinrich Hertz was a prime example.

By this time, the game in front had driven off the adjacent tee so Bob walked over and hit his second drive which, although it was not as cleanly hit as he'd hoped, hopped and skipped the ball onto the fairway and it ended up around fifty yards short of the green. Alec followed with a fairway wood and his ball finished a few yards beyond Bob's. They both chipped onto the green, two putted for a half and moved over to the fifth tee from where they could see down the length of the shortest par four on the course.

Club members have long considered that for the average player the long fourth was really a par four-and-a-half which was nicely balanced by the fifth being effectively a par three-and-a half. They sat in the buggy as the team in front played their shots to the green which Bob still had high hopes of being drivable, even by an old duffer like him.

Fifth Hole 295 yards par 4 - Tak' me Doon.

This is a straightforward hole that takes you back down to the same level as the previous tee. It's played from a high teeing area, down a steep hill to a generous fairway with a pronounced right to left slope. The green's driveable if you can pick the correct line and get your ball to swing in between the two large bunkers guarding the green. Both hit good drives but were disappointed when their balls ended up just short of the rightmost bunker. They climbed into the cart and motored slowly down the steep path to the fairway.

Alec – You mentioned Heinrich Hertz, I take it that he's nothing to do with the car rental company?

Bob –No, he's not that Hertz, but he's at least equally famous. You'll have come across his abbreviated name as the little Hz sign you see after electric frequencies. They used to be called cycles per second, but now, for better or worse, they're Hertz.

Alec – Did he invent something important and forget to tell anyone about it?

Bob – It's even worse than that. Back in 1888 he was the first person to produce and detect radio waves travelling thru' the air but when he was asked several times what his equipment might be used for he replied, "It's of no use at all." When he was pressed to re-consider it he answered. "No, nothing. Nothing I guess."

Alec –Way back when I was gainfully employed in the Bank I developed a habit of checking newspaper analysts' stock market tips and I clearly remember that on New Year's Eve 1999 quite a few of them gave their top tips for the coming century as 'quoted companies who are big in wireless transmission'. I remember asking you what it meant and you telling me it was bits of kit that are sometimes used to connect electronic devices together without needing wires.

Bob – Yes I remember you asking me if I thought there was a future for it and I think I said that it'll come in useful in some areas, but I couldn't see it as a major advance.

Alec – You're some tipster. Look at it now, it's everywhere. If only I'd bought into some of their recommendations I'd be a rich man now.

Bob – That 'if only' remark reminds me of your Auntie Sally, the one you used to call peely-wally Sally.

Alec – Old Auntie Sally, she was a real character. She got that name when she wasn't feeling too well at work one day and her boss told her "You'd better go and see the doctor as you're looking awfully peely-wally, Sally."

Bob – It's funny how nicknames stick, but didn't she have a saying she used every time someone trotted out that 'if only' plaintive cry?

Alec – That's right, she always came out with "Yes, and if only I'd a pair of testicles I'd be your uncle."

Bob – She never married did she? When I was courting Alice she advised me several times, "Never marry son and bring up all your children the same way." She was a supervisor on the central telephone exchange switchboard and I've got a lot my life's direction to thank her for. She told me several times that they were looking for apprentices and I was just the type of lad they needed. I dithered 'til one day she handed me an envelope with a name, address and time on it and said, "Make sure you're neat and tidy and take that to the man at the address on the front. And don't worry son, I've already done the interview for you." Along with marrying Alice it was the best move I made and it was all down to her.

Alec – You'd get a good understanding of electromagnetism when you were working there.

Bob – Telephones and computers are just progressions of Faraday and Maxwell's insights, but going back to electromagnetism's early days, a serious problem with Maxwell's equations popped up and for a while it looked as tho' they were completely wrong.

Alec – Maxwell and Faraday were wrong?

Bob – No, Faraday's experiments were gold plated, but Maxwell's equations describing them didn't agree with reality. They'd been initially accepted as 100% OK, but then a problem popped up which showed that they couldn't be correct. It wasn't that they were just a wee bit out, what they were predicting was impossible!

Alec – Maxwell had got it impossibly wrong, was it a slip up in his maths?

Bob – After the equations were published they were tested and re-tested successfully by scientists all over the world. Then one day a baker comes along and insists, 'no matter what Mr. Maxwell's says, his equations don't apply inside my baking ovens'.

Alec – Do you mean a chap in flour covered overalls and a white puffed hat stops Maxwell in the street and says –
'ere mate, 'em equations of yours are rubbish?'

Bob – I don't think it was quite like that, but someone somewhere flags this up as a problem. The nub of it was that the equations were predicting that ovens all over the world would start to heat up but wouldn't stop when they reached their operating temperature, they'd continue heating up to infinity. Checks were made and science had to take a step back and agree that Maxwell's equations didn't apply inside baking ovens.

Alec - Hmm, a bit of a let-down. It would appear that Mr. Maxwell should have checked them with his local baker before publishing. What did he do to correct it?

Bob – I assume he tried to get a handle on the problem, but he was no further forward when he died in 1879. Had he lived he might well have resolved it but that was left to a respected scientist who twenty-one years later had what amounted to little more than a lucky guess.

Alec – Was this the guy who suggested that light isn't continuous but comes in chunks and why did Maxwell's problem only apply to baking ovens?

Bob – It was quickly realised that it wasn't just with ovens as his equations should apply to, it was anything that's gaining or losing heat. Faraday had proved that light was a wave of energy and the heat inside an oven will be made up of energy waves of many different frequencies. At that time it was known that light frequencies went from infra-red, the lowest, to ultra-violet, the highest, and in between them there are many billions of frequencies. In Maxwell's theory they could all be present inside an oven at the same time and there was nothing in his equations to limit the number of different frequency waves that ovens could contain. According to his equations the waves would be continuous and keep adding heat 'til the total energy in the oven approached infinity. As the problem got worse when the most energetic waves were included, it became known as the 'Ultra Violet Catastrophe'.

They parked the buggy beside the next tee and Bob selected his wedge, lobbed the ball over the bunker and was a bit disappointed when it failed to stop on the green. Alec, trying to compensate, hit his wedge too softly and the ball ended up in the bunker. They left the buggy at the side of the green and Alec splashed out to about 10 feet short of the hole. Bob hit his approach chip a bit too firmly and they both two putted to half the hole. As they walked the short distance to the next tee they were unsurprised to see that the game in front was still ball-searching in patches of rough either side of the green so they sat back in the golf cart and waited for them to play out and take their tee shots on the next hole.

Alec – Ultra Violet Catastrophe, it couldn't have done much for Maxwell's reputation.

Bob – In 1895 things went from bad to worse when Roentgen discovered X-Rays which extended light's energy spectrum upward and a few years later it got even worse when Marie4 and Pierre Curie topped out the frequency chart with gamma rays. Going into the twentieth century we had lights complete spectrum beginning with the lowest frequency waves of 30 hertz up to the highest, gamma rays, which started at one with nineteen zeros after it.

Alec – That's quite a range. Where does our bit of visible light fit into this?

Bob – Our eyes can detect frequencies between 430 and 750 trillion hertz, or cycles per second, and starting with the lowest we see waves of them as red. As the frequency rises they change thru' all the colours of the rainbow to violet. I tend to think of light in frequencies rather than wavelengths because as the frequency rises so does the energy that each wave carries.

Alec – Very interesting I'm sure, but did any of this shine a light on Maxwell's problem. I assume that this is where a young Albert Einstein comes galloping to the rescue.

Bob – Albert needed another insight to get him onto the right track and that came at the turn of the last century when he was twenty-one. The guy you're looking for was a German theoretical physicist called Max Planck and he was studying how solid matter gains and loses heat. After a few years of work he came up with an equation which he very firmly believed couldn't be correct as it violated one of the basic laws of science. Being a diligent scientist he published the equation and told everyone to ignore it, then eighteen years later pocketed a Nobel Prize for it!

Sixth Hole   148 yards par 3 - Mugdock.

The sixth hole is a short par three played to an upturned saucer green with deep bunkers on either side with a short length of fairway just before the green. Alec played first but his shot was a fraction too long and the ball bounced off the back verge then rolled halfway to the next tee. Bob replied with a nice easy swing and his ball stopped on the apron just short of the green. Alec's pitch back was looking good but, with green sloping away from him, his ball trickled down the green and stopped near Bob's. Feeling good about his game Bob played a chip and run which he almost holed. Alec's putt to half the hole looked in all the way, but stopped an agonizing couple of inches short. As they walked off the green he pulled a face and signalled to Bob that he was back to two holes down so they climbed back into the buggy and watched the game in front searching for yet another wayward shot.

Alec – Max Planck, I've heard of that name.

Bob – As well as being a scientist Max was a world class singer, pianist and organist who almost took to music as a career. When he was a freshman at the University of Munich he asked one of his professors about the likely prospects of him having a future career in physics. The professor, Philipp von Jolly, famously replied, "In this field almost everything's already discovered and all that remains to do is to fill in a few insignificant gaps. If it were me I'd stick to music."

Alec – I take it he ignored this advice.

Bob – He did and in 1900 after three years studying how metals radiate heat he came up with a very precise equation which said that energy doesn't come as a continuous wave, but as small discrete chunks. This solved Maxwell's heating up to infinity problem because if heat comes in packets of energy then the energy they contain must be linked to their frequency. Energy rarely comes in very high frequencies because there isn't enough energy to create them. Max was a scientist of the old school who believed that only equations which described events which can be observed should be allowed. He tried several solutions to explain why metals change colour as they heat up but always came up with an infinite answer. In desperation he tried a solution which treated the particles as a unit and that worked perfectly. His reasoning was that this result must be a mathematical curiosity as there's no way that it could be correct. He checked and re-checked his work but couldn't find a flaw. Being a very precise scientist, he named the fictitious group of particles as quanta's of energy and published the result, but advised everyone to ignore it as it contradicted the Second Law.

Alec – Second Law, isn't that the one about entropy and how eggs lying smashed on the floor never jump back onto the table and re-assemble themselves? I've always had problems understanding this law as it talks of the smashed eggs in terms of entropy which it says must always increase. But increase from what to what?

Bob – Maybe the best way to understand entropy is to think of it as things wearing down, or how they change in time. As things wear down they use up energy and their entropy increases. If you leave something like a house or a car to its own devices it'll eventually crumble to dust or rust. Dust or rust never re-assembles into houses or cars, does it?

If you leave something like a house or a car to its own devices it'll eventually crumble to dust or rust. Dust or rust never re-assembles into houses or cars, does it?

Alec – I can see that's OK for inanimate objects, but what about living things like us?

Bob – All living things live because they get energy from the Sun and when our Sun's energy finally disappears so will we. We're able to stave off entropy for a time by eating things that've been solar powered, but eventually time and entropy will always win out.

Alec – So Max's view of entropy was proved to be wrong. Is this finally where Einstein comes in?

Bob – By this time Einstein had left university and was teaching in a school when he heard of Max Planck's work. He was puzzled by the idea of 'quanta's of energy' and he wasn't the only one. It appears that most scientists were too puzzled by it to even consider proposing an explanation. Einstein was convinced that there was something very basic in the equation and beavered away trying to understand what it really meant with the result that a few years later he was able to pick it up where Max had left off.

Alec – Did you say that Einstein started out as a teacher? I assumed that he'd always been a high-flyer.

Bob – As a child he was far from being a precocious genius and was very slow to speak. His parents even thought that he might be backward as he was neatly three before he started to talk to them. When he was five, and altho' he was Jewish, his parents enrolled him in the local Catholic school which he hated. One day when he was off school with measles his father gave him a magnetic compass to play with and he became intrigued by it.

He was fascinated by the way that an unseen force could control the needle no matter which way he pointed it.

Alec – Didn't do baby talk and sensed there was something magic about a compass. That sounds more like the real Einstein!

Bob – When he was ten years old a Jewish tradition and a young medical student combined to change his life forever. The tradition was that middle class Jewish families would invite an impoverished student to have dinner with them and the student, so a Polish chap called Max Talmey, dined with the Einstein's once a week. As well as training to be a doctor, Max was interested in science and he discussed the latest ideas with Albert as tho' he was an adult. He lent Albert some of the latest popular science books, introduced him to algebra and, for his twelfth birthday, gave him a book on geometry. Later in life Einstein described reading this book as the single most important factor in making him wanting to be a scientist. Within a year he'd worked his way thru' the entire mathematical syllabus of the school and, as couldn't see the point of learning subjects like Classical Greek, he quickly gained a bad reputation. On one occasion The Principal summoned his father and told him that Albert was a troublemaker. When his father asked, "In what way," he was told, "Albert sits at the back of classes and smiles."

Alec – Wouldn't behaviour like that scupper his chances of going on to university as he would need good grades in subjects other than mathematics?

Bob – Things came to a head when he was fifteen. The family electrical business was in financial difficulties and his father decided to re-locate to Italy leaving Albert behind to complete his education. This was a decision he really hated.

Alec – How did he manage to get from there to Switzerland? I know that he was a student at Zurich University.

Bob – Another thing he hated was that every German male had to do military service so he decided that his only option was to find a way to leave school, re-join his parents in Italy and renounce his German citizenship. He talked his maths teacher into writing a letter saying that he'd progressed as far as he could with school maths and took it to the principal to inform him he was leaving school. The principal knew he was coming and beat him to it saying, "There's no need for the letter Albert, we're expelling you for being a disruptive influence." Six months after being left behind, Albert turned up at the new family home in Milan.

Alec – Had he renounced his citizenship by then and become an Italian citizen?

Bob – He probably saw Italy as another militaristic country and decided that his safest bet was to become a Swiss citizen so he moved there to live with a relative. When he was sixteen and back on a visit to Milan his father asked what his future plans were and was assured that in the autumn he intended to take the entrance exam for the Zurich Federal Polytechnic. This was a new type of university that specialised in educating teachers and engineers and he was so cocksure that he would easily walk into an institution with relatively modest standards that he got a real shock when he failed the exam. He later found out that he'd been lucky to be allowed to sit it in the first place as the normal age for entry was eighteen and he was still six months short of his seventeenth birthday. He was also informed that another requirement for entrance was a high school diploma.

Alec – Leaving his German school early and being branded as a troublemaker wouldn't have helped his cause.

Bob – Fortunately the director of the ETH, the initials of the Polytechnic's name in German, recognised his potential in the maths part of the exam and suggested that he should enrol in a Swiss High School, get his diploma, and re-sit the exam the following year. Einstein followed his advice, and as they say, the rest's history.

Alec – It's not quite tho' is it? How did he get from training to become an engineer or teacher to becoming the greatest scientists that's ever lived? After all, his father had an electricity supply company in Italy, why didn't he want to join him in it?

Bob – Einstein later recounted, 'What appealed to me most at the time was that science would give me a certain amount of independence.' He also recalled that he spent a lot of his time puzzling over Maxwell's claim that if he could run at the same speed as light and switched on a torch, the light from it would still be flying away from him at light speed and not double light's speed!.

Alec – That's quite an advanced thought for a boy of sixteen, where did he go from there?

Bob - Once he'd settled in at the ETH he quickly realised that physics rather than pure maths was a better match for his temperament. In 1900 he graduated first in his class but as two of his professors had taken a dislike to him he was unable to stay on as an assistant lecturer. He survived on some temporary teaching and tutoring work and two years later a friend of the family got him a job in the Swiss Patent Office at Bern as an Examiner Third Class. He later said that this was the best stroke of luck he had in his life.

Alec – You have to wonder again how it might have turned out if he'd not annoyed his lecturers and the university had accepted him as an assistant lecturer.

Bob – Who knows, but he certainly wouldn't have had the time that he had in the Patent Office to think thru' to his relativity theories. I'm sure he would've eventually worked them out, that's assuming no one else got there first!

Alec – Supposing relativity had been delayed by ten or twenty years, would we be where we are now?

Bob – At this time Einstein was working outside the European scientific circle and was one of the few people who accepted Maxwell's equations and Planck's energy quanta as being gospel. He realised early on that if he could complete his patent office duties expertly, but more important quickly, he would have time and a bit of peace to think thru' to his scientific speculations. He later said, "Discretion was necessary for though the authorities may find slow work satisfactory, the saving of time for personal pursuits was officially forbidden." For this reason he did most of his speculating on small slips of paper that could be quickly slid into a drawer which he called 'The Department of Theoretical Physics' as soon as he heard footsteps approaching. He knew that the Director of the Patent Office was a strict positivist who would laugh at him as well as being very angry. This way he started thinking thru' Maxwell's proof that light can only ever travel at light speed and never faster.

This way he started thinking thru' Maxwell's proof that light can only ever travel at light speed and never faster. His way of working was to sit back and get a visual picture of the problem then come up with some thought experiments that he could mull over until he could see through to the basics.

Alec – How did he think his way thru' to the speed of light problem?

Bob – Every morning he travelled to the Patent Office by tramcar and one day as it was trundling past the famous Bern Town Hall clock he noticed that it had stopped and the hands weren't moving. Something clicked and he realised that he would get the same result if the clock's hands were moving, but the tram was travelling away from the clock on a beam of light. To the people walking past the clock it would show them the correct time, but to him and everyone on the tram the clock's hands would be standing still during their journey.

Alec – It sounds almost too simple when you say it like that, but what a lot of connections he had to make.

Bob - Another of his thought experiments was the problem he'd considered back when he was sixteen. If he was sitting in a tram travelling at light speed and a beam of light was travelling alongside him, Maxwell's equations said that the beam of light would be still moving away from him at light speed. He turned this around and realised that because the speed of light isn't infinite, it's perfectly possible that a person who was watching two spaced out events would see them happening simultaneously. But a second person watching the same two events from a different angle would swear that one of them was happening before the other and both of them would be correct! Another connection he made was to consider what light travels thru' when it's coming to us and that helped him to solve a problem that had bugged people since Democritus back in Ancient Greece.

Alec – Was that what's light made of and what does it travel thru'?

Bob – It was, and Faraday had already solved the first part of the problem.

Alec – So that left him with the puzzle that had stumped people over the ages, what does light really travel thru'.

Bob – It was quite simple when you think about it and it's amazing that no one had thought this way before. Faraday started it with his experiments of a conductor moving thru' a magnetic field and creating electricity. Einstein's first statement in his General Relativity paper started with, 'The observable phenomenon depends solely on the motions of the conductor and the magnet'. What he's saying is that it doesn't matter whether it's the magnet that's fixed in place and the conductor's moving past it, or if it's the other way around, either way an electric current will always be created in the wire. The important point he took from this is that one of them has to be stationary with respect to the other. If they're both stationary, or are moving at the same speed, no current's created and this proves that the only thing that matters is their movement relative to each other. In Einstein's words, 'They'll do this whether or not there's anything present and therefor the concept of something like the aether is redundant as there's no requirement for it.' Einstein wrote this up and sent it off with the title 'On the Electrodynamics of Moving Bodies'.

Alec – Solving his boyhood problem in the process!

Bob – His Moving Bodies paper was published in September 1905, but he kept thinking about relativity throughout the summer and sent in an afterthought which was published in November. In his previous paper he'd used pulses of light and showed that for them to tie in with his relativity theory the source that's emitting the pulses must lose some of its energy and, if it is losing energy, it must also be losing some of its mass. Mass and energy must therefore be two faces of the same thing and be related to each other by the simple equation $E=mc^2$. He called this paper Mass and Energy which explained, along with lots of other things, why the Sun shines. That's the first half of his masterwork delivered.

Alec – The Sun certainly shone on him, but I've read various pieces which claim that he built his theories using simple high school algebra because maths, apart from geometry, had never been important to him.

Bob – Sorry, that's completely wrong. Einstein was a very competent mathematician.

Alec – Later on didn't he also have to get help with his General Theory?

Bob – Where the confusion comes from is that his first relativity theory was an extension of an earlier work by a Dutch physicist called Hendrik Lorentz whose calculations were in a relatively simple algebraic form. Einstein was a more than capable mathematician as his doctoral thesis shows. In 1906 he submitted it which described a better way of working out how many molecules a certain amount of a gas will contain. Back in 1811 an Italian Count, Armedo Avogadro, published a law stating that if you have two equal volumes of gases under the same conditions of temperature and pressure they'll contain an equal number of molecules.

Alec – That sounds to me like a statement of the bleeding obvious!

Bob – At first glance it seems that way, but it's what the law leads on to that's the big deal. Later chemists used this simple idea to come up with a number that acts like a bridge linking chemistry in our classical world directly with physics in the atomic world and they named it Avogadro's number in his honour. In chemistry things are measured by their size and weight, but when the same thing's measured from an atomic perspective it's all about the individual atoms and how they link up. Avogadro's number connects these two things and allows scientists to explore atomic level molecules by measuring their quantities in the classical world. In practice it's a very big deal.

Alec – What did Einstein contribute to this?

Bob – His thesis described a better way of working out Avogadro's number which made it much easier to calculate how many molecules there are in a sample when you mix a given amount of them with a liquid. The two professors who reviewed his doctorate paper expressed a high regard for his mathematical ability. One wrote in his report 'The arguments and calculations to be carried out are among the most difficult in hydrodynamics and could only be approached by someone who possesses understanding and talent.' His colleague commented, 'The mode of treatment demonstrates a fundamental mastery of the relevant mathematical methods.'

Alec – That shows just how much of a genius Einstein was. He's able to explain complex subjects using Lorentz's simple maths, but that doesn't imply that he couldn't have done it if it required more complex maths. What did Lorentz discover that was so important to Einstein?

Bob – Lorentz picked up on an idea proposed by George Fitzgerald, an Irish physicist, who wrote, 'For the speed of light to remain constant throughout the Universe, things like rulers must shrink in the direction they're travelling'. Fitzgerald didn't produce any proof to back up his revolutionary statement and his theory was laughed at by most of his colleagues. Lorentz came up with the same idea while he was studying how to synchronise clocks that are a distance apart from each other, but this time he produced a proof that showed how this ruler shortening works.

Alec – So the stage is set for Einstein to burst into the world.

Bob – Yes. His years of hard thinking came together in 1905 when in seven months he submitted and had published his ground-breaking papers. His second paper proving the existence of atoms was the basis of his doctoral thesis which was accepted the following year.

Alec – So when his historic papers were being published he's just plain Herr Albert Einstein.

Bob – His doctorate was awarded in 1906 and three years later he was installed as Assistant Professor of Physics at Zurich University where he went from being Herr Doktor Einstein to Herr Professor Einstein.

Seventh Hole   445 yards par 4 - The Whangie.

The seventh's a slight dogleg par four. Down the right-hand side and halfway to the green are a series of bunkers which if you can clear shortens the hole. It had been many years since Alec or Bob had attempted the short route, so they aimed their drives down the left half of the fairway which left them with longer second shots to the green. Both hit reasonable drives but as they neared to where their balls should be only one was visible. They checked it and to Alec's surprise the ball had Bob's identification marks on it. Looking around Bob noticed that there was a ball plugged in the up-slope of the first fairway bunker.

Alec - How on earth did my ball get to there, I was certain it was a good ten yards to the left of that bunker. Are you sure it hasn't been relocated over the winter?

Bob – That bunker's been sitting right there since you and I were juniors but that's a tough break. You took the same line as me and I was sure that both our balls would be sitting side by side. Yours must've hit one of the humps on the fairway and bounced sideways into the bunker.

Alec sighed – Golf bounces are more fickle than a woman and I should know, I'm married to one.

Bob - Away wi' you, you've got the perfect lass there and you with your golden wedding anniversary this year.

Alec – Don't remind me, it's anything but fair. You only get twenty years for first degree murder and if you put in a wee bit of good behaviour you're out in ten. But marriage, that's a real life sentence!

Bob – Maybe that was true in our day, but marriage seems to be slipping out of fashion. Nowadays it's mostly this 'try before you buy' method.

Bob was still shaking his head when Alec played his bunker shot. "Well out" he said, but as the ball was on the up-slope it didn't fly very far. He suggested that they wait 'til the green was clear as he thought he could just about reach it. "Aye, maybe twenty-five years ago" came back the smiled reply as Alec joined him in the buggy.

Alec – Einstein's well on his way now. He's had four papers published in one of the most respected scientific journals in Europe in five months. The sky's the limit!

Bob – So you would've thought, but the patent office's overwhelming response was a pat on the back and promotion to Examiner Second Class. He stayed in that position 'til 1909 when he left to take over the Chair of Theoretical Physics at the University of Zurich.

Alec – That's some jump. Examiner Second Class to Associate Professor and it's amazing when you think about the chain of events that led to it. Gravity falls out of Kepler and Newton's thinking about why planets stay in place and travel in elliptical orbits. Maxwell's intention was to put Faraday's electromagnetic results into mathematical form and the speed of light falls out of them. Then the world's most famous equation jumps out of Einstein accepting that the speed of light's a constant and Planck's quanta equation is correct. Did Einstein have any contact with Planck when he was developing his special theory?

Bob – Planck was the first major academic to get in touch with him, but that wasn't 'till after they were published. Altho' Einstein's photoelectric effect paper was proof of Planck's non-theory, he initially argued against it.

However, after reconsidering it for a short time he came round to Einstein's way of thinking and became one of his major supporters as well as a good source of academic contacts. As per usual Einstein's papers didn't get immediate acceptance and Planck's support and promotion of them was crucial in helping Einstein into the mainstream of European physics. But talking of professors, didn't one of his maths lecturers back in his Institute days have a pretty low opinion of him?

Alec – Yes that was Hermann Minkowski who called Einstein, 'A lazy dog who skips most of my lectures.' When he read Einstein's papers he's reputed to have said, "Oh, that Einstein. I certainly never would have thought he could do it." Something in the lazy dog's theory sparked him off and he dug out a paper by a great German mathematician, Bernhard Riemann, who'd published a geometric theory fifty years previously on how to work in more than three dimensions of space. He knew that another scientist, Ernst Mach, had questioned Newton's static version of the Universe and Minkowski reasoned that if Einstein was correct then the Universe couldn't be static and time must come into it somewhere. He added time to Reimann's equations of the existing three space dimensions and came up with a totally new concept, a four-dimensional block of something which he called spacetime.

Bob – I remember reading about Minkowski's announcement of spacetime at a major conference. It was a brilliant piece of oratory, but I thought it was a bit flowery and more suited to the stage than a scientific conference.

Alec – I'd forgotten about that. Minkowski was a bit of a hero with Prof and I think the theatricality of it appealed to him. Minkowski started off his lecture, "The views of space and time which I wish to lay before you today have sprung from the soil of experimental physics and therein lie's their strength. They are radical. Henceforth space by itself and time by itself are doomed to fade away into mere shadows and only a kind of union of the two will preserve an independent reality."

Bob – I don't think Einstein was best pleased with this and at first he regarded it as a mathematical trick, but he soon came to realise that this four-dimensional view of space geometry provided him with a whole new map of the Universe to work with. He was fully aware that his 1905 paper on Special Relativity was only half the theory as it didn't include the effects of gravity. Spacetime along with a brilliant insight helped him to complete it.

Alec – I've heard of Einstein's great insight. Didn't he call it the happiest thought of his life, although it didn't start out that way, did it?

Bob – If the story's true, it certainly didn't. The way it's usually told has him sitting at his desk trying to think of a possible scenario he could use to measure gravity when a sudden movement outside caught his attention. He glanced up and saw that a workman who's repairing the roof of a building opposite was in trouble and watches in horror as the workman slid down the roof, just managing to grab onto a pipe which stopped him from falling several stories to the ground. He gave a sigh of relief then started to think about the forces that the roofer would have felt if the pipe hadn't saved him. He considered various explanations and came up with a solution that could be checked. His reasoning was that if the workman had slid off the roof he'd be in free and the force that was causing this was gravity. If he could find a way to measure free fall it would be the same as measuring gravity. He reasoned that weightless free-fall would be experienced by people standing in a lift when the cables holding it broke. It would accelerate downward under the effect of gravity, and if the lift floor was replaced by a weighing scale that would show that all the passengers were weightless during their descent because their free-fall was cancelling out gravity. Therefor acceleration and gravity must be the same thing.

Alec – Was this falling roofer explanation a fact or another thought experiment explaining Einstein's way of processing his thoughts? Like the ones he had about sitting in trams travelling at light speed?

Bob – It seems to be like Newton's falling apple, a nice story to illustrate a point. Einstein first explained his thoughts about this in a 1922 lecture he gave in Japan. He gave the story away by saying that one day in 1907 he was sitting in his office when a sudden thought occurred to him that a person who's free falling wouldn't feel his own weight during the fall. This simple thought made a deep impression on him and he started thinking towards a more complete explanation of gravity.

Alec – There already was a theory that described gravity, Newton's. Why wasn't that the complete theory?

Bob – Newton's gravity describes what happens in a flat universe. A flat universe is like a map hanging on a wall where the angles of a triangle always add up to 180 degrees. What Einstein was looking for was a geometry that described the universe the way it really is, curved like the map of the Earth on a globe.

Alec – There's an entire branch of maths that describes the geometry of curved surfaces, why didn't he use that?

Bob – He wanted the description of a dynamic universe where everything's constantly changing. Newton's universe is flat and unchanging and everything continues to do what it's always been doing. Einstein knew the then current view was incomplete and Minkowski's addition of time to the three fixed dimensions pointed the way to how a curved dynamic universe would change in time.

Alec – It takes real genius to have a simple thought like that and build a second world changing theory from it. I remember hearing that when Einstein died his family gave permission for his brain to be examined and it was found to have an unusual pattern of grooves.

Bob – I don't remember hearing about that. Was it any bigger or heavier than normal brains?

Alec – Apparently it was much the same weight, but it was 15% wider than an average brain. What was more important was that it had a groove missing that normal brains have and this enabled him to make more and better connections in the areas of the brain that's involved in computing things. Getting back to his General Theory, working out the maths wasn't a straightforward task was it?

Bob – No it certainly wasn't and even with a lot of help from Marcel Grossmann, a mathematically gifted friend, it took ten years of hard slog to get to the final answer. Shortly before he cracked it Einstein gave a series of lectures at Gottingen University and David Hilbert, the Maths Professor there, attended them. He agreed with the theory and got involved in the part that Einstein was having trouble with. They corresponded and while Einstein was nearing the end of his series of weekly lectures on what he was now calling General Relativity, Hilbert wrote to him telling that he was on the brink of solving the last remaining problem. Einstein was concerned that Hilbert might pre-empt him so he got stuck in and solved it just in time. You can see the headline 'After striving for ten years, the world's cleverest man is beaten by a number-cruncher'.

Alec - That's a bit hard, but I know what you mean. David Hilbert's up there with the very best, but it would've almost been a crime if he'd pipped Einstein at the post and taken any of the credit.

Bob – Einstein's General Theory of Relativity starts with Ernst Mach's contention that space and time aren't static and fixed forever. The theory describes gravity as the bending of space and time in the areas around mass. The greater the mass, the more spacetime around it bends. John Wheeler, one of physics great's of the last century, paraphrased it as, 'Spacetime tells matter how to move, matter tells spacetime how to curve.' The theory tells us precisely how we, the planets, suns and galaxies interact with each other, but it doesn't give a physical explanation of how this happens other than it being the result of mass constantly accelerating!

Alec – Is this the problem they call quantum gravity?

Bob - Scientists currently work with two very successful, but very different, theories describing how the Universe works. Einstein's General Relativity explains it up to the largest level while quantum theory describes the interactions inside atoms down at the smallest level. Einstein's theory gives very precise answers to questions about how matter from atoms up to the scale of the Universe interacts, but quantum theory's only able to give probabilities of what's happening inside those atoms.

Alec - That's them cleared the green at last. Come on big boy, let's see what the new Bob can do!

Bob was quite proud of what he considered his best effort so far, but as he said when it was only halfway there, "Sad, but true, time and tide waits for no man" and his ball finished a good thirty yards short. Alec played a similar shot for his third, but his ball also finished just short of the green. They chipped and putted out and Bob won the hole with a five against Alec's six who, with three fingers pointing downward, said, "You're hitting that ball really well today and it's time I got my game back up and running." They got back into the golf cart and rolled fifty yards to the next tee.

Eighth Hole   365 yards Par 4 - Tam's Goat.

Their next hole's a relatively short par four. The fairway curves to the right and about a hundred yards in front of the tee there's a small bush covered hillock which blocks out the view of the left half the fairway. The best line is to drive over the hillock without going too far left which'll land you in some fairly heavy rough. As they got out of the cart and walked onto the tee they noticed that one of the players from the game ahead was standing in the middle of the fairway and inviting them to play through. After a quick glance at each other they waved back that they were in no hurry and quite happy to wait.

This is as good a time as any thought Alec and going over to his golf bag he took out a small leather case, opened it and handed a glass to Bob with, "Perfect time for a wee snifter, this one's from your local distillery." Bob replied "Ah, uisge beatha. Somebody recently told me it's the Gaelic translation of the Latin 'aqua vitae' meaning the water of life. Apparently it was monks in the Middle Ages' who introduced it to us, not that we needed any introduction!

As they sat sipping their whisky Bob turned round and re-read the plaque inset in the backrest of the bench they were sitting on. He remembered when he was Club Captain and was asked if this bench could be located here to the memory of a Past Captain of the club whose favourite hole this was. It wasn't his favourite hole for the view Bob remembered, but as the hole that he came within inches of getting a triple birdie, or a hole in one. Bob could still picture him, a really friendly chap, about average height and a very fast swing. One day while he was waiting to go out with his father he was told to watch this chap's swing. "Phil hits the ball further than we go on our holidays" and maybe it was because he'd been able to drive the green that a few years later a new tee was built and the hole lengthened by about forty yards. Still to drive over three hundred yards with one of the old wooden headed drivers was awesome. No wonder he was known in the club as Biff Smith!

Bob – Cheers Alec, lovely bit of whisky. Anyway, going back to Max Planck, it's been to the benefit of science that he took his 'sod you Professor Jolly' decision and went on to win a Nobel Prize for his equation which is now one of the nine basic constants of science.

Alec – I've heard of this 'little left to discover' bit of advice being given to other successful scientists and the people giving it must that thought that science had nearly reached the end of the road.

Bob – Planck had a long active life and in his obituary notice The New York Times called him one of the immortals of science. But it's his non-theory that he's best remembered for because without realising it he'd set science off on a completely different course for the new century.

Alec – We were watching a quiz program a few weeks ago and one of the questions was 'Who invented quantum mechanics? I said to Brenda that's easy, every schoolkid knows that and was a bit miffed when the contestant answered, "That's Max Planck." Can't say I know very much about the gentleman though I've heard his name mentioned in connection with a space research program.

Oh, and isn't there also an institute named after him?

Bob - Max had very productive life, but a rather tragic end. His only son, Erwin, was hanged in 1945 as a member of the gang who tried to kill Hitler with a bomb and it left Max a broken man who died not long after. The European Space Agency named an observatory that they sent into space in his honour and there are now over eighty research institutes named after him. Not bad for someone who didn't believe in what he'd discovered.

During this wee whisky and chat interlude the players in front had given up searching on the left side, moved across the fairway and were looking for a ball among trees on the other side. After a fruitless few minutes they gave up and the remaining two players hit their second shots toward the green. After waiting till they were on the green Bob and Alec hit good drives and, as they rolled up to them, the golfers ahead were walking off the green and over to the next tee.

Bob - May as well wait till they've all driven. We wouldn't want to slice the ball and conk someone on the head, would we Steady Eddie?

Alec assumed his usual penitent face whenever Bob trotted out this ancient quip as he knew fine well that his pal didn't hold him in any way responsible for the accident. He winked back at Bob and, taking the eight iron from his golf bag, had several practice swishes with it.

Alec - Quantum theory, I've only the vaguest idea what it's all about. The only thing I can remember was that it was responsible for a long-running argument which I think Einstein lost and it's full of uncertainties!

Bob – If you start with Max Planck's constant at the beginning of the century, it took twenty-seven years for quantum theory to come to fruition. To get it there had required considerable efforts by some very bright people and, altho' he played a big part in setting it on its way, one of them wasn't Albert Einstein.

Alec – I thought that it all started with Einstein, are you quite sure that he didn't play any further part in it?

Bob – He's recognised as a forefather of quantum theory and it was his 1905 photoelectric effect paper which was crucial to getting it started. Some of his ideas were crucial to it, but for ten years he was almost fully committed to finding the solution to his General Relativity theory. Quantum left him behind in 1911 when it began to come together with a young Danish physicist called Niels Bohr travelling over to England and hoping to study with a scientist called J. J. Thomson. Back in 1897 Thomson had discovered electrons and proposed the first model for the atom, even though atoms hadn't been an accepted part of reality by almost all the European physicists. J. J. was friendly towards Bohr, but instead of offering him a place he pointed him to an ex-student of his, Ernest Rutherford, who was a New Zealander. Bohr spent two years with Rutherford and together they introduced a second model of the atom in which the electrons swirled round a tiny central nucleus and were being held in place by the electric force of attraction between them. Thomson's initial model had been called the plum pudding model of an atom and the Rutherford/Bohr one was dubbed the planetary model.

Like Einstein, Bohr was a firm believer in Planck's theory that energy isn't continuous and he realised that this should also apply to the electrons inside the atom. When he went back home to Copenhagen he proposed an improved model which incorporated this.

Alec – Was this just before the First World War started?

Bob – This was in 1913 and just nine years later it won him a Nobel Prize. Although the model was mostly correct, it didn't give an exact explanation of the different colours we see when things are heated. Between 1918 and 1923 he worked on a much better second model and, at the same time, worked on a theory that brought in General Relativity. But within two years both his models were obsolete.

Alec – Again, I'm a bit confused. J. J. Thomson proposed a model for the atom whose existence wasn't generally accepted 'til Einstein proved it eight years later. How come?

Bob – I'm guessing a bit, but I think the most likely explanation was the different philosophical cultures in the UK and Continental Europe. Nearly a hundred years earlier a Manchester school teacher called John Dalton had more or less proved the existence of atoms with his chemical theory.

Alec – And European scientists wouldn't accept this as proof?

Bob – Philosophers in Europe, particularly in Austria and Germany, considered themselves to be the elite and top of the science tree. Their view was that it was OK for others to assume the existence of atoms, but they only dealt with rigorous proofs rather than concepts that fitted in with some chemical experiments. A casualty of this philosophy was an Austrian physicist who in 1877 proposed a constant which correctly matched the temperature of heated objects to the atoms they're made of. The physicist was Ludwig Boltzmann and altho' he didn't call them atoms his constant didn't go down well with his colleagues in Vienna. They insisted that it must be wrong as it wasn't in full agreement with the Second Law. Incidentally, this was the constant that solved Maxwell's heating up to infinity problem!

Alec – Why did it matter what his colleagues thought?

Bob - In the second half of the 1800s Vienna, as well as being the centre of the Austro-Hungarian Empire, was also the centre of a philosophy which was later called logical positivism which insisted that if you can't observe it then it doesn't exist. A society called 'The Ernst Mach Society' was formed and named after him as he was one of its prime movers. Mach was the person who explained, among other things, why police sirens change note as they race past and he put their philosophy succinctly. 'Just because things in the real world behave as tho' they're made of atoms, it doesn't prove that atoms actually exist.' He famously put Boltzmann down with, "Atoms, have you seen one yet?" After an 1897 lecture by Boltzmann at the Imperial Academy of Science in Vienna, Mach declared "I don't believe that atoms exist!" Eventually Boltzmann couldn't take any more of his colleague's rejections and he hung himself the year after Einstein gave conclusive proof that Mach was wrong. A few years ago his constant was made one of the constants which have exact definitions by the Worlds' Standards Body.

Alec – That's really sad, but it highlights the importance of timing in life. If he'd waited a few years he could've been a hero and given Mach the two-fingered salute!

Bob – Einstein's work was inspired by some of Mach's earlier ideas in which he criticised Newton's description of an absolute space and time and in 1930 he said, "It's justified to consider Mach as the precursor of the General Theory of Relativity."

Alec – It just shows how some people can be brilliant in some areas and blind in others as he turned out to be!

Bob – Then in 1900 Planck discovers that energy comes in tiny chunks and suggests that everyone should ignore this as it doesn't agree with the Second Law. Could the real reason have been that he was afraid to stick his head above the parapet and take the chance that, like Boltzmann, he'd get it blown off!

Alec – Why's the Second Law so important?

Bob – The basic notions of heat and temperature were well understood by the sixteen-hundreds and scientists back then correctly thought that heat's associated with the motion of the smallest bits of matter. In the seventeen-hundreds this was disputed and was replaced by heat being something that flowed. Experiments in the 1840s put this in doubt and ten years later it became accepted that heat's simply a form of energy. This relation between heat and energy was very important for the development of steam engines and in 1850 two scientists, Rudolf Clausius and Lord Kelvin, came up with the First and Second Laws of Thermodynamics. The First Law says that energy can be passed around, but the total amount of it in the Universe never changes, in scientific terms it's always 'conserved'.

The Second Law was originally quoted in terms of the basic fact that heat never transfers from a cold body to a hotter one. Lord Kelvin was aware of some further implications for this so the Second law settled down as, 'When energy changes from one form into another, or when matter moves freely, the total amount of disorder in a closed system always increases'. As we said this increase is referred to as the systems' entropy.

Alec – I've seen entropy mentioned in several places and I accept what you said earlier, but I still don't fully understand what it means.

Bob – I'm a bit like that myself so I stick with the idea that it's saying that no action, including time, can be truly reversible. Eggs can't un-splatter and we're not allowed to go back in time and murder our grandfathers. I've also read it described as the amount of 'used up energy' in a system that's no longer available to do any work.

Alec – So three years before Planck' discovery scientists in Britain have accepted that atoms do exist while their counterparts in Europe are still insisting that they don't!

Bob – Seems that way, but remember Britain had gone thru' the Industrial Revolution and were busy exporting steam power to the world. The continental idea of splitting hairs about whether or not atoms existed wasn't a big issue.

Alec – Did Einstein consider any of this before he sent off his four papers for publication?

Bob – I don't think that it was a problem for him as he wasn't part of the European physics community. He didn't have a reputation to protect when he blew the logical positivists position apart with his photoelectric paper proving that atoms are an essential part of the Universe.

Alec – So the facts had been in place since the 1870s when Boltzmann published his equation.

Bob – Boltzmann worked on an earlier paper by Maxwell which described how energy spreads thru' gasses and he applied it to solids. His problem was that if his colleagues had assumed his constant was correct then they would also have to accept the existence of atoms which they said didn't agree with the Second Law. To them anything that offended this law in any way was totally unacceptable. What Boltzmann had actually proved was that while the law always applies to large collections of atoms and molecules, it doesn't necessarily apply to each and every individual one. Nowadays it's considered to be a statistical law rather than a universal one.

Alec – And the Viennese philosophers didn't like this approach. They wanted rigorous proof that atoms existed before they would accept any details about them.

Bob – They didn't give up easily. Right up to his death in 1916 Mach was still insisting on the non-existence of atoms and not even the introduction of Bohr's atom three years earlier shook his opposition. Both Einstein and Planck paid tributes to Mach's earlier contributions, but added that he'd also played a large part in delaying continental science by a good few years.

Alec – The main reason I can remember Bohr is that after winning the Nobel Prize he got the gift of a house from Carlsberg, the international brewing company, and it included free beer for life.

Bob – That's probably why you remember it. Tho' he wasn't actually gifted the house, just the right to live in it for life. Calling it a house doesn't do it justice, it's a sizeable mansion. The Danish Government was keen to encourage new sciences and built a physics research institute with the sole purpose of giving Bohr a suitable environment to work in. Then, as you said, Carlsberg chipped in with a pension and the right to live in their Carlsberg Honorary Residence for life. The mansion comes with a pipe dispensing free beer and, as Bohr was a very gregarious person, I'm sure that lots of very merry times were had by all.

Alec – Your own institute, a mansion and free beer for life! They must have thought he was exceptional.

Bob – They weren't the only ones because years later Richard Feynman, one of the most distinguished physicists of the last century, visited Bohr in Copenhagen and was very impressed with him saying, "Even to the big shots Bohr was the great god." Incidentally, I've just remembered that Bohr didn't get the house straight away. He'd to wait till 1932 when his physics professor vacated it feet first.

Assuming that your drive is on the fairway, the main problem on the Eighth hole is the second shot. Some thirty-odd yards in front of the green the fairway slopes up to a large bunker which crests the top then slopes back down to the green. The bunker obscures a full view of the green and only the top third of the flagstick was visible to indicate where the hole was located. Alec's practice swings worked well and his shot covered the flag all the way. Although they couldn't see where it finished both know that the ball was quite close. Bob played the same club, but miss-hit it slightly and watched it plop into the bunker. After taking two shots to extricate it, Alec's four feet putt was conceded and they walked across to the golf cart parked beside the next tee.

Alec – Looks like they've cleared the hill, is the bell still in operation?

Bob – Yes, but back on the green I noticed a chap standing just over the top and waving us back. Maybe they didn't see the notice.

Alec – What's the tie-up between Plank's energy quanta, Bohr's atom and quantum theory?

Bob – Bohr's model proposed that the electrons in an atom can't whiz willy-nilly around the central nucleus, but can only go round it in fixed orbits. His crucial insight was that atoms gain energy and heat up when their electrons absorb loose photons that has been pumped into the system and step up to orbits at a higher energy level. The electric force from the nucleus is always trying to pull them closer to it, so if there's an available lower orbit they'll drop down to it and release a photon with the difference in energy between the orbits. Actually stepping up or down's the wrong description as electrons simply disappear from one orbit and immediately reappear in their new one. Planck's constant showed that charcoal must be emitting different coloured quanta of energy as it releases heat and Bohr proved that this is caused by the charcoal's electrons dropping down orbits. However there was a slight problem with Bohr's model in that it only worked successfully for hydrogen which is the lightest atom with only one electron.

Alec – Sounds like Bohr's almost there. Is this where uncertainty comes in?

Bob – Uncertainty came a bit later. In 1925 one of Bohr's associates Wolfgang Pauli, a Viennese wonder-kid with the sharpest tongue in the business, showed that the only way to make sense of Bohr's atomic structure is if no two identical electrons are allowed to be in the same orbit at the same time.

Alec – I thought an electron was an electron and that was all there was to it. In what way can electrons not be identical?

Bob - By then it was known that moving electrons generated their own little magnetic field and act like tiny spinning balls of magnetic charge. They don't physically spin as they're not miniscule lumps of matter. They're electromagnetic waves and, just like waves in the sea, they have a phase as the wave goes up and down. Pauli reasoned that two electrons could only share an orbit if they balanced out each other's magnetic charge by going round the nucleus with opposite phases leaving each orbit containing only the electric charges of the two electrons. He used this to prove that an orbit can only contain one clockwise and one anti-clockwise 'spinning' electron at the same time. His insight, called the Pauli Exclusion Principle, showed that electrons are fuzzy waves spread around an atom and not the solid little balls they're normally shown as. The way to look at opposite phases is that one wave is the mirror image of the other wave.

Alec – I can see Faraday's proof that moving electrons create magnetic fields, but how can that possibly work? I'm imagining the nucleus being surrounded by layer after layer of two electrons stretching away from it and the electrons jumping up and down the layers as they absorb and emit photons.

Bob – There's a couple of concepts that helped to explain it to me and the first is to picture an atom in three dimensions rather that the two it's normally depicted in. The second one's to think of the electrons not as little solid balls, but as continuous electric waves of energy wrapped around the nucleus in layers.

Alec – The picture I'm getting now is like an onion where you can peel layers away down to its central core. But how do the electrons know where to slot into each layer?

Bob – Electrons inside an atom aren't allocated their own little parking space to flit in and out of. Every electron's a wave of negative energy that's being attracted by the positive nucleus to the lowest energy space available to it. Atoms are stable when the positive electric charge of the nucleus is balanced by all the electrons negative charges and the electrons opposing magnetic fields are cancelling each other out.

Alec – I know that the protons' positive charge is balanced by the electrons' negative charge and that atoms bond by sharing their outer electrons, but are you saying that they also act like little storage heaters?

Bob – An electron absorbs energy by capturing photons of a particular frequency and jumping up energy layers. As higher energy layers are physically longer than lower ones they contain more energy which causes the energised atoms to vibrate more. The more photons its electrons are storing, the more energetic, or hotter, an atom becomes. The energised electrons are still being attracted down by the positive protons and each one is trying to shuck off photons in an attempt to get back down to be as near to the nucleus as possible. Every electron's sole aim in life is to get back down to the lowest energy level available to it. A very important point in all this is that the photons they absorb are different from the electrons they gather in in that they don't obey Pauli's Exclusion Principle. You can pile as many photons into an electron as it'll take, always with the proviso that if you pile in too many the horse shoe you're shaping will melt!

Alec – So when I boil a kettle of water what's happening is that electrons in the water atoms are jumping up orbits and when I switch the kettle off they drop down and try to get back to where they started.

Bob – What you're doing is heating up the element inside the kettle which is releasing more and more energetic photons into the water molecules whose electrons absorb them and heat up 'til they boil and change into water vapour. When you switch off the supply of heat the hydrogen and oxygen atoms release their stored energy into the surrounding atmosphere by dropping down energy orbits 'til the temperatures inside and outside the kettle are balanced.

Alec – I thought it was too simple to think of electrons going up and down slotting into layers as they go.

Bob – It's quite logical and it all fits together when you think of the next step.

Alec – Which is?

Bob – What happens when the electrons jump up orbits?

Alec – Do you mean they'll cause the atom to expand?

Bob – You can see this happening in a metal bar which expands as you heat it up. Steel rail tracks have to build this in as they expand enough to buckle in summer and contract during the winter.

Alec – As the atoms expand is there still the same positive electric force on electrons as they move further from the nucleus?

Bob – The protons binding force decreases with distance and this gives the outermost electrons more freedom as they move further away. Heat's another name for energy and the more energy you pile into an electron the more the atom will heat up and the further away its electrons will move from the nucleus. This is the basis of chemistry as energy in the form of heat allows the outermost electrons to mingle and form molecules then compounds.

Alec – Will we ever be able to see electrons jumping between layers?

Bob – This is why you can't picture them as tiny particles orbiting the nucleus, it only works when you picture them as waves. The first thing to consider is that waves of any type have a wavelength and layers in an atom can only exist at the distance from the nucleus where an exact number of waves fit around it without overlapping and it forms what's called a standing wave. As only two electrons with opposite phases can co-exist in an orbit, and to differentiate them from orbits which could be anywhere around the nucleus, these fixed length orbits are called orbitals to avoid any confusion.

Alec – That seems quite a complicated structure. Are you saying that these orbitals occur naturally at the distances from the nucleus where complete waves fit in? What's in the bit between them?

Bob – As far as I'm aware there's nothing between orbitals, it's just masses of empty space.

Alec – Do the orbitals combine into layers like onion

skins?

Bob – They do and the first layer out from the nucleus can contain only one orbital made up of two 'contra-rotating' electrons. Layers going out beyond the first can contain multiple orbitals and to give them a better descriptive feel. Scientists refer to a layer of orbitals as a shell. Shells are much like your picture of an onion with each 'skin' containing orbitals with the same frequency, or energy. Because they're waves and not particles they can't physically move between shells. When it gains or loses energy an electron wave simply disappears from one shell and instantly appears in another one. This is referred to as 'jumping' and it was described by Albert Einstein in 1916.

Alec – How many shells are there?

Bob - The first shell contains one orbital with two electrons. The next shell, being further away, can hold up to four orbitals with eight electrons, four spinning clockwise and four anti-clockwise. This is where your onion gets messed up a bit as the third and succeeding shells can get quite complex. Their orbitals don't all go round in nice circular orbits and some of them can even follow a dumbbell shape around the nucleus.

Alec - Why such a strange arrangement and not just anywhere in the shell that's got space?

Bob – This is where we need a degree in quantum theory to understand why atoms are built this way.'

Alec – Is there any way we can experience electrons without getting an electric shock when we touch a bare wire?

Bob – We experience electrons all the time and the seat you're sitting on depends on them. If they weren't doing what the outermost electrons are supposed to do we'd fall thru' the seat to the ground. It wouldn't be able to support us either so we'd end up in the core. Everything we think of as being solid only acts that way because all electrons have a negative charge and like electric charges always repel each other. We can walk thru' the atmosphere because the atoms there have a much smaller negative charge than ours. We can swim thru' water for much the same reason, but I don't think it's necessary to walk into a brick wall in order to check which of us has the greater negative charge.

Alec – So an electron's a wave when we're not looking at it and becomes a particle when we interact with it?

Bob – That's probably not 100% technically correct, but that's the only way I can make some sense of it. Everything that moves does so as a wave, and if it's not moving I think of it as a particle of matter.

Alec – It's a bit mind-boggling, but it seems quite logical.

Bob –You can't be absolutely sure where you'll find an electron's particle properties in a wave 'til you interact with it. The wave is the electron and the particle has the potential to be anywhere, or almost everywhere, in it at the same time. In quantum's early days one of its founders, Werner Heisenberg, struggled with these thoughts 'til one night he went for a stroll in a nearby park and was sitting on a bench puzzling about where electrons go between jumps. As he sat thinking about it darkness fell and the park was in complete darkness except for where an occasional lamppost was shining a circle of light downward. Suddenly he sensed that someone was walking thru' the park and was only made aware of it by seeing a figure suddenly appear in a circle of light then almost instantly disappear into the darkness. The person eventually left the park and Heisenberg reasoned that if substantial objects like a person walking thru' a park could disappear then reappear somewhere else then why couldn't electrons and other sub-atomic particles do the same?

Alec –That again seems almost reasonable. The person walking thru' the park was the particle when they interacted with each circle of light, but they disappeared when they were in between them.

Bob – If you think about it, the park that Heisenberg was sitting in could have been an inner-city parks connected to a number of streets with paths running thru' it in all directions and only the occasional circle of light to guide people. Had Heisenberg been sitting there in darkness he would see people popping in and out of existence and be totally unable to see which paths they were following thru' the park and at which gate they were exiting it .

Alec – So you're saying Heisenberg might see the park as tho' it was sub-atomic particles popping in and out of existence and re-appearing only when they interacted with something. In that case all he could do to make sense of it would be to treat it statistically and assign to each person, or particle, a probability of where they would exit the park. Or in the particle case, leave the quantum field!

Bob – Do you remember the kids' TV series where the Roadrunner's going along the road towards one of Wile E. Coyote's cunning traps and he's moving so fast that a cloud of dust billows out behind him? Imagine we're watching a quantum version of the cartoon and Wile E's in for a shock.

There's a cloud of dust approaching him that stretches 'way back down the road, but he can't spot the Roadrunner at the head of it. In fact the Roadrunner doesn't exist as a roadrunner while the cloud's moving and only appears when the dust settles down. While the dust cloud's moving the Roadrunner's nowhere and everywhere in it at the same time!

Alec – I know I said that it seems almost reasonable, but I can see why people think that the whole quantum area's weird!

Bob – I can't see it being any weirder than watching people walking thru a park in darkness, but calling it weird is what grabs people's attention. I'll agree the way the Universe works seems strange at first 'cos we're used to thinking of solid objects as being solid and space being empty, but we now know that neither's strictly correct. Was that someone ringing the bell?

Ninth Hole   436 yards par 4 - Halfway.

The halfway hole starts with a blind drive and the first hundred-odd yards of it are up and over a hill strewn with scrub bushes then onto a downward sloping fairway. Even with a good drive you're left with a long second shot to a green guarded by bunkers on either side. Fifty yards before you reach the green a small stream crosses the fairway to catch a miss-hit shot.

Alec admitted that he hadn't heard the bell and suggested that it would only take a couple of minutes to drive up to the top of the hill and check things out. Coming over the top they could see that a delay had built up in front of them. The four players from the game ahead were standing in the middle of the fairway watching the game in front of them putting out while the four in front of them were ball searching in heavy rough just a short distance off the next tee. They motored down to the players standing on the fairway and after agreeing that finding balls in the rough wasn't easy, they asked them to ring the bell when they approach the green. Then they turned and motored back to the tee

Alec – Is this where we leave understandable physics and head into Fuzzyland?

Bob – 'Fraid so. Fuzzyland, or Quantum Mechanics as science calls it, describes what's happening at the sub-atomic level. As well as proposing the uncertainty principle Werner Heisenberg has a cut named after him and, although he probably didn't suggest it, it's an idea of the point where the classical world meets the quantum one. Over the years various string theories have been proposed which treats everything at an atoms lowest level as tiny vibrating strings of energy and I've been told that the equations describing them are considered to be among the most elegant in maths. Beautiful they may be, but the problem's always been that they only work if space contains six or seven extra dimensions and we're not allowed to detect them!

Alec – If the equations make sense what's holding science back? If it's lack of knowledge about what's happening at the string level why don't they build a particle smasher the size of Europe and make sure that we've discovered and measured everything that's needed?

Bob – To measure and be sure of everything would take a good bit more than that. Scientists have now lowered their sights from a Theory of Everything and are aiming towards a Grand Unified Theory of the universal forces which will unite gravity along with the other three.

Alec – So the big ToE's out of the question and we've lowered, or maybe raised, our sights to the GUT. Has string theory given us any pointers in this direction?

Bob – Although string theories still haven't made any predictions that can be tested, they're still sitting quietly in the background waiting for some new insight which'll put them back in pole position. One thing that I almost forgot is that all the various string theories predicted that we're not alone. They say that our universe is just one among billions and billions of similar universes, but most of them are unlikely to have exactly the same laws as ours.

Alec – So Heisenberg's got a cut and an uncertainty principle named after him and you said that his cut's just a vague idea. Does that also apply to his principle?

Bob – Sort of. Uncertainty loses a bit in its translation from German and should really be referred to as The Inexactness Principle. But it's uncertainty that grabs people's attention so uncertainty it is. The way that I look at it is that Thomas Young proved that Newton's 'corpuscles' were acting as waves. This was confirmed by Faraday and Maxwell who described them as continuous waves of energy. Planck changed the continuous waves into tiny discrete chunks of energy which implied that they were back to something like particles. Up pops Einstein with his $E=mc^2$ equation and says 'If matter and energy are interchangeable then so must be the waves which make up the energy and matter particles. Heisenberg's Uncertainty Principle ties these waves and particles together by saying that there's a fundamental limit to what we are allowed to know about any quantum system.

Alec – Who or what decides the limit?

Bob – As we said, sub-atomic items like photons, electrons, etc. have two properties, wave properties and particle properties and we're only allowed to measure the exact state of them one property at a time.

Alec – Why's that?

Bob – Basically because what you're measuring can only be a wave or a particle. It can't be both at the same time.

Alec – What's stopping you measuring both states separately and combining them?

Bob – Problem there is that sub-atomic particles are always on the move, so if you're a wave you can't stand still. Let's say you put a bag of sugar on a scale to weigh it. You come back ten minutes later and the weight's still the same and, as the bag hasn't moved, you know that its speed and direction is zero. However, if you want to measure a sub-atomic particle the same way, its wave would be in constant movement relative to the scale. You can measure it as a wave and get the speed it's travelling at and the direction it's heading, or you can measure it as a particle and get its exact position inside the wave. But as waves can't stand still and the particle in it is constantly moving, you can never get both results at the same time.

Alec – I can see that, but why can't you measure both of them separately and put them together?

Bob – This is where uncertainty comes in. Heisenberg says yes you can do that, but if you do you have to accept a trade-off. The more accurately you measure one property, the less accurately you're allowed to measure the other one.

Alec – Wouldn't you get a better outcome by measuring them both to 50% accuracy?

Bob – You can't do that either because you would then be measuring them as both a wave and a particle. 50-50 implies that they're waves and particles at the same time.

Alec – Doesn't that create an unsurmountable problem?

Bob – If you want the logical positivist's reality then the straight answer's yes, but there's a sort-of way round it. If a sub-atomic system has two quantities that are related to each other, the theory allows you to measure the first one with a bit of inaccuracy. This then lets you to do a follow-up measurement of the second property up to the accuracy left over from the measurement of the first one. Let's call them A & B and if you measure A with 75% accuracy, you're only allowed to measure B with the remaining 25% and that's the Uncertainty Principle in a nutshell. The more that you allowed to know about one part of the pair, the less you're able to find out about the other one. Also because you're dealing with moving waves and stationary particles it's extremely unlikely that you'll get the same answer each time you repeat the measurements. This is where quantum theory comes to your rescue and gives you a range of the probabilities you'll get in the final measurement. So if you want to get 100% certainty you have to collapse the wave so that the particles moving properties are reduced to zero speed and direction, just as we had when we weighed the bag of sugar!

Alec – Is this as close that quantum theory can get to reality? Couldn't it be that there's more information in there, but we're not allowed to know what it is?

Bob – Bohr and most of quantum theory's founding fathers insisted that this is as close to reality as we're ever going to get because reality at the quantum level is only what we're allowed to know. This was the core of the dispute between Bohr and Einstein and Bohr's take was that it's pointless to talk of what's going on in the quantum world 'til you take your measurements and force the waves and particles to reveal themselves. Up 'til then all you can get is a range of probabilities, one of which will be confirmed when you make your final measurement.

Alec – Did Heisenberg just stumble across his quantum theory?

Bob – Getting to the theory was quite a painful journey for him as he had to go to a very small island to get the solitude to work on it!

Alec - What did Einstein make of Heisenberg's theory?

Bob – Einstein and Erwin Schrodinger, who wrote the equation that became known as wave mechanics, were both dyed-in-the-wool realists and refused to accept Bohr's probability interpretation, but both were quickly side-lined by the tide. Loads of bright students flocked to Copenhagen to study with Bohr because they wanted to be part of the quantum revolution. Bohr and his associates educated most of the students who by the mid-1930's made up a large part of the world's physics professors. As there was no credible opposition at the time it was Bohr's view of the quantum world that prevailed.

Alec – You said that Heisenberg went to a small island to work out his theory. That seems a strange place to go.

Bob – His main reason for going there was because he was suffering very badly with hay fever and the island, called Helgoland, had very little vegetation and almost zero pollen. It used to be called Helegiland, meaning Holy, or Sacred, Island and there he worked on a theory with the strict proviso that only those things that we can see, or observe, should be part of it and any attempt to form a picture of what's actually going on inside an atom would be forbidden. He had the intuition that the answers to this puzzle lay in manipulating something called matrices, but what they are is as clear as mud to me.

Alec – A matrix is quite simple, you use them almost every day.

Bob – How come.

Alec – A bus or a railway timetable's a matrix with a column down the side showing the bus or railway stations and the times that they arrive are across the top. If you want an answer to your 'what time do I catch the next train or bus,' then it's where the columns and rows intersect.

Bob – I can see that, but Heisenberg's matrices must do a lot more than that.

Alec – Heisenberg was trying to find a way to calculate Bohr's theory that electrons circulate around an atoms nucleus in defined orbits with nothing in between them and used the matrix as a table of numbers to describe the movement of the electron in each possible scenario. This is where it becomes difficult to describe as the result of multiplying two boxes in the matrix depends on the order that you multiply them! Multiplying box five by box eight gives a different answer to multiplying box eight by box five. After several weeks of relentless toil it started to give him answers so he went back and spoke to Max Born, his university professor telling him that he's written a crazy paper and couldn't decide whether or not to publish it. Born saw the importance of the theory and sent it off for publication while getting one of his students, Pascual Jordan, to put some order into the paper. All three worked feverishly on it and in a few months they'd put together the structure of a whole new system of mechanics to replace Newton's theory.

Bob – That's amazing, but it's still as clear as mud.

Alec – Heisenberg's theory provided tables of every possible position that an electron can be in as it jumps about inside an atom. Even more amazingly the papers publication caused a young Englishman called Paul Dirac to send Born a short essay with results that agreed with theirs, but was constructed using an even more abstract mathematical system.

Bob – So including Bohr, there was a gang of five people responsible for the original quantum theory.

Alec – There was a sixth, called Wolfgang Pauli, who was a brilliant, if arrogant, mathematician and he worked out the most difficult calculations.

Bob – So in a nutshell the Copenhagen Interpretation says that quantum mechanics can't give you a description of what's actually going on down in the murky sub-atomic depths as it's just a recipe to give you the probabilities of how an experiment will work out. The interpretation explicitly says that if you're looking for a full description of reality you're wasting your time. Just accept these equations as gospel, do the calculations and you'll get the correct results. Anyone foolish enough to doubt this was referred to a book on Quantum Theory written in 1931 by John von Neumann supposedly proving that this interpretation is the only valid one possible. Anyone who doubted the theory was advised that if they wanted to have any future prospects in physics its best that they 'shut up and calculate' and that's what most did. At the time Von Neumann was regarded as the nearest thing to a mathematical god and the only person who dared to challenge his theory was a German mathematician called Grete Hermann and she, for some reason completely unrelated to her gender, was totally ignored.

Alec – I know a fair bit about Johnny von Neumann and he really was one of the world's greatest ever mathematicians. He's justly famous for developing the 'Cold War' game theories and was part of a group of brilliant Hungarian mathematicians who were accused of being aliens as they were so far ahead of pack. I imagine Grete must have been among the bravest of the brave daring to challenge von Neumann.

Bob – What was so important about a theory of games?

Alec – It wasn't games as in chess or snakes and ladders, this 'game' was predicting how many people on either side would survive in an all-out nuclear war. Fortunately its predictions have so far indicated that there isn't a scenario where either side could come out of it as winners!

Bob – So it's the nuclear option that's dictating why we have to learn to live with each other.

Alec – That's why it's called a deterrent and my hope is that it's the ultimate guarantee with which future generations will also have to learn to live with!

Bob – If we've learned anything out of the last century it's that in the long term wars solve nothing and discourse is the only way forward. But going back to your question about people doubting quantum mechanics, everyone who did was faced with the hard fact that although it only works after a fashion, it does so surprisingly well

Alec – Has there been any successful challengers to it?

Bob – Back in 1924 a French Duke called Louis de Broglie proposed in his Ph.D thesis that electrons are actually electromagnetic waves that can display both wave and particle properties at the same time. Six months after Heisenberg's theory, Erwin Schrodinger, on Einstein's advice, took de Broglie's thesis with him on a weekend skiing trip and one afternoon remained in his hotel room where he wrote a much simpler equation describing how he thought an electron wave should behave. His approach was to treat the wave by using the equations that worked for normal sound or sea waves.

Alec – Was this similar to Heisenberg's equation?

Bob – No, they were totally different solutions.

Heisenberg used a series of complicated mathematical matrices whereas Schrodinger more or less dreamt his up from a mixture of existing wave theory along with bits of classical mechanics. He was never able to fully explain his reasoning for what was part intuition, part imagination and part lucky guess, but whatever it was, it worked. However, when he published his equation it caused a great deal of consternation, because how can you have two totally different equations that describe the same event?

Alec – How did that play out?

Bob – Heisenberg and a few others came to the rescue by showing that both equations gave identical predictions and it was just that both had approached the problem from different angles. It's now recognised that only Heisenberg's equation that gives some description of the quantum actions. Schrodinger's equation is only a mathematical calculation which gives the same answers as Heisenberg's, but is much simpler to work with and makes it possible to practice Quantum Mechanics without having to fully understand what's going on.

Alec – So Heisenberg has six months of glory then along comes this guy with a simpler explanation and takes it all away. Was this before or after he came up with his Uncertainty Principle?

Bob – This was before his Uncertainty Principle, but he'd a double downer. To get to his theory Heisenberg had spent weeks on a small island off Germany's coast, whereas Schrodinger worked his out part-time on a weekend skiing trip with a lady who wasn't his wife.

Alec – Surely there must've been more to it than that?

Bob – Nope, that's the way it was and that left Heisenberg with a problem which Einstein helped him solve.

Alec – How?

Bob – After he developed his theory Heisenberg gave a presentation of it and Einstein was in the audience. At the end of it Einstein invited Heisenberg to come back home with him, possibly for a snifter of schnapps and once there he cornered Heisenberg and insisted that his theory had a lot of holes in it and therefore it couldn't be the complete article. Although Heisenberg was taken aback, he asked Einstein for advice and explained that he'd received two job offers. One was to take up a full professorship at the University of Leipzig and the other was to go to Copenhagen and work with Bohr. Which one would Einstein recommend he took?

Alec – Hmm, bit of a poser. Did Einstein have an ulterior motive before he replied?

Bob – Not that I know of, I don't think skulduggery was in Einstein's nature.

Alec – Safety and a tenured professor for life or take a chance with Bohr, I think I'd go with safety.

Bob – Einstein said the opposite. "Go to Copenhagen" and he did. Heisenberg probably assumed there was plenty of time left for professorships.

Alec – Then along comes Schrodinger, steals half his glory and the Leipzig job's gone. Must have thought he'd made the wrong decision.

Bob – Heisenberg was made of sterner stuff than that. He buckled down and came up with the Uncertainty Principle to regain top spot.

Alec – Good on him. He went with Bohr and helped to develop the complete quantum theory. Or should it be called half a theory as it doesn't correspond to reality.

Bob – You could say that, but it's given us large parts of the modern world and without any doubt it's the most successful theory we've ever had.

Alec – Let me get this straight. Bohr sorts out the atom, then Schrodinger and Heisenberg provide two different descriptions for it. The first generation of professors are trained in Bohr's interpretation of quantum theory and they go out and train the next generation who start to produce the goodies we have today.

Bob – That's how it worked out. A group of people following known patterns used their intuition plus a bit of guesswork and came up with what eventually became known as 'The Copenhagen Interpretation of Quantum Physics'.

Alec – Why eventually? It started out and most of it seems to be linked to Copenhagen?

Bob – It was never actually called that 'til after the Second World War when Werner Heisenberg tried to re-integrate into the physics community by claiming that he was a major player in what he called 'The Copenhagen Interpretation,' even though none of the others had referred to it that way.

Alec - Does this mean that the people involved weren't all singing from the same hymn sheet?

Bob – No. The name's a bit of a misnomer as there never was a fully agreed interpretation of Quantum Physics. This Copenhagen Interpretation then became a very ambiguous term that was used to convince new physicists that

Schrodinger's Quantum Mechanics will give them all the answers they'll ever need without having to trouble their heads about what's going on at the basic level. It became the name that was applied to a set of rules and interpretations on how to practice the art of Quantum Mechanics without actually knowing what it's based on. In a way it's like riding a bike without knowing how it manages to remain upright. Is there still no mathematical challenge to Heisenberg and Schrodinger's version of quantum mechanics?

Alec - Right at the beginning there was de Broglie's proposal saying it's a wave and a particle at the same time, but Niels Bohr and Wolfgang Pauli, both very forceful men, convinced him that his theory must be wrong. A similar theory resurfaced twenty-five years later, but it was also talked out of court. The fundamental problem with either of the proposed replacements is that altho' they took the, 'having to make a measurement before you get a result' part out of the process they gave exactly the same results as the existing theory. Their theories said that both the wave and particle are present and the function of the wave is to guide the particle on to its final destination. We're over a hundred years further on from Bohr's original proposal and there's still no sign of a theory that'll give a deeper explanation.

Bob – I read recently that many scientists are coming to the belief that the wave is a wave of the probabilities of where an electron, or photon, might land when it ceases to move and it's not a wave that contains an actual photon or electron.

Alec – So we need someone to come up with some simple insights like Einstein with his relativity theories.

Bob– The problem with simple insights is that some of them which seem simple on the surface turn out to be anything but. Take our Rules of Golf for example and you'll remember what dear old Henry Longhurst, the original golf commentator on the box, thought about them. It was Henry who turned golf commentating into an art form, but he always managed to let you know that he was ever so slightly superior to you!

Alec – Henry Longhurst, once heard never forgotten. His apprentice, Peter Allis, claimed that Henry was such a snob that he once refused to get into the same Rolls-Royce as his driver. His love of golf was obvious from his commentary, but he used to get really worked up as the game's slower players got slower and slower. Henry reckoned that slow play was spoiling the game for everyone else and the pro's should be setting a much better example. I wonder what he'd make of some of today's players.

Bob – That's right, but as well as complaining about it Henry had a solution. His suggestion was that the rules of golf had become far too complicated and should be simplified right down to being able to be written on the back of a fag packet.

Alec – His version was that you put your ball down on the tee and don't touch it again 'til you lift it out of the hole. Touch it anywhere in between and you incur penalty shots.

Bob – Very logical, simple and straightforward till you come to the dreaded word penalty. Because of penalty we now have several comprehensive volumes called The Official Rules of Golf, The Official Interpretation of the

Rules of Golf and a mass of others trying to explain both.

Alec – Any day now I expect we'll get notice that there's a new out one called The Official Interpretation of The Official Interpretation of the Rules of Golf!

Bob – Wouldn't surprise me at all me old mate. Your average golfer's quite happy to stick to something like Henry's rules until they get into a position that they can't, or don't, want to. play their ball from and that's when a lot of time wasting begins.

Alec - You can say that again. We've both played with people whose interpretation of the rules takes some imagination. Someone once told me that golf's got more rules than any three other major sports put together!

Bob - Remember Seve, he was a real wizard with the rules. His drives often found parts of courses that other players didn't even know existed. The number of times he would call over an official and inform him that he was entitled to relief as his ball was lying in a patch of animal scrapings or something similar.

Alec - I'm sure Henry would've answered Seve with something like, 'Prove to me which animal made those scrapings Senor Ballesteros and I'll grant you relief.'

Bob – If you mention the rules to some golfers they'll rummage about in their golf bag and come out with a dog-eared booklet that's already two revisions out of date. Then they'll happily discuss convoluted rules that tell them it's OK to move their ball rather than accept their due punishment for a badly, or unluckily, hit shot. Did you know that Einstein had a brush with golf the year he was awarded his Nobel Prize?

Alec – No, I've never heard of that. What happened?

Bob –In 1921 he went to the U.S. of A on a fund-raising tour to help build a Hebrew University in Jerusalem. The day he arrived he got a request from the New York Times for an interview, but it must have been a busy news day because they sent Henry Crouch to interview him. Henry was their golf correspondent and he hadn't the faintest clue what Einstein was talking about, but he did have a nice line in myth-making. The following day he assured readers that Professor Einstein had come over to promote his book which only three people in the world would be able to understand. The story was covered over here and a journalist asked Sir Arthur Eddington, Britain's top scientist, if this was true. Eddington was silent for a few moments and when the journalist said, 'Will I put that down as no comment Sir' he replied 'No, I'm trying to think who the third person might be.'

Alec –Wasn't Eddington the chap who proved that Einstein's theory of gravity was correct by taking photographs during an eclipse showing that the light from a distant star was being bent round the Sun by its massive gravity?

Bob – Yes, that was him and he published several books on the subject. One of them, his Mathematical Theory of Relativity, was considered by Einstein to be the best presentation of General Relativity in any language. J. J. Thomson who had proposed the Plum Pudding model of the atom said that Eddington had persuaded multitudes of people that it was possible to understand what relativity and quantum mechanics were all about.

Alec – Didn't J. J. have a son called George who was also awarded a Nobel Prize for physics?

Bob – That's one of the strangest coincidences in Science. Dad got the prize in 1906 for proving that electrons are particles then thirty-one years later his lad got the same prize for proving that they weren't.

Alec – I remember a few discussions we've had over the years, mainly about those weirder predictions of quantum theory. Like how can particles possibly be capable of being in two places at the same time and why is a photon able to fly twice round the moon before coming back to go thru' both of Young's pinholes. Then there was the idea that particles are able to tunnel thru', or jump over, quantum walls by borrowing energy from somewhere as long as they immediately paid it back!

Bob – Last year I got a good overview of quantum theory when I played a match against a chap who'd just re-joined the club. His name was Ian but I can't remember his surname. When I told him that I'd started here as a junior he said "ditto." I mentioned dates but he couldn't place me so he started mentioning names and yours was in the first few that he came up with. Tall, still got a mass of fairish hair and a good golfer. He played off four and beat me out of the park.

Alec – Would that be Ian Donaldson? In my last year here I stepped in to partner him in the Dad and Son Cup and we came first, altho' we were unable to win the cup and it was awarded to the pair who came second. Ian had only joined the club a couple of weeks previously and hadn't even played a full round. They drafted me in at the last minute when his dad had to call off and, as he hadn't an official handicap, they gave him the maximum of 36. You'll remember his dad Tom, been club champion a couple of

times. Ian turned out to be a natural like his dad and played well below his 36 handicap. Apart from one hole my only contribution was to point out where to aim and I advised him a few times which club he should hit
for his next shot. I met Ian again some years later when he came into the bank looking for funding to expand his business, which if I remember correctly was involved in supplying equipment to archaeologists. We'd a bit of a rushed meeting and never got around to chatting about golf.

Bob – That's him and he mentioned archaeology during the round. Said he'd been lucky as it had been his passion as well as his work. Said his golf over the years had been an occasional round here and there, but now he's semi-retired and intended to play more often. He asked me what I'd done for a living and how I passed the time now that I'm retired. I told him my job had been with telephones and computers and since I stopped working I've found that more often than not I run out of time before I run out of things that I want to do.

Alec – It's funny how life changes when you retire. When you're working it's quite daunting to think of all the extra time you're going to have and how you'll ever manage to fill it. I remember Brenda saying to me "Now you're a free man we'll take one day every week to ourselves and do the things we've always wanted to do. We'll jump into the car on impulse and go somewhere that we've never been to before for lunch. Or we could go and play a game of bowls, or take the grandkids and play rounder's or cricket on the beach." The problem's been that we never seem to have a spare day at the same time so we keep putting it off and saying that next year we'll get better organized.

Bob – Same here. When I retired I was presented with a painting of Famous West-End Pubs. When I got home Alice took one look at it and said, "Eleven famous pubs in one small area, seems to me like a great excuse for a pub crawl." I agreed and told her that the next sunny day we'll drop everything and go for it. Five years later we finally got around to it and everything went well till the fifth or sixth pub where we got involved with a wedding party and I had to phone for one of the kids to come and collect us. Three or four times a year I still get, "And when are we going to finish off that pub-crawl."

Alec – I think the secret's having a fixed aim and timetable and I'll suggest that to Brenda next time she mentions it. Get her to say what she really wants to do and we'll go for it before we're both in our wheelchairs.

Bob – Ian asked me about my other interests and I told him that the family, a bit of golf, gardening and trying to keep on the right side of my owner takes up most of my waking hours. He asked me about my other interests and I told him that I'd given up reading fiction and tended to read books that kept me up to date with the world. But I admitted that over the last thirty years it's been mainly the popular science variety. I told him I've always been a curious person and as I get older I want to know more about how everything around me fits together. He asked if I had joined any societies or been to any science lectures and I had to admit that the furthest I got was an occasional discussion with you. He said that at school science had been his favourite subject and it meshed nicely with his hobby which he'd been lucky enough to turn into a business supplying tools to archaeologists all around the world. I told him that for the past few years I've been trying to get my head round quantum mechanics, but the more I read the less I seem to understand it.

Alec – Did you tell him that you considered the whole quantum area weird?

Bob – I did and he asked me if I knew anything about Radio Carbon Dating. I told him the only dating I knew anything about was when I was in my teens. I said that I was aware that we are a carbon based society and it breaks down over time so you can tell the age of something by counting the number of carbon atoms that remain in it. He asked me if I thought this was a weird process and I had to admit that it seems to be a straightforward process, but wasn't it more of a chemical process than a quantum one?

Alec – We've had that sort of discussion several times.

Bob - Ian said RCD, as he called it, works because carbon's a very special atom that's present in the atmosphere in three varieties. Carbon-12, carbon-13 and carbon-14 and it's the C-14 atom that does the breaking down. C-14's are naturally produced by neutrons in cosmic rays from the Sun reacting with nitrogen atoms which in turn react with oxygen atoms to produce carbon dioxide molecules and that bit of it is chemistry. The reason they're called C-14 atoms is because their nucleus is made up of 6 protons and 8 neutrons makes it slightly unstable, or as he called it, radioactive. All three varieties of the carbon atoms are present in our lower atmosphere and they're absorbed into plants by photosynthesis, some of which are eaten by animals and us. While it's alive anything that's eaten or absorbed the carbon atoms exhales them back into the atmosphere, but when a plant, animal or human dies the atoms remain locked in. As the C-14 atoms are unstable radioactive decay starts to chip away resulting in two of the neutrons being kicked out of the atom which then changes into a stable carbon-12 atom.'

Alec – I can understand that, but why isn't it a chemical process?

Bob – That's exactly what I said to him.

Alec – And.

Bob – He said sorry he'd missed out two words and should have said, "It starts to become carbon-12 and that's where the processes in the quantum world comes in."

Alec – OK, but how does knowing this help us?

Bob – Ian said that without quantum theory we'd be stuck with the knowledge that there's a process which changes carbon-14 atoms into carbon-12 ones and that would be very useful to know, but it wouldn't be of much help to archaeologists.

Alec – Radio Carbon Dating's all about telling how old a bone or a bit of wood is, isn't it?

Bob – Ian said that the key thing is that the C-14 atoms decay at a steady measurable rate so a sample can be dated by counting the C-14 atoms remaining in it. Quantum mechanics describes how this decay happens and gives archaeologists a fairly accurate calculation of the time it'll take for half of them to decay into C-12 atoms. He said that because we're dealing with all the C-14 atoms in a sample at once, RCD can only be a statistical theory. It's a bit like counting the number of heads and tails when you repeatedly flip a coin in the air! I said that's all very well, but flipping coins isn't a quantum effect.

Alec – Did you ask him if we could get the same result by counting the number of C-14 atoms on two different occasions and subtracting one from the other?

Bob – I didn't think of that and it would probably work. But wouldn't the interval between the counts have to be hundreds of years to get anywhere near an accurate answer?

Alec – So we're stuck with the quantum.

Bob – Looks like it 'til something better comes along.

Alec – Did Ian say how Radio Carbon Dating can give a fairly certain date to a bone sample when the theory's governed by the uncertainty principle?

Bob - I asked him why if the theory can tell us the duration of half lifetimes, what's stopping it from telling us which atom will be the next one to go pop. He said "It can't do that as the Universe isn't static with actions happening one at a time so Quantum Mechanics has to be a predictive theory that deals with groups of particles. Equally it can't tell us which pair of the eight neutrons in an atom will decay, only that two of them will. In fact, according to the theory some atoms in the sample will still be C-14's when our solar system flares out five billion years from now." His take was that Quantum Mechanics may not be telling us the whole story, but it's able to tell us why and at what rate two neutrons will disappear from an atom and leave behind a stable carbon-12 atom.

Alec – We've now got two loose neutrons floating about. What happens to them?

Bob – Apparently the theory also says that they'll be expelled as high-energy electrons, not neutrons!

Alec –So we're back to quantum mechanics only telling

us half the story and unable to give one hundred percent correct answers.

Bob – Ian said that QM's predictions have been backed up by experiments and, like all statistical theories, it only deals with the whole sample and can't tell us anything about individual actions within it.

Alec – OK. We can have confidence that the answers we get are one hundred percent correct, but is that as close to reality we're ever likely to get?

Bob – 'Fraid so and much to Einstein and Schrodinger's disgust the answer after a hundred years still seems to be an unqualified yes.

Alec – Say I'm able to establish the precise location of an electron, is that all I'm allowed to know even if the information about where it's heading is available?

Bob – Quantum mechanics states that to get the precise value of one of the two related properties you have to give up all knowledge of the other. Regardless of whether or not you think it's a fudge, that's quantum mechanics for you. It's given us the modern world from transistors to life-saving scanners. It explains why stars shine and why one day ours will run out of atoms to burn and it'll be goodnight Vienna for us.

Alec – Now there's a nice cheery thought, tho' to make it even worse, I've read that a million years before that happens our nearest galaxy's planning to join up with us!

Bob – I read that too and this is where quantum theory comes in very handy as it's able to predict the exact day that'll happen. Apparently our meeting with Andromeda's scheduled for a Sunday with a quantum probability of three days either way!

Alec – That's always assuming that some of our descendants will be around to witness it. But here's another thought, if the space between us is supposed to be expanding, how come Andromeda's moving towards us?

Bob – Galaxies like our Milky Way come in local groups which merge into clusters which are really massive. Sometimes clusters combine into superclusters but for some reason that's as far as they seem to go. Our wee planet's a part of a relatively small local group containing just over thirty galaxies with Andromeda, which is three times the size of ours, being by far the largest. Local groups, clusters and superclusters contain enough gravity within themselves to out-muscle the dark energy that's attempting to push them apart.

Alec – Makes you think doesn't it? Andromeda's two and a half million light years away, but one day it'll join us to form what, Milkomeda or maybe Andromilk. Did Ian say how far back they can go with Radio Carbon Dating?

Bob – I asked him that and it's valid for up to 60,000 years. After that time potassium's naturally found in our body and it's got a half-life of 1.3 billion years. I asked him why it was called Radio Carbon Dating and he said that it really should be called Radioactive Carbon Dating, but back when it was being developed radioactivity had a bad press so it was shortened to make it more acceptable.

Alec – And this all this comes from a half theory dreamed up by Heisenberg, Born Jordan and Dirac and using the 'strange' idea of limiting your knowledge to only what you can observe has never yet been proved to fail It's the only fundamental theory about the world that's never been proved wrong and we've still a long way to go to find its limits. That's definitely the bell, it's safe to go now.

Some years earlier Bob had a very near miss at this hole. He was walking across the fairway after helping his playing partner to search for his ball when another one driven from the tee whizzed past his head. His immediate thought was that being hit once in a lifetime's already once too many so he offered to pay for a bell to be placed where it could be rung just before players crossed the burn on their way to the green. This was backed up by a notice on the tee warning golfers to be sure not to play until they heard the bell.

They drove off and both balls cleared the hill comfortably and ran down to the middle of the fairway leaving them second shots of just under two hundred yards to reach the green. As they came over the hill they could see that the game in front had played out the home and were waiting on the next tee so they motored to where their balls lay and Alec got out and played first. "That swing was your smoothest and best one yet, a swing of real beauty" said Bob. "It looked effortless as you just wafted the ball onto the green." He tried to follow with his rescue club, but was well short and his ball trickled into the burn. They motored down, Bob retrieved his ball and took a drop saying "The team in front's just moving off the tee, so I may as well see if I can hole this and at least make you putt." His chip was weak and finished well short of the flag so with, "I make it back to one-up at the turn and would you pick up my ball as well," he walked over to the bench at the side of the tenth tee carrying a paper bag which he offered to Alec in exchange for his golf ball. Alec took a piece of fruit from it and sat down beside him munching on an apple.

Tenth Hole   408 yards par 4 - Dumgoyne.

Bob – Twenty years after Boltzmann proposed his constant, J. J. Thomson announced at a conference that he'd discovered electrons. It was so unexpected that he was later told by a distinguished colleague that most people in the audience thought he was playing an April Fools' Day joke on them. Fourteen years later Ernest Rutherford fired positively charged particles at very thin sheets of gold foil and, although almost all went straight thru', a few bounced back. As Rutherford later described, 'It was as if we'd fired fifteen inch shells at tissue paper and some of them rebounded.' Rutherford showed that atoms are mainly empty space which allowed most of his positively charged particles free passage, but the occasional one hit the bull's eye and was repelled by the positively charged nucleus.

Alec – Apart from providing a charge to balance the electrons there doesn't seem to be much going on with the protons and neutrons in the middle

Bob – As Ian said, if atoms want to be stable they must be electrically and magnetically neutral and apart from that I don't think that the quantum pioneers gave the nucleus too much thought. Incidentally it wasn't until 1932 that neutrons came into the picture when James Chadwick announced that the nucleus also contained a second particle which had no electric charge. Since the obvious name to match up with protons as neutrons it meant that masses of undetectable particles which had been proposed earlier by Wolfgang Pauli had to change their name to neutrinos.

Alec – Try me with that one again, an undetectable particle called a neutrino!

Bob – Pauli proposed them in 1930 as the solution to problems where atomic experiments were mysteriously losing mass and the First Law insisted that's impossible.

Alec – I'm sure the girls would love to know how that's done!

Bob – Unfortunately neutrinos aren't the answer to the current obesity pandemic and in any case billions of them are passing thru' the tip of your nose every second without you having the slightest reaction.

Alec – You're joking! What important function do they perform that needs so many of them?

Bob – It's no joke 'cos we know they're there, but we don't know why they are, nor why they're around in such massive quantities. Even as we speak countless gazillions of them are being sprayed out of the Sun and are passing right thru' our planet without as much as a 'by your leave'.

Alec – How have they been detected if they can pass right thru' the Earth without reacting to anything?

Bob – A very few have been detected and considering their numbers that's a very, very few of them. It takes massive underground tanks filled with bleach and surrounded by detectors many years just to catch the odd neutrino. They've even installed strings of detectors buried kilometres deep in the ice at the South Pole to search for them. They're so tiny that it takes half a million of them to add up to an electron and as they've no electric charge and just the faintest smidgeon of mass they're virtually undetectable.

Alec – In that case how did Pauli know that they we're there?

Bob – He knew that at the end of every experiment all the resulting bits and pieces are carefully added up and that should equal the energy mass that the experiment started with. It quickly became obvious that this wasn't happening and a tiny bit was consistently missing. As mass energy in the Universe can't be destroyed Pauli realised that there must be particles getting created that we were unable to detect and he called them neutrons. When James Chadwick discovered the neutral particles inside the atoms nucleus a famous Italian scientist called Enrico Fermi suggested that the tiny missing particles should be renamed neutrinos which is Italian for little neutral one and the ones inside the nucleus be called neutrons to match the existing protons.

Alec – So it appears that Einstein, Bohr and some others had different views about what constituted reality, how would you describe it?

Bob – For me reality's what I can see probably coupled with what I'm experiencing right now.

Alec – I'd say that my personal description would be that reality is what's here and now.

Bob – I'd go along with that one, reality must be what's real at this present moment.

Alec – The reason that I asked was a book I read recently implied that the present moment doesn't exist for us humans. It seems that we always come to the party a fifth of a second late.

Bob – That's a new one for me. Is it a proven fact or just a prediction?

Alec – Apparently it's a fact and it's all to do with the way our eyes and brains work together to protect us. If it is true, and I've no reason to doubt it, reality's different from what we're seeing!

Bob – Is it connected with how the optical nerve feeding the signals from our eyes to our brain blocks out a small part of what we see and our brains have to fill the in the gap?

Alec – It's in that area, but it's all to do with the signals that are sent from our eyes to our brain taking a fifth of a second to travel there!

Bob – So you're saying that we're always a fifth of a second behind reality.

Alec – It's gets even stranger than that. Because our brains receive sound signals quicker than visual ones, it computes possible scenarios of what's likely to happen in that fifth of a second and if necessary it warns us in advance to take evasive action. This gives us time to tense our muscles and that's what causes the involuntary twitch we sometimes get.

Bob – Do you remember where you got this information from?

Alec – It was in a book I got last birthday called The Body, written by Bill Bryson. It explained the advantage this gives us if a large beast, or more likely nowadays a truck, is hurtling toward us. Getting warned that fifth of a second early could make the difference between life and death.

Bob – So our brains are checking scenarios at the same time our eyes are seeing it. Where does the fifth of a second come in?

Alec – No, our brains are forecasting plausible scenarios a fifth of a second before the signals from our eyes reaches them. It's reckoned that the delay's to do with the signals from our eyes taking twenty times as long to reach our brain as the sound signals coming in thru' our ears. Our brain makes forecasts depending on the sounds it's receiving so what's reality? Is it when our brains receive the sounds or a fifth of a second later when it processes what our eyes saw?

Bob – So it's the screech of the brakes that we react to rather than our eyes seeing the truck heading towards us that might save our life. That must add a whole new meaning to how we describe consciousness and our concept of now.

Alec – I'm still struggling to get a picture of photons travelling thru' space! Do they come to us as waves or as 'particles.' Or do they switch back and forth as they travel along?

Bob – Photons are waves all the way 'til our eyes get in the way of them and pass on the information that the photons were carrying. Physicists have labelled this action as 'wave collapse' and at no point in a photons journey is it a particle that's creating the wave.

Alec – Even from distant suns?

Bob – Photons emitted by them billions of years ago travel and reach us as energy waves. Most are too few for our brains to register so we need telescopes with long exposure cameras attached to enable us to 'see' them. Surprisingly frogs are able to register photons one at a time, but we need a stream of around thirty of them to comprise a signal and that's all down to the different environments we've had to survive in. However, what the telescopes are seeing now is a snapshot in time of where the suns were billions of years ago and they're most unlikely to still be where the photons say they're located. That's if they still exist!

Alec – Do these photons travel on forever?

Bob – Photons are different from other types of particles in that they're unable to decay spontaneously and turn into other types of particles. Assuming that we live in an expanding universe each photons wave will be getting stretched out and dropping down to a lower and lower frequency. As red is the lowest frequency we can see, the photons are said to be getting red shifted and unless it interacts with some form of matter, the poor photon will eventually get red shifted into oblivion.

Alec – Are there any physical effects when the wave collapses to a particle? Is it something like waves in the ocean pounding onto the beach?

Bob – What makes up 'wave collapse' has been a hot topic over the years. Ian reckoned that calling it that gives the wrong impression and he prefers to say that the wave has been localised. While it's travelling as a wave each photon contains all the information about itself including all its probabilities and this bundle's called the photon's 'wave function'. However, what collapses isn't the entire wave function, it's all the probabilities except one, and that's the point where the photons been localised. This wipes out all the other probabilities and the photons probability value goes to 100%.

Alec – That explains quite a lot, but does that include when we measure its position or momentum while it's moving?

Bob – This is where we bring the problem of ourselves

into it by trying to make things personal. particles have been wave collapsing without our help since day one of the Universe!

Alec – OK, but what if we want to measure something?

Bob – You can't measure something when it's travelling as a wave without interacting with it. Natural interactions are happening all the time and even spontaneously like Ian's radioactive decay.

Alec –So back to the old chestnut, how much does this view of the quantum world reflect reality?

Bob – We're back into yes and no territory and it's all to do with quantum theory's founding fathers, an occasional mother, Nazi persecution of the Jews, the Second and the Cold wars, the Space Race and hard-nosed Americans.

Alec – That's some line-up, but I'd have thought that the scientific community would've plumped for Einstein's view of reality as he'd given them four cast iron proofs. Did Bohr and his merry men use any of them to predict the actions in their quantum realm?

Bob – It would only be fair to consider Planck's non-theory in 1900 as the starting point of the quantum revolution, but the real break-through was Einstein's paper five years later on the photoelectric effect showing that light has both wave and particle properties. He showed that by shining a light on some metals you can create an electric current which depends solely on the amount of energy in the light you shine. You can shine a low energy red light from now 'til eternity, but it'll never produce an electric current. It's only when you increase the frequency, or energy, of the light to near ultra-violet that the current starts to flow. This proved that the electrons needed to be given a certain amount of energy before they're able to shake loose from their atoms.

Alec – Einstein proposed this in 1905 and six years later Rutherford proposed his Planetary Model, why didn't either of them develop the quantum theory?

Bob – Einstein contributed a bit, but he was almost completely immersed in his General Theory of Relativity and Rutherford concentrated on the nucleus where he described nuclear reactions including radioactivity. He also suggested that the nucleus could be split and this would provide a great deal of energy. When Bohr left Rutherford and returned to Copenhagen he couldn't have had inkling of the revolution he was starting. Once he settled in he used Planck's quanta of energy, Rutherford's circling electrons and Einstein's wave/particle nature of light along with some standard physics and came up with a theory which correctly predicted the range of colours that we see when hydrogen atoms are heated.

Alec – When you talk of their range of energy, do you mean like the colours of the rainbow?

Bob – Back in the Iron Age people would've been aware that the colour changes a piece of metal goes thru' is a reliable guide to how hot it is. Bohr showed that this is because the electrons inside atoms collect energy on the way up and shed it on the way down. We see this as the different colours that metals shine out going from dull red to white hot. Before Bohr's theory there had been a lot of attempts to explain this but they were all vastly complicated. His model with the electrons moving up and down orbits acquiring and emitting energy at each stage was a relatively simple and elegant solution.

Alec – I can see that trying to predict the energy of electrons if they're moving around all over the place would be well neigh impossible. Did Bohr concentrate on the colour change of hydrogen atoms as they've only one electron bouncing up and down?

Bob – Ian said that Bohr's model should've been able to describe this for all the elements, not just hydrogen. But it seems that there was something stopping it called the three-body problem.

Alec – The three body problem, I know about that as we covered it in our fifth year at school and it's a major stopper. If you have three bodies that are close to each other and let them move randomly there's no way we can predict where they'll end up. There are some special cases, but usually the only way to solve this is to keep one of the bodies stationary and let the other two move relative to it.

Bob –I remember you telling me about this a long time ago and I thought it would've been resolved by now.

Alec – A Frenchman called Henri Poincare, one of the world's greatest mathematicians, thought that he'd solved it as part of what sounds like a fairy-tale.

Bob – I've heard his name, but it was never in relation to anything like that.

Alec – It's a classic maths story with what turned out to have a very important sting in the tale.

Bob – Go on, I'm all ears. I like fairy stories.

Alec – In 1889 King Oscar the Second of Sweden and Norway organised an international prize competition to celebrate his sixtieth birthday. Being mathematically minded he said that the winner would be the person who submitted the best solution to the Three-Body Problem.

Henri entered it and won.

Bob – Didn't you say that it still hasn't been solved?

Alec – Henri thought that he'd solved the problem by the brilliant idea of replacing one body with a tiny speck of dust and working out solutions for that. The organising committee agreed with him and The King presented Henri with the award at a grand ceremony but then the gremlins struck. Henri discovered a flaw in his workings which put him in an embarrassing position as his solution was due to be published on the day of the King's sixtieth birthday. Being an honourable man he admitted his mistake.

Bob – Did he have to hand back the prize?

Alec – No, he added a hundred pages of workings and a new manuscript was published in time for the Kings next birthday. To save everyone's blushes the King changed the title of the prize to 'The Most Innovative Solutions to the Three-Body Problem'. Henri got to keep the gold medal and the pile of dosh.

Bob – Is that the sting in the tail?

Alec – It wasn't, but no one recognised it at the time, Henri had laid the groundwork for what is now called Chaos Theory. The Three-Body Problem's still hanging out there and maybe they'll need a new type of maths to solve it.

Bob – Chaos Theory, is that the one that says you can't predict the weather for more than five days ahead?

Alec – And what has become known as the 'butterfly effect'.

Bob – I've read about that. Didn't someone propose that a butterfly flapping its wings could be the root cause of a major storm weeks later?

Alec – In 1972 an American meteorologist called Edward Norton Lorenz was due to give a talk on Chaos Theory to the American Association for the Advancement of Science, but forgot to provide his lecture with a title. A colleague, Philip Merrilees, stepped in and suggested, 'Does the flap of a butterfly's wings in Brazil set off a tornado in Texas?' Although the concept of a, butterfly flapping its wings has remained constant, the poor wee thing's location and the consequences have varied widely over the years. I remember reading an old poem about it. 'A butterfly fluttered by, on a warm summer day'. 'The flutter by the butterfly, blew up a storm over old Mandalay'. But going back to Einstein, he didn't see eye to eye with Bohr about his quantum theory and came up with some proofs which were supposed to show that it couldn't be the complete theory.

Bob – That he did, but their disagreements were very gentlemanly affairs as they had a genuine respect for each other.

Alec – Did they make any attempts to come to a compromise?

Bob – All thru' the years Bohr stuck to his guns while Einstein produced several problems that he considered highlighted quantum theory's inconsistencies and his main grouse was always its inability to predict individual events. In his replies Bohr repeatedly told Einstein that the Universe doesn't come in a series of individual events and you're wasting your time if you expect to use it to look for individual actions. On several occasions Einstein was told that he had to accept that what you've measured is all the information you're ever going to get. He countered this with 'Reality is the business of physics.' On one famous occasion he told Bohr "The theory says a lot, but it doesn't bring us any closer to the secret of the Old One, and I at any rate am convinced that He is not playing at dice." What Einstein wanted was a complete description of atoms, electrons and light as particles rather than waves so that he could build a classical picture of reality in the atomic world.

Alec – Isn't Bohr taking a pretty unsustainable position as he's saying that the present theory takes us as far as we'll ever be able to go and Einstein's wasting his time looking for a deeper explanation!

Bob – I don't think Bohr's saying quite that. His argument was that to understand atomic physics you need a new way of thinking what science is all about.

Alec – Is this where the probabilities come in?

Bob - Bohr said that there's a basic contradiction between quantum mechanics and the way we regard the classical world. Every time we perform a quantum measurement we get a well- defined result, but the theory isn't describing these individual events. It can only give you the probability of the event you're measuring happening in a particular way. The next time you measure it you'll be disappointed if you're expecting to get the exact same result.

Alec – Didn't Einstein highlight a problem with quantum mechanics that he called 'spooky action at a distance' and it backfired?

Bob – He did, and along with two young physicists, Boris Podolsky and Nathan Rosen, pointed out to Bohr that quantum theory was proposing something that Maxwell said was impossible. Their starting point was the obvious one that the closer together two particles are the quicker they're able to interact with each other. However quantum theory was saying that the two particles needn't be sitting side by side, they could be separated by any distance in the Universe and they would still interact as tho' they were sitting side-by-side. EPR, as the trio was named, said this is impossible because for that to happen signals sent from one particle to the other would need to have travelled faster than the speed of light and, as Bohr must surely agree, that's impossible.

Alec – What was Bohr's reply to that?

Bob – For a while it really worried him and he came back with a bit of obscure reasoning saying it was EPR's picture of reality that was at fault. The problem was called The EPR Paradox. It was raised in 1935 and it was nearly fifty years before it could be tested and proved correct.

Alec – Was this taken as the ultimate proof of quantum theory and what's the gist of the argument that made it such a big issue?

Bob – As an example, take the two electrons that are spat out when one of Ian's C-14 atoms undergoes Radio Carbon Decay. They'll be identical except for having opposite spins as they're vibrating with opposite phases of the energy they're carrying and this can be detected. The spin of each electron is superposed in their waveform at birth so when you measure one electrons spin and find it to be 'spin up' you'll automatically know the other electron will be 'spin down'. The distance they've moved apart is irrelevant.

Alec – That's a strange concept. Are you saying that 'almost twin' of an electron that's here on earth could be on the far side of the moon yet there's an instantaneous connection between them.

Bob – The whole point is that there's no connection between them as Einstein had supposed. Each of their local waveforms carries the full information for both of them.

Alec – And this has been proved?

Bob - Since the first proof of it in Paris in the 1980s where the particles were separated by less than ten metres there's been many more sophisticated confirmations of this action which is called 'quantum entanglement'. Here on Earth it's been checked by particles spaced 175 kilometres apart on two separate Spanish islands and the proof's never failed. It's also planned to test it out in deep space, so it appears that we have to take waveform superposition and entanglement as facts of life.

Alec – I'd still say that if someone hit me with that proof I'd probably go with Einstein's spooky action and say that it's too weird to be true. Was this his last attempt to prove the quantum theory wrong?

Bob – For the rest of their lives Einstein and Schrodinger believed that quantum mechanics wasn't complete and that a deeper theory would bring a form of classical reality into the quantum world.

Alec – Did you ask Ian if we're any closer to one?

Bob – I didn't ask him directly, but several times he said that it was his impression that physics still has a long way to go which reminds me of a hoary story he told me about Bohr and Einstein.

They meet by chance at a street corner and after exchanging pleasantries Bohr takes a coin out of his pocket and says, 'Watch this Albert, I've just discovered a great new wheeze.' He flips the coin up in the air, puts out his hand and two coins drop into it. Albert inspects his hand and says, 'Show me that again Neils.' Bohr repeats the trick and Einstein examines the two coins. He goes into his pocket and takes out a coin saying, 'The one you're tossing up must be a trick coin. Show me it happening with this one.' Bohr flips it and this time three coins come down which he hands to Albert. Einstein looks at the three coins, shakes his head and asks for the correct explanation saying, 'Although I've seen it with my own eyes it can't be real because reality doesn't work that way.' Bohr shrugs, shakes Einstein's hand and tells him, 'It works every time for me Albert, so that must prove this is as close to reality as we're ever going to get' and, pockets bulging, he walks off down the street.

Alec - So Bohr's won and Einstein's lost?

Bob – Don't worry about poor old Albert, he did alright for himself. It was just that all his life he'd been a realist and what he wanted was a simple realist solution. He couldn't agree with Bohr's interpretation of a theory he'd a hand in giving birth to.

Alec – I remember reading that back in the 1930s physics students at European Universities travelling back home on weekend trains were being advised that it was a waste of time studying their course as only one more equation was required and then there would be no further need of their services.

Bob – By then quantum mechanics must have been in full swing and given physicists the confidence that the end of the road was just round the next corner

Alec – Did you ask Ian what's stopping us from getting a quantum theory of gravity?

Bob – Ian said that funnily enough the main problem with gravity is that it's a one-way action and all types of matter only feel it acting on them in one direction.

Alec – What's funny about that?

Bob– If you think about it gravity's a secondary force and that makes it different from the other three. It's the force that matter generates for itself as it constantly accelerates thru' space.

Alec – You've mentioned that lumps of matter are heavier and lighter. Shouldn't they be lumps of mass instead of lumps of matter, or are they interchangeable?

Bob – Sort of, matter and mass is usually considered as the same thing, as is energy. Energy and mass have consistent scientific definitions, but matter is more a poetic term and its meaning can depend on the context you're using it in. Newton's apple was mass attracted by gravity which pulled it off the tree and caused it to fall straight down and he used this simple action to prove that gravity's one of the universal forces. The fundamental difference between the universal ones is that electromagnetism and the strong nuclear force can attract and repel, whereas gravity only ever acts as an attractive force.

Alec – I've always found gravity a conundrum. It's said that it's so weak that we can't measure it yet if I tried to leap over a bar six feet above the ground it would take all the force that I could muster and I'd still be three feet short. You said that electromagnetism's also a force throughout the Universe, in what other way does gravity differ from it?

Bob – Mainly that gravity's a field with a force in it that's everywhere and as we said it's always a plus force so it can't be cancelled out like the other forces. The electric force is a field that can be zero or plus or minus and even where it's zero the field's still there but there's no force present at that point in it. Remember that magnetism's a separate force which is caused by matter moving thru' a charged electromagnetic field and surprisingly, there's no such thing as a universal magnetic field

Alec – If gravity's always a plus force, how is it possible to be weightless in space?

Bob – You only get to be weightless when two or more gravitational forces pull on you equally. No matter where you are in the Universe, there's always some level of the force of gravity present.

Alec – Why then are the astronauts in the Space Station weightless?

Bob – That's a good example of Einstein's general theory. Earth's gravity is tugging the Space Station towards us and its momentum's trying to make it whizz off in a straight line into deep space. The astronauts are weightless because Einstein proved that a constantly accelerating body like the Space Station cancels out gravity and this applies to everything inside it as well!

Alec – If gravity can do all this, why is it such a weak force?

Bob – I think it's likely to be because of the distance that it acts over. Gravity's force diminishes as per the four square rule, but I think there's enough constantly accelerating matter in the Universe to ensure that there's no point within it that wouldn't have a smidgen of gravity present.

Gravity's spread out everywhere in the Universe whereas the electric field only has the potential to be everywhere. The other two forces are massive by comparison as they're limited to acting inside an atom's nucleus. It appears that gravity affects all three of them due to the universal speed limit and Einstein's $E=mc^2$ equation.

Alec – I know that at speeds approaching light speed strange things start to happen, but I didn't think that it would have any effect on gravity!

Bob - Einstein proved that when any mass approaches 186,000 miles per second it's time slows down and, according to someone watching from a distance, it's mass appears to be bulked up to compensate for it taking less time. Right now we're in this golf cart which is our spaceship and we've pushed its speed up to 99.999% of the speed of light. What do you see happening?

Alec – As I now understand it my watch is running at the same time as it was back on Earth. But the people back there are whizzing about and they need a calendar to tell them the time.

Bob – We're aging in time with the buggy's moving clock and the people back on Earth are ageing according to their 'static' clocks. In other words our metabolisms are running at different speeds. Our bodies are being timed by our moving clock and although we get to live to be many years older by Earth's clock, we peg out on the same day and at the same age no matter where we are. But has anything else happening to us?

Alec – Everything appears to be normal, but the buggy's using up an awful lot of gas. I'll switch on the turbo and see if there's enough left to take us up to light's speed.

Bob – I felt a jolt as the turbo kicked in and I can see we've added some more 9's on the speedo. If there's any gas left in the tank boost it and we'll go for the ton.

Alec – That's it I'm afraid. The tanks dry, we've run out of energy.

Bob – That means we've hit the impenetrable barrier. If it was possible to reach light speed we'd have to burn an infinite amount of energy to get there and keep burning it to stay there!

Alec – And that's impossible.

Bob – Maybe we're looking at it from the wrong angle. If you turn it around that makes what we've just experienced easier to understand, but still has equally profound consequences.

Alec – Are you saying that the reason we can't accelerate the buggy up to light speed is because anything that travels at light speed can only do so if it doesn't have any mass?

Bob – Spot on Mr. Spock, we're looking at it upside down.

Alec – Do you mean that our actions make more sense if we start with the speed of light?

Bob – Important as it is it's not light's actual speed that's really important. It's the hard fact that 186,000 miles per second marks the unbreakable speed limit of the Universe and it's the fixed speed that 'particles' without any mass must travel at. Conversely, for anything to travel slower than the speed of light it must contain mass. If we wanted to exceed the speed limit we'd have to be made of negative mass and gravity being only able to act positively makes that impossible. The other side of the coin is that anything travelling at the speed limit can't take up any time and everything that travels slower than the speed limit must have its internal clock set to run according to the amount of mass it contains!

Alec - What about us travelling just below the speed limit? Wasn't there something about this aging slowly having an effect on a pair of twins?

Bob – Someone worked out what would happen if a pair of twins got separated by one becoming the pilot of a spaceship that zipped out round the galaxy at 75% of the speed of light while his younger brother remained at home. While he was travelling the space exploring brothers' metabolism would be running slower than his younger sibling who would be in for a shock. When he welcomes his big brother back home after travelling for sixty years, he'll find out that his 'older' brother is now twenty years younger than he is!

Alec – Wouldn't there be a problem there. I would think that if they wanted to meet they'd both have to be in the same time zone, not ones that are twenty years apart?

Bob – You're absolutely right, meeting anyone who's in a different time zone would appear to be impossible.

Alec – That's the chaps in front finally moved on. I've got it back to one down at the turn, the fightback continues.

The first hole on the back nine is probably the trickiest on the course and it favours players who can reliably hit their drives with a slight hook. From the tee you're faced with a quite severe hillside sloping down from your left and an out of bounds wall on your right which runs all the way up to the green. As the tee is located at an angle fifty yards from the wall this leaves you with a gap of about twenty yards between the base of the hill and the wall and unless you can drive with a consistent hook you have to take on the sloping hillside which has heavy rough between it and the tee. The green's only a few yards from the wall so most players drive up and over the hillside and come in at the green from an angle. Alec played first and aimed his ball about halfway up the hillside and onto the fairway leaving him with about two hundred yards to the green. Bob took a lower line and with his slight slice he was left with a shot parallel to the out of bounds wall. They got into the golf cart, motored up to the corner and saw that the players in front were pitching onto the green, so once again they sat back and waited.

Alec – Why does the speed of light come into physics so often?

Bob – There's another effect that balances the space buggy's clock slowing down. As we travelled faster and faster it would appear to people back on Earth that, like the Irish physicists ruler, our buggy's getting squashed down in the direction we're travelling and that's directly as a result of us being unable to reach the universal speed limit. If we had been able to reach it the buggy would disappear from their sight and we'd have been squashed down to nothing. Well not nothing, we'd become pure energy!

Alec – I didn't notice us or the buggy being squashed when we were scooting along at almost light speed.

Bob – We wouldn't notice it as we're moving at zero speed relative to the buggy. For us its length has stayed the same as it was when we started. The squashing down would only be apparent to someone watching us from back on Earth.

Alec – That seems very unintuitive. How does light speed affect our cart's apparent length?

Bob – A relatively easy way to understand it is if you imagine I'm on a supersonic train and you're standing on the platform as I whizz past you. I'll make the train one of the new super-duper hypersonic plus ones that can travel up to very near the speed of light.

Alec – And I'm expecting to see the train getting shorter as it passes by me. OK, I'm standing on the platform waiting for the train, what am I looking out for?

Bob – Take this camera and I'll get on board the train with a light clock.

Alec – Light clock as in not heavy. Is that so it won't be affected by gravity?

Bob – No, it's light as in a clock that works by light pulses. It's the simplest possible type of clock and I made it by attaching a mirror at each end of this old metre stick. The mirror at the bottom has a small pencil torch which, when I switch it on, sends a thin beam of photons that'll bounce up and down between the mirrors as we flash past you. I know it's going to be hard to see things when I'm passing by at speed, so to make it easier your camera's got a very high definition movie mode. I'll put the clock on a table next to a window so you can see what's happening and I'll paint a line across the window where the top mirror is. I'll make half a dozen increasingly faster runs past you and then we'll examine the movies.

Alec – Leave the photography to me and enjoy your trip.

Bob – That was quite exhilarating, let's see what we've got. When the train was stationary the light's bouncing straight up and down. In this next run the movie's slightly different. As I flashed past you the top mirror and bouncing photons were starting to lean forward in the direction the train was travelling. These later movies show that as the train gets faster the forward lean increases and this last one shows that as we pass you at the fastest speed the photons are bouncing up and down like the teeth on a saw.

Alec – What surprises me more is what's happening to your metre stick. As the train speeds up your stick's getting shorter and shorter and this last one shows quite a gap between the line you painted and the top of the stick!

Bob – As George Fitzgerald said and Hendrik Lorentz proved, when the train moves faster the ruler must shorten and that's the direct consequence of not being able to exceed light's speed limit. As the train speeds up for each 'tick' of the photons, the top mirror has moved slightly forward in the very short time it takes for the photons to bounce between the two mirrors. Because the distance between the two mirrors has got longer only one of two things can happen. Either the photons have to travel faster than the speed of light, or the distance they have to travel stays the same. As the first solution's impossible we're stuck with the second and the metre stick has to get shorter giving the light clock enough time to complete each tick. It's not only speed that slows down clocks though, gravity has the same effect on them.

Alec – Has this been proved?

Bob – Some time ago two scientists flew atomic clocks around the world in opposite directions and compared them to an identical clock back on the ground. The effect on time at these very, very slow speeds was miniscule, but still measurable. They proved that if you flew one way around the world you'd step off the plane a tiny fraction of a second younger than if you'd remained in the airport lounge and similarly if you'd flown around the other way you'd have aged very slightly more.

Alec – So it's true then that clocks will actually stop running at the speed of light.

Bob – Strictly speaking the answer has to be no. Clocks, even atomic ones, have mass so they can't exist at light speed.

Alec - Does that mean that a massless photon travelling at light speed to us from a galaxy thirteen billion light years away hasn't had thirteen billion birthdays on the way?

Bob – It's worse than that for the poor photon, it hasn't even celebrated its first birthday. Sorry, day, second, or whatever time interval you want!

Alec – So the consequence of being massless is that you're also timeless! This is where I get screwed up when I try to fit it all together.

Bob – When Ian was explaining this to me he said that I was looking a bit dubious and that there's a quite simple concept that is often missed out, or not explained simply enough, and that's something called reference frames.

Alec – Go on.

Bob – It goes back to Newton and his insistence that clocks only ever tick at one second per second and in our reference frame this is what happens. The problem with this is that, due to the way we evolved, we're naturally selfish and tend to think that our reference frame applies throughout the Universe which we now know isn't true.

All the weird things we've talked about are weird mainly because we look at them as tho' they're all happening in our reference frame.

Alec – And you're saying they're not!

Bob – What Ian said is that while we might be masters of our wee planet, we're certainly not masters of the Universe where everything that's happening does so with reference to us.

Alec – So the poor birthday-less photon loses all its birthdays 'cos it's travelling in no time whereas we see that it has travelled for thirteen billion years. How's that possible?

Bob – Basically I look upon it as whoever is doing the measuring is doing so from their reference frame.

Alec – Do all actions have a reference frame?

Bob – Even simple thing like watching a ball rolling down a street. It has a reference frame and we can measure its movements as the ball and us are both in the same reference frame. As Galileo pointed out, the lady on shore and the man on the boat were stationary in their reference frames, but moving in each other's reference frame

Alec – I still don't get it, who decides the reference frames?

Bob – You do, but you can also put yourself in another reference frame and look at things from its point of view.

Alec – I see. I could also look at it from the photons point of view and see things from its perspective.

Bob - If we look at it from the photons reference frame then it's stationary and we're travelling to it from thirteen billion light years away.

Alec – So we're nothing special and things seem weird to

us because we're trying to picture everything as tho' it's all happening with reference to us!

Bob – I think one of the problems we have is that terms like 'reference frames' makes it sound much more difficult than it is.

Alec – Going back to universal forces, what's the difference between the strong one and the weak one?

Bob – They both work inside the nucleus, but the weak force doesn't have a field as it interacts directly with particles that are unstable. It really should be called the Weak Interaction.

Alec – How does that work?

Bob – Amongst other things it reduces atoms down to their most stable state.

Alec – In other words, it's the weak force that helps unstable atoms to become stable ones.

Bob – The strong force is a strange one. It's carried by aptly named gluons which are only active at the very short distances inside an atom's nucleus. In terms of strength, the strong force is by far the most powerful force in the Universe and it's followed by the weak interaction, electromagnetism and then gravity.

Alec – Are all the three forces that act inside atoms interlinked?

Bob - The weak force has no electric charge and while the strong force works very hard to keep protons and neutrons bound together, the weak force does its best to chip away at unstable neutrons. Just as the electric force is carried by photons, the strong force has its own carriers which are called glueons. They're only able to act over the shortest of short distances inside an atoms nucleus and that's why their force is so strong. Electromagnetism works inside and outside a nucleus 'tho' it's only the electric part that's active outside the nucleus. It's been shown that at high energies electromagnetism and the weak force are two faces of a joint field called the electroweak force.

Alec – I've heard of that. Isn't it likely that one day they'll be able to show that this electroweak force, the strong force and possibly gravity are all part of the same overall field?

Bob – I think it's generally reckoned that at the very highest energy levels that were present during the Big bang, three of the four forces were united. But I haven't read of any suggestions that gravity might soon join them. The weak interaction, despite not being a force like the other three, has one of the most important jobs in the Universe. As well as reconfiguring atoms, it works with gravity to create all the suns in the Universe and they're responsible for creating most of the elements. Without the weak force our universe would be a very boring sterile place filled almost completely with hydrogen and a puff or two of helium.

Alec – OK, let's put them in order. The strong force binds three of what you call quarks together to form protons and neutrons and they make up every atom's nucleus, except for hydrogen. The weak force is constantly trying to eject any extra neutrons and along with gravity it gives us sunshine.

Bob – Another important point is that when scientists say that every proton and neutron is made up of three quarks, that's exactly what they mean. Protons and neutrons are three 'herded together' quarks and not three quarks inside a protective bag! Outside the nucleus it's the positive electric charge from the protons acting on the negatively charged electrons that keeps them in order and enables them to move up and down energy levels by capturing and releasing photons. The immediate advantage of this model was that it solved the big problem they had with the earlier theories, why don't atoms lose energy and spiral down into the nucleus?

Alec – And Bohr worked all this out?

Bob – With the help of Rutherford who showed that electrons are free moving and that electricity was the primary force inside the atom. Most atoms are happy little bunnies which if left alone will last until eternity, whenever that is. Fortunately for us there are other actions taking place in an atom's outer shells which create the amazing variety we see all around us.

Alec – I remember that bit from school. Most atoms don't have enough electrons to complete their outer shells so they try to fill them by sharing some electrons with other atoms and that's how molecules are formed. I can see why the electrons inside atoms move as waves, but when are they particles?

Bob – One of the original quantum gang, Pascual Jordan, insisted that the electrons inside an atom are nowhere 'til we look for them and it's the act of us looking for them that turns them into particles. His thinking was that particles represent some form reality whereas waves don't. The best description of what's going on in the sub-atomic world was by a physicist who asked an online group for a five word description of quantum theory and the best answer he got was 'Don't look waves, look particles'

They watched as a member of the group in front replaced the flag and as others walked over to the next tee he remained standing beside the green. Alec decided that the bunker in front of the green and the out of bounds wall behind it made a shot to the green too dangerous so he laid up. Bob reckoned that a three wood would do the job, but his slice came back with a vengeance and, with one bounce on the road, his ball vanished into thick bushes on the other side. He played a second ball hoping that he might put it on the green and one-putt his way to a five but it followed the first one. He said, "I should've played short like you instead of throwing away the hole." Alec replied "Your game's come on a lot since you had that op, but it's when you try to force it that you've still got that tendency to slice." Bob nodded his agreement and they drove up to the green where the chap was waiting patiently for them. Alec chipped onto the green and holed a curly twelve footer for his four before joining Bob and the visitor who greeted him with, "I was telling your friend here how sorry we are to be holding you up. I organised this outing as I played here at your member-guest competition a few years ago but I didn't realise how much difference it makes not having someone with you who knows the course. You're welcome to play thru' and as you come to each group they'll also step aside". Bob told Alec that he'd tried to explain that they'd been doing us a favour as we're old pals from schooldays and we don't often get a bit of time to ourselves to have a good chat. Alec had a momentary vision of his mum saying to Bob's mum 'Look at them, they're like a pair of old men chatting away' before he said, "Too true mate" and the visitor turned away shaking his head.

Eleventh Hole   368 yards par 4 - Craigallion.

Bob – That's us back to all square then. You've come onto your normal game over the last three holes, altho' I haven't helped myself with my shot selection.

Alec - Have a wee tot of this whisky. I remember you telling me that that it's distilled in the Highlands and aged in the Lowlands. How does that come about?

Bob – In the distant past Scotland was formed from six different parts. Five of them joined to make up the Highlands and the other bit came up from the south to form the Lowlands. There's a distinct border where the rocky stone of the north meets the rolling hills of the south and a road near here marks part of that boundary. Glengoyne Distillery straddles the road so the water comes from Highland hills and the spirit's distilled there before being pumped under the road to mature in casks on the Lowland side. As you can taste this gives it a softer, more refined pallet.

Alec – I suppose having one foot in the Highlands and the other in the Lowlands must be pretty unique. On holiday last year we did the tour of a distillery up north and I was amazed at how much whisky tourism's moved on since our last visit to Glengoyne.

Bob – They're getting very popular. My cousin Gina and her husband Andrew came up from Winchester last autumn and stayed overnight with us on their way to do the North Coast 500 run in a beautiful Morgan sports car they'd just bought. I thought they'd appreciate a tour of the distillery, but when Alice phoned to book a time she was surprised to find how few slots were left.

Alec – Going back to what you were saying about electrons, do they also exist outside atoms?

Bob – In some materials like copper, the outermost electrons are so loosely bound that room temperature's enough to give them the energy to leave their atoms and float around. Metals generally have loosely bound electrons while other materials like glass have their electrons more under control and it takes a lot of energy to detach them. An electric current's just a one directional flow of electrons caused by pumping in an excess of them at one end of the wire and retrieving them at the other end. The torch on my light clock is a prime example as it's just a battery connected to a light bulb thru' an on/off switch. The battery's a chemical store of free negative electrons which are let loose when the switch is closed and the bulb lights up.

Alec – So an electric current's just a flow of these electrons down a wire?

Bob – Sort of, but surprisingly it's not the electrons rushing down the wire at light speed which causes the current to flow. Each individual electron saunters along the wire at less than walking pace.

Alec – That's not the way I've experienced it. If I'm in a long tunnel and switch on the lights they come on immediately, not as I'm walking past them!

Bob – The way to picture electrons travelling down a copper wire is to think of them as being like your practice golf balls and the plastic tube you use to pick them up is the copper wire. When the tube's full and you push down to retrieve a ball, the one at the top instantly pops out and it's the same with an electric current. A battery pushes electrons in at one end and they form a stately queue waiting their turn to pop out at the other end. If the wire's connected to the mains alternating electricity which changes polarity fifty times every second, it's likely that most electrons will never make it out of the wire.

Alec – So is an electric current's just these electrons flowing slowly down the wire or alternatively jiggling about in it.

Bob – Incoming electrons displace existing electrons which displace neighbouring ones and so on down the wire. The displacing is done at light speed so the current moves just like your ball tube. An electron pops out at the positive end as a new one is pushed in at the negative end so the direction of flow is actually negative to positive. This anomaly came about because Benjamin Franklin, one of the early American Presidents, rubbed two dissimilar materials together and created static electricity. He said that an electric current flows from the 'positive' donor material to the 'negative' receptive material. When it was later confirmed that the actual flow is in the opposite direction, it was too late to change and the decision was made to keep the positive to negative convention as reversing it would cause too many practical problems.

Alec – Apart from electrons having opposite spins what other differences are there between them and photons?

Bob – The only similarity they have is that they both travel as waves, but apart from that they're totally different animals. Electrons are energy with mass and photons are energy without mass. Photons must zip everywhere at the speed of light and are able to circle the Earth seven times in a second. By comparison, electrons would take around eighteen seconds to complete the same journey.

The eleventh hole's flat for the first hundred yards, but then slopes up steeply to a green perched on top of the hill they played to before. The hill's called Mount Zion and three holes and tees are located at the top. When the course was being laid out two burial urns were uncovered dating back 5,500 years to the time when the first cities were built, the wheel was invented and the Sumerians developed the first written language. Unfortunately one of the urns was badly damaged, but the other one was in pristine condition and it's on display in a special glass security case in the clubhouse. It shows that there was a late Neolithic settlement around here with the hilltop as their sacred burial ground.

If you want to drive the direct line to the green you have to carry a large bunker halfway up the left half of the slope. Unless you can clear the bunker your options are to play short of it or drive up the right half of the fairway. Taking this line leaves you with a more difficult second shot as you have to carry a large bunker guarding that side of the entrance to the green. Alec opted to play a lesser club and drove to just short of the fairway bunker. Bob, trying to out-think the course, aimed straight at the bunker expecting a slight slice.

Bob – That's typical. If I allow for a slice the ball goes straight and when I want to hit it straight it slices. Where's the logic in that?

Alec – That's the way it goes old pal, some you win and some you slice. A wee while ago you said something about quantum mechanic's founding fathers, Nazis, Jews, world wars and some other things. Where does all that come in?

Bob – One of the unexpected things about the quantum revolution was the speed it took over the physics world. In a few short years the students who'd flocked to Bohr and Heisenberg became professors who decided the direction physics was heading in. As a result of its successful predictions most of them championed Bohr's theory and all the objections were swept aside leaving universities to teach only Bohr's version of quantum theory. However, most of the quantum action was taking place in Middle Europe where there was lots of political turmoil left over from the Great War and this led to the Nazis gaining power in Germany.

Alec – Yes and their anti-Jewish dogma caused many of the foremost physicists in Europe to leave. I assume that included a lot of the quantum ones?

Bob – A large portion of them upped and settled in Britain or America to where at the beginning of 1939 Niels Bohr paid a visit with the news that a German Physicist called Otto Hahn had, by a very lucky fluke, split the atom. With the help of John Wheeler, one of his US students, they started to think about the implications of this. The size of an atom makes it difficult for us to get even a rough idea of what they were dealing with. The nucleus of a typical atom is 100,000 times smaller than the cloud of electrons that surrounds it and that is about a million times smaller than the width of a human hair. Also it's not the whole atom they're trying to split, it's just the bit in the middle which accounts for around 99% of an atom's energy!

Alec – Knowing that the Nazis had already achieved this must have been a great concern to those in the know. I think that Heisenberg remained on the German side and he must have been aware of the potential use this had as a bomb. But did Germany have the resources and enough brainpower left to see the project thru'?

Bob – At the beginning of the war the expanded German Empire certainly had the resources. Czechoslovakia was occupied in 1939 and it had vast uranium deposits. If they'd poured all their efforts into developing a nuclear bomb at the beginning of the war I doubt there's not much we could've done to stop them.

Alec – That would have been a terrifying prospect. Half a dozen bombs carried by their rocket planes and missiles then exploded over Britain and Russia would've had us suing for peace at any cost. But with the Jewish physicists demonised and chased out did they have the human resources to see it thru'?

Bob – I don't think there was any lack of brainpower, look how far ahead of us they were in technology by the end of the war. They'd developed guided missiles, rockets, super tanks and jet planes, but it now seems that it was partly the Nazi's own philosophy that saved us!

Alec – Philosophy determined the course of the war, surely that can't be right!

Bob – Not philosophy alone, but I think it played a role in how it was fought.

Alec – How come?

Bob – Between the two wars, Europe was seething with ideas about philosophy and politics. In Middle Europe philosophy was regarded as the top of the science tree with physics on a lower branch. One result of this was that it was easier for Jews to gain entry into physics which was often referred to by the Nazis as Jewish Science. Before the war started most of these physicists had left Europe and the centre of world physics moved with them. Some came to the UK but the major beneficiary of this was the USA. But when they got there they quickly found out that hard-nosed results were valued more highly than philosophical musings.

Alec – The 1914 – 1918 war seems to have left as many problems as it solved, if not more!

Bob - In the 1930s European philosophy had two opposing branches, Circles in Vienna and Berlin verses National Socialism. The Circles were left wing democratic internationalists whereas National Socialism promoted extreme right-wing nationalism along with persecution of those who were deemed unfit to be included in their brave new Germanic World.

Alec – I see what you're getting at. Nuclear was physics and stained as Jewish science, so it couldn't be allowed to play any part in the final victory. Do you think it's possible that's what helped to decide the fate of the world!

Bob – I don't think it's the entire story by a long chalk, but given their other engineering achievements I'd reckon it's perfectly feasible.

Alec – Surely Hahn splitting the atom must've caused consternation in the Western Powers.

Bob – It didn't seem to as it was quickly realised that there was a massive logistical problem to be solved before you could even start to think about building a working bomb. The major problem was that to make a successful one they needed uranium.

Alec – What's the problem with uranium? I know it's

radioactive and very heavy, but what else is unique about it?

Bob – It comes in several different types, or isotopes, and the best one to build a successful bomb is Uranium 235 as it's the one that splits open relatively easily. That's easily with a big accent on relatively and that gave the bomb builders a very big logistical problem.

Alec – Is this U-235 very hard to find?

Bob – Uranium's most common isotope is U-238 and there are also a few others. U-235's mixed in with these and accounts for less than one percent of the total amount. The major problem was how to separate out the U-235 from all the other isotopes to at least 90% purity giving them what's called 'enriched uranium'. The actual bomb theory is pretty simple. You split open a U-235's nucleus and the energy this releases causes two or more of the other nucleus's to split and that keeps building up in a chain reaction. The problem is that if any isotopes other than U-235 gets' in the way they put a stop to the chain reaction spreading. Bohr highlighted the problem during his visit when he worked out that to get the required amount to make viable bombs, a large area in the United States would have to be turned into a factory and in the end he was proved very nearly correct.

Alec – Back to U-235, why?

Bob – To make a bomb out of a chunk of uranium you need to start a chain-reaction among the atoms and because it's the easiest to split the U-235 nucleus is the one that's most capable of keeping it going. Getting the actual chain-reaction started was the least of the problems. Keeping it going by getting enough 90% enriched U-235 was a much bigger headache.

Alec – Doesn't Einstein's $E=mc^2$ equation tell us that we can get an enormous amount of energy from a tiny mass. Why couldn't they use a small amount of U-235?

Bob – You would think it would work that way and that would be the case if you could get 100% enriched U-235, but since they only had 90% it worked out to be almost the opposite. A small bomb containing one kilogram of 90% enriched uranium isn't enough to sustain the chain reaction and they settled for a minimum of fifteen kilos. The first bombs were very inefficient as they only released the energy of 3 grams of U-235 and that's about the mass of a penny out of a warhead of over twenty kilos. They were called dirty bombs as the vast majority of unused uranium was scattered all around as radioactive radiation.

By this time they'd driven up to their golf balls and Alec once again hit his seven iron a bit too thin and, although they couldn't see it, his ball bounced on the green and rolled off the back. Bob's drive had landed short of the fairway bunker then rolled into the front of it leaving him with a nice flat lie. From there he nipped an eight iron off the top of the sand and was disappointed when it landed just short of the green. Alec chipped back to a couple of yards beyond the hole and Bob stroked a long putt to within inches of it. When Alec missed his return putt he conceded the hole by signalling to Bob with his index finger once again pointing down. As they climbed into the buggy they noticed that there were golfers on the two greens between them and the next tee so they sat in the golf cart and waited once again.

Alec – I've read about the race to build the first bomb and the essential contributions made by a significant number of the European physicists who fled from Hitler. Did Einstein have any part in it?

Bob – Just before the war started Einstein, along with three other prominent physicists, wrote a letter to President Roosevelt warning him about the destructive effect that a nuclear bomb would have. Their pleas were ignored 'til a couple of months before Japan declared war on the USA. From that late starting point it took four more years to make the bombs that were dropped on Japan.

Alec – Did The Nazis have any idea that the allies were building a bomb?

Bob – During the war Hitler was made aware that nuclear weapons were a possibility. In a 1942 meeting with Albert Speer, the Minister of Armaments and War Production, Heisenberg made a reference to the amount of U-235 that was necessary and caused a small sensation when he used the word 'bomb' as most of the scientists and officials present weren't aware that this was a possibility. Hitler later suggested to Speer that such a bomb 'Would throw a man off his horse at a distance of over three kilometres.' Thankfully they never got to grips with it and, along with their National Socialism dogma, the project never got off the ground. At the end of the war Heisenberg and nine other German physicists were rounded up and held in a Manor House in England. The house was liberally spiked with eavesdropping microphones and the prisoners were supplied with good food, newspapers and radio access. They talked freely amongst themselves saying that they would be alright once things settled down as there

204

would be a great demand for their advanced nuclear expertise. They were gobsmacked when the news came thru' that the US had dropped the first bomb as they were totally convinced that German science had been much further advanced than the Allies.

Alec – Unfortunately the war was hardly over before the world was caught up in the Cold War which started another arms race.

Bob – Which lead to a massive requirement for highly educated quantum physicists to keep pushing the boundaries with the accent on creating end products that had a practical use. Get results and get them quick was the hard-nosed American mantra and anyone questioning the basics of quantum theory was met with the 'shut up and calculate' response!

Alec – It certainly worked 'cos in 25 years they'd put a man on the moon. Three of them in fact!

Bob – That was an amazing feat, but it was only made possible by developing German rocketry and microelectronics based on quantum theory.

Alec – It was round about then that you moved into computers wasn't it?

Bob – The day I started working with them I had a meeting with Bert, my manager. After a getting to know each other chat he passed over a paperweight and showed me my very first integrated circuit chip. I told him that I'd heard of them, but never actually seen one and he told me "What you're holding in your hand is the future of computing." He pointed to a picture on the wall showing two circuit boards and continued, "That wee black square in the middle contains more transistors than fifty of those circuit boards." He retired a few years later and in his farewell dinner speech said that the world of computing was changing too fast for him. Bert got a laugh when he said that in next to no time we'll be able to hang up our soldering irons and instead of rooms full of mainframe computers everything would be contained on a few chips. I said to the chap sitting next to me that he's probably right, but his time-scale's way out.

Alec – Yes but it wasn't, was it! It didn't take long before the Commodore Pet came along and we started playing games on them. Then in what seemed no time at all the Pet's had morphed into desktop computers.

Bob – I bought a Pet in the late 70's, but it was only good as an educational toy or to play simple games on. It was the introduction of the Commodore 64 in the early 80's along with a simple way to program them called Basic that enabled the development of software packages like Word and Excel. From that quick beginning desktop computing's taken over the world.

Alec – A chap in my department at the bank went to USA on holiday and brought back a Commodore 64 and we were all amazed when he said that he'd bought it in a local supermarket for less than $600. We were incredulous that you could go into a local shop and get a working computer for about a quarter of what we were paying for the machines that just punched the holes in the cards that fed them.

Bob – Away back when I started in telephones they all had a rotary dial to make calls within your local area If you wanted to speak to anyone further away you had to dial '0' for a switchboard operator to connect you. Now with one click on her mobile your Auntie Jean in Sydney can call you and ask if you would read out the greetings on the birthday email you sent as she's mislaid her specs again.

Alec – It's certainly a whole different world out there from the one we were born into!

Bob – With Mr. Bohr's half-a-theory we've moved on from the machines that Alan Turing built to decipher the unbreakable German codes during the war to computers that can consistently beat the finest chess grandmasters. It's probably true that the development of integrated circuits is as great an invention as the wheel and it's now reckoned that in the future the number of internet connected computers will be more important than the number of transistors in any individual computers integrated circuits.

Alec – That's what's led to the growth of the Internet isn't it?

Bob - Alan Turing didn't actually build the Enigma machines and it's a bit like the Maxwell and Faraday story of electromagnetism. The company where I started as an apprentice was at that time called the Post Office Telephones and one of their researchers called Tommy Flowers built the machines out of existing telephone exchange components like relays, selector switches and vacuum tubes. Turing called Flowers a mechanical genius, but most of his colleagues looked down on him and now he's been almost completely written out of the story. Without the Turing and Flowers partnership it's possible that the War could've dragged on for at least another year.

Alec – Fame's a very fickle thing, but you were saying something about the Internet

Bob – Early computers communicated with each other

using modems which were connected one-to-one by direct, or dial-up, telephone lines and messages were sent as long strings of zeros and ones. That worked reasonably well but it suffered from the problems of slow speed and poor line quality. There was a bit of error checking to make sure the message wasn't distorted, but any disruption to the long string of characters meant that you had to go back to the beginning and send the complete message again. In the mid-sixties the technology was becoming available to split these long strings into packets of data so that if one packet was jumbled up you didn't have to re-send the entire message. But even then the messages were still being sent slowly one-to-one and it wasn't 'til 1989 that Tim Berners-Lee, then working at the European atom smasher called CERN, tackled the direct connection problem. He sketched out a system where the local telephone lines are connected to switches called routers which read the address of the computer you're sending the packet to and passes it on to the next router. It on-passes it and the data packet 'hops' along 'til it reaches its final destination. This was called The World Wide Web and was limited to CERN, the participating universities and the companies working with them. In 1995 it was thrown open to the world and re-named The Internet. Now individual packets of your Internet traffic can go by any route around the world before getting to their final destination and this way of routing messages is what's now called 'The Cloud'

Alec – Does this all happen when I request a page over the internet?

Bob – That and lots more and all due to CERN wanting to exchange information with researchers around the world quickly and securely.

Alec – Do the messages sent to me in packets have to come in sequence?

Bob – No and that's the beauty of the system. Each individual packet's got the recipients internet address and its number in the messages sequence. Messages for you arrive at your computer in any order and it checks and assembles them into the correct sequence. You can see that it's an extension of the World Wide Web by the initials www in front of the name of the site you're connecting to.

Alec – Is the internet address those four numbers with a dot between each of them?

Bob – That's called the IPv4 system or to give it it's full name, Internet Protocol version 4, 'cos it uses four groups of numbers and provided 4.3 billion internet addresses which engineers were confident would be sufficient for at least a century. But after only twenty years it started to run of numbers so in 2015 a new system called IPv6 was introduced with six groups of numbers and letters. This gives around 340 trillion, trillion, trillion combinations, so the hope is that it will last a bit longer this time!

Alec – 4.3 billion seems a lot of internet users. Where did they all come from?

Bob - At the end of 1995 it had 15 million users, or 0.4% of the world's population. Twenty five years later it's grown to over 5 billion users and that means that almost 65% of the world's population are now connected together, but the addressing system doesn't stop with individual computers. Almost anything, including your car or cows in a field, can have an internet address and be contacted if you have its Internet address and password.

Alec – How did the Internet manage such growth in a relatively short time?

Bob – The Internet as we now know it couldn't have been built out of the technology that was around when Berners-Lee developed it, another method which had a much greater bandwidth was required. Bandwidth's just like the flow of water down a pipe which increases when you use a wider pipe. Instead of sending electrons down copper wires, fibre optics was developed to send streams of photons zig-zagging down thin fibreglass strands at around 70% of the speed of light. When the technology was being developed in the late eighties and early nineties money was plentiful and the favoured investment was in new technology companies whose stock market prices kept soaring at ever increasing rates. Most of these high tech companies used this torrent of money to upgrade their copper wire networks to the new fibre and as there wasn't much difference in the cost of fibre, they put in ten's, hundreds or even thousands of strands rather than one or two. When the bubble burst with the 1998 Stock Market crash the world was awash with cheap fibre optic capacity and the Internet was the ideal home for it.

Alec – When did computers as we know them come into the picture?

Bob – Back in 1950 Alan Turing wrote a paper on the interactions between humans and computers called The Turing Test and the same year he built the Pilot ACE which was the first computer that we could interact with. A few years later transistors replaced electronic valves, but that gave rise to an unexpected problem. For the next couple of decades we had computers that could run much faster than we could get the information into or back out of them.

Alec – So we had what looks like a great tool, but couldn't get full use of it. Is that not still the case?

Bob – It wasn't the computers fault, it was the programs that ran on them. They could only run one program at a time so in the late 1970's Bell, the American telephone company, introduced a more useable programming system called UNIX. They trademarked it and expected the world to pay to use it and for a while it looked as if Bell was going to be holding the computing world to ransom. This provoked a software engineer from Finland called Linus Torvalds to write a comparable system which he called Linux and offered it to the world for free.

Alec – What's the advantage of UNIX and Linux?

Bob – A chap who's a software developer told me they were computer operating systems that did all the housekeeping jobs for you leaving programmers like him to turn a computer into whatever they wanted. He said that they both worked like a circular coat-stand where you can hook up coats, jackets, anoraks, jumpers, scarfs, or in this case different software programs, and know where to find them when you want them to run.

Alec – Is the Windows system on my laptop a UNIX or a Linux operating system?

Bob – Windows is Microsoft's own operating system which only allows you run programs one at a time. UNIX and Linux are multitasking operating systems which makes better use of computers by enabling them to run multiple interacting programs at the same time. Linus Torvalds wasn't a big fan of Microsoft and he's well known for some of the quips he's made about theirs, and some other operating systems. A couple of his more famous ones are 'Software's like sex, it's better when it's free' and on Microsoft 'In my opinion they're much better at making money than making good operating systems.'

Alec – He sounds a switched on chap. Was it UNIX and Linux that helped the computer world to get up to speed?

Bob – It was and they're still running huge, complex, key applications for companies that absolutely, positively need those apps to run. Despite rumours of their imminent death, use of both is still growing and they've helped to produce much of the modern world. Then just when we thought that we're getting near that last turn in the road and are closing in on the ultimate knowledge, astronomers come along and give our self-esteem its biggest ever shock. It now seems that all the solid matter we see throughout the Universe only adds up to one sixth what's actually there. The other eighty-odd percent appears to be made up of something that so far we've been unable to detect.

Alec – Is that the dark matter that was found when they weighed the Universe?

Bob – It is and apart from watching various film and TV astronauts calling it the last frontier, I doubt most of us give space a second thought. Most of us regarded it as just that empty bit of inconvenient distance between planets and galaxies. Surprisingly tho' the idea that there's a lot more to it goes back to 1884 when Lord Kelvin, then the top scientist in the UK, gave a talk. In it he said that there must be a great number of unseen bodies in the Milky Way because when he added up all the bits that he can see, there isn't nearly enough mass to keep our galaxy stable. His conjecture was that if what we see in our solar system is all there is then our wee solar system would've been ejected from the Milky Way long ago!

Alec – I imagine that most people would've assumed that there must be something wrong with the old boy's calculations, so we'll sit back and wait for further proof before bothering our heads about it.

Bob – If they did they had a long wait. It wasn't 'til 1922 that a Dutch astronomer called Jacobus Kapteyn, then Jan Oort ten years later, did the same calculations and announced that there must be loads more matter present in space than just the bits they were able to detect. A year after Oort a Swiss astrophysicist called Fritz Zwicky, who'd spent years studying galaxy clusters, made the strongest case that this unseen matter must exist everywhere throughout the Universe. Dark matter's existence was finally proved in the late 1970's by Vera Rubin and Kent Ford using a much improved spectroscope made by Kent Ford. It'd taken eight-six years since Lord Kelvin's proposal, but now we know that we have to deal with dark matter as a fact of life.

Twelfth Hole   162 yards par 3 - Carbeth.

This short downhill hole is the first in a triangle of three holes that takes you down, round and back up Mount Zion before lining you up for the final stretch back to the clubhouse. The four golfers in front were searching again, this time in a group of trees to the right of the green, so Bob and Alec sat on a bench and took in the view. It was a beautiful clear day and Bob pointed out various local landmarks.

Alec - This view's been here since I was a boy and it's only when I got older that I start to appreciate it.

Bob - I was the same. Too busy thinking of my last shot, next shot, what was right or wrong with my swing and a hundred and one other things to have any time to spare for all these natural beauties around us. Wasn't it Ben Hogan who said, 'Play golf, but take time out to smell the flowers on the way round.'

Alec – I've still got the book and I'm sure it was actually Walter Hagen who said it. He was a contemporary of the great Ben Hogan.

Bob – Hagen or Hogan, no matter who said it, it's a noble sentiment. Life and rush were too often equal partners for me before I grew to appreciate what I was missing.

Alec – I'm looking up and trying to visualise what it would be like if there was no dark matter. Would the stars at the outer edge of our Milky Way galaxy be the first to leave us?

Bob – It now looks likely that if dark matter had never existed there wouldn't be any galaxies, suns or planets to peel off into the darkness. The current theory is that when they were being formed it was dark matter that provided a sort of scaffolding round which the visible matter congregated.

Alec – When Lord Kelvin measured the amount of dark matter our galaxy needed to provide the balance, did he come up with a figure?

Bob – I don't know if he calculated an actual amount, but modern astronomers have and they've concluded that the total amount of dark matter that's there must be about five times more than the mass of all the visible stars and planets in the Universe. As well as this dark matter being everywhere inside our galaxy, it also forms a large halo around it which extends outward for over a million light years and that's getting on for nearly halfway to our next-door neighbour, Andromeda.

Alec – That's quite a thought, but why can't we detect it?

Bob – The simple answer is that it doesn't produce photons nor does it interact electromagnetically with anything else. The real answer's likely to be much more complicated and it's hoped that one day CERN will be able to produce enough of it to study and hopefully make some sense of. Astronomers have been keeping tabs on a pair of galaxies that are merging out in deep space and they've noticed that the clouds of dark matter that surround each galaxy are passing right thru' each other without appearing to create any interactions. It looks as tho' dark matter doesn't even interact with itself!

Alec – Could Andromeda and our Milky Way be getting pulled together by the dark matter and not by the visible galaxies?

Bob – I don't know, but it looks as if dark matter's acting like a form of gravity so I wouldn't be surprised if it was.

Then there's dark energy and we've also got no clues how and where it comes into the picture.

Alec – Is dark energy dark because it doesn't produce any light?

Bob – Dark energy's a totally different concept and it looks more like being a giant reservoir of energy built into the fabric of the Universe. It's different from dark matter because rather than contributing to the Universe's gravity pulling us together, dark energy's creating a repulsive energy which is pushing matter in the Universe further and further apart!

Alec – Is this dark energy what's causing space to expand.

Bob – That's a popular misconception, but Space hasn't an independent existence of its own. There's no way it can be measured as there aren't any markers attached to it. It's not expanding or contracting or doing anything else as it's not a physical substance and that way it can be considered as the only thing that's truly infinite. Dark energy's causing matter to expand into an infinite Space and the distance between a pair of well separated galaxy's is increasing all the time!

Alec – How did dark energy come about?

Bob – Like a lot of things dark energy started with Albert Einstein, but at the time he called it 'the greatest blunder of my life.'

Alec – I suppose even the best of us can make mistakes. What did he do to rectify it, change his calculations?

Bob – Five years after Einstein presented his great work, a Russian physicist called Alexander Friedmann found a solution to his equations which suggested that the Universe must still be expanding in all directions. He sent a letter to Einstein explaining this, but Einstein returned the letter saying that he thought the workings were suspicious. At the time he was on a lecture tour with Werner Heisenberg in Japan and didn't seem to take Friedmann's solution seriously. Friedmann died of typhoid a couple of years later and, with Russia being in turmoil after the revolution, his solution wasn't widely reported in the West.

Alec – Didn't someone around then who'd access to the world's biggest telescope make observations which also suggested that the Universe is expanding and they added that the further away galaxies are from us, the faster their expansion is speeding-up!

Bob – That was Edwin Hubble. Seven years after Friedmann sent his calculation to Einstein Hubble came up with his photographic evidence showing the spectrums of light coming to us from distant galaxies.

Alec – What did they tell us?

Bob – Here on Earth we're lucky as our atmosphere blocks out almost all the harmful high energy photons which could cause us damage. Groups of lower energy photons are absorbed by the gases that are present in our atmosphere and, as each different gas absorbs the photons that are vibrating at its particular frequency, black bands appear where their frequencies should have been. These black bands and their positions in the spectrum were well known as scientists had used them to identify the gases that make up our atmosphere. Hubble's photos showed that distant stars and galaxies have similar black bands which indicated that their atmospheres contained gases just like ours.

Alec – It must have been reassuring to see that other parts of the Universe are like us!

Bob – That's true, but maybe what he saw wasn't so reassuring. The missing frequencies were there sure enough, but the difference was that they weren't in their correct place! Each band was at a lower frequency than the ones we see here on Earth, and not only that the further the stars were away from us the lower the missing frequencies were shifted.

Alec – Does that mean that the light's getting dimmer because it's coming from further away?

Bob – Dimness or brightness is simply the number of photons that reach us and the further away a galaxy is away from us, the dimmer its light will normally be. There were already some proven ways to measure the distances between us and various galaxies and Hubble's photos showed that the more distant a galaxy was, the more its tell-tale markers were red shifted. Hubble never said that his photos showed that space was expanding. He left that decision up to others to make what they wanted out of it!

Alec – If he didn't say it who did?

Bob - In 1927, two years before Hubble made his redshift announcement, there was a conference that all the A-listers of science attended. It included Bohr, Einstein, Dirac, Heisenberg and Marie Curie along with others that weren't household names.. At it a Belgian priest, Georges Lemaître, presented his Ph.D thesis which predicted that the Universe was expanding and he got a respectful hearing but very little support. After the presentation he'd a discussion with Einstein who told him 'Your calculations are correct, but your physics is atrocious.' Einstein didn't question his maths, but he couldn't accept what they were saying. After Hubble showed astronomical proof of Lemaître's theory Einstein came round and became one of its main supporters. He said, "It looks crazy, but it's a completely sound idea." Lemaitre's work became the basis for the Big bang Theory, but for the rest of his life Hubble remained doubtful about this interpretation of redshift.

Alec – So that's what leads us to the Big Bang Theory?

Bob – Yes and it's the theory that takes us back through all the stages of the Universe to its very beginning as a primeval super-atom, or singularity, 13.8 billion years ago. But now some scientists are casting doubts that we can go back as far as that.

Alec – Singularity, what's that all about?

Bob – It's the point where all the known laws of physics break down making it impossible to measure anything.

Alec – Over the years we've had a few discussions about The Big Bang and I think you've always had some reservations about it.

Bob – I don't think that the Big Bang's a completely done and dusted deal yet, especially now we know that it only accounts for 5% of what's there. Almost everything I've read gives the standard view about the Universe starting from a microscopic dot and expanding extremely rapidly. The theory says that the energy it started out with was converted into matter and when it finished there was a tiny bit left over which we see today as the Cosmic Microwave Background Radiation.

Alec –That's what's usually referred to as the CMBR isn't it? Wasn't that taken as conclusive proof that the Universe must have started out from a Big bang.

Bob – It was the discovery of the CMBR that clinched the argument in Big bang's favour against a rival Steady State theory. But recent work has suggested that the Universe's creation didn't all take place at the singularity starting point. Some now say that the actual beginning took place 380,000 years later after the universe had gone thru' an era of very rapid massive expansion called inflation.

The game in front had played out and moved over to the next tee so they both hit seven irons from which neither ball found the green. Alec, although only half Bob's distance away from the hole, had the worst lie as his ball had once again plugged in the bunker. Bob's ball had a clean lie in the bunker on the other side of the green so he took a three quarter swing and his ball hit the flagstick then dropped into the hole. Alec dug his ball out of the sand, but unfortunately it finished as far from the hole as it started. As he picked Bob's ball out of the hole and handed it to him he said, "That's me two down again. Playing golf at this pace obviously suites your game." Bob replied "It's not the pace that matters, it's the pain I get from you hanging onto my ten-bob note for far too long!"

Alec – I've heard of this space inflating theory, but why start the Universe from there?
Bob – I think it's mainly because that's as far back in time as science can provide proof of. They say that that the only thing which can be proved with any degree of certainty is that the state describing the Big bang came about after the inflation period ended.
Alec – How certain are they about this inflation theory?

Bob – The current consensus seems to be that although they don't know everything about it they're fairly certain that inflation or something very much like it must be the cause of the very flat state that we see all around us today. When they say flat they mean that regardless of which way we look out at the universe we see similar views and the same laws. To back that up the temperature of space all around us has been measured to be flat to 99.997%.

Alec – Does that affect the CMBR?

Bob – No it's still the view that it's the cooled-down heat that was left over 380,000 years after the singularity.

Alec – Does this new Big Bang theory throw any light on dark matter or energy?

Bob – Ian Donaldson said that scientists were convinced that the results they got the first time they added up all the visible matter in galaxies must be wrong so they checked and rechecked their figures. They then checked them again using whole clusters of galaxies and they were amazed when the exact same results came back each time.

Alec – Puts us down a bit doesn't it? In a few short years our beloved matter universe has gone from being almost all there is to just a miserly five percent of what's actually there.

Bob – Science now seems to be in agreement that it's roughly a two third, one third split with somewhere around two-thirds of it being dark energy. Of the remaining third, five-sixths is dark matter and the remaining one twentieth is what we once thought of as our complete universe.

Alec – Could it be anything to do with Einstein's $E=mc^2$ equation and all the dark energy that's locked up in visible matter?

Bob – No. That energy and matter's accounted for in our five percent of the Universe, it's the remaining ninety- five percent that's the problem. Over the last few years I've watched bits on the telly and read quite a few books, but apart from refining the percentages up and down a bit we don't seem to be any nearer to a proposal that could make a start at resolving it.

Alec – Does the current Big Bang theory say anything about this dark 95% of the Universe?

Bob - I've often wondered about the Big Bang starting from a singularity, but I think that one of the main reasons it's so readily accepted is because it provides us with a very convenient cop-out.

Alec – You've said that before, but a cop-out of what?

Bob – The cop-out that gives us a comfortable history which is readily acceptable to most people, races and religions. We get handed a nice clean start with the possibility of there being a creator who organised and gifted it to us without having to explain where it came from.

Alec – Are you suggesting that the Universe might not have come into existence with a Big Bang?

Bob – Unless it's eternal in the truest sense of the word the Universe must have come into existence somehow. The current Big Bang theory describes the start as exploding from an infinitely dense, infinitely hot, singularity and if we're to make any sense of that we have to assume that the present laws of physics, or something very much like them, were in existence before the Big Bang started. That leads to an idea that The Big Bang might've sprouted out from a form of energy that was part of space itself. Apparently the possibility for an energy dominated universe to sprout is there all the time and, unlike the current theory, it doesn't need a singularity to sprout from.

Alec - Run that past me again!

Bob – There's a theory which says that the Universe could have resulted because of an energy field that eventually contracted and kept concentrating its energy 'til it reached a tipping point.

Alec – Doesn't that contradict the First Law?

Bob – It could, but only if you end up with a different amount of energy than you started with. What the theory proposes is that all the energy space contained was being compressed for whatever reason and it gets denser and denser until it erupts!

Alec – I suppose that's possible, but how could it be proved?

Bob – At the moment I don't think that there's any way to do that, but if it's ever proved that the massive inflation can be linked to string theory, who knows. It might suggest that our universe will continue to expand then contract and start all over again. Or again maybe it's as string theory proposes, our universe is just one of many similar universes with each one having slightly different laws.

Alec – How would we ever know?

Bob – Some string theories propose that we're part of a 'multiverse' while others refer to ours as being just one among many gazillions of universes that's out there.

Alec – Our tiny 5% of something seems to be shrinking all the time.

Bob – I think that loads of multiple universes that we'll never be able to see or contact may be pushing the boat out

Is a bit too far, but we could be looking at it the wrong way.

Alec- Do these proposals that there might be a multiverse or multiple universes come from the currently unproven string theories?

Bob – Yes and they all freely admit to being pure speculation.

Alec – In that case I'd go back to several of Prof's lectures that I attended and stick to his dictum which was, never confuse mathematics with reality. Let's start at the beginning of string theory, are these strings supposed to be the very basic bits of energy in our universe or do they include matter as well?

Bob – Strings were initially proposed as the basic starting point for everything. All the matter, forces and energy in the Universe is made up of these strings and not the other way around.

Alec – You said that string was meant to be the theory of everything, what everything?

Bob – In the 80's and 90's various theories dominated the attempts to combine general relativity with quantum theory and at the beginning they looked logical solutions. But like Henry Longhursts' attempt to simplify the Rules of Golf, they all ran into difficulties by proposing that there's parts of our universe that'll be forever out of our reach.

Alec – I take it that was the extra dimensions problem?

Bob – It was and all the various theories needed a universe that seems very different from ours by having six or seven extra dimensions that only the little vibrating strings are able to experience. As you said, string theory's still a mathematical exercise so it doesn't need to prove anything or be based on reality. The way the system works is that scientists propose theories and mathematicians prove whether they're correct or not. Not the other way around!

Alec – More's the pity. Strings looked a really cool way to solve the logjam between relativity and quantum mechanics.

Bob – String theorists kept developing and over the years they've come up with five different versions that gave conflicting answers and, probably much more importantly, all of them only work in a universe without time. Undaunted, they've kept beavering away and found some unexpected connections between the five theories. It came to a head at a conference in 1995 where Ed Witten combined the best bits of the five different theories, tacked on one extra dimension and presented an updated version which, for some reason unknown to science, became known as M-theory.

Alec – Would that be M-theory as in Magic theory?

Bob – Or maybe Ed Witten's secretary had a miss-type when they were inputting the documents for a conference and started a paragraph as M theory instead of A theory and it stuck. The new M-theory has been further developed by replacing the strings with tiny vibrating loops and, as the main aim of all the theories is still to unite the quantum with general relativity, the new theory's unsurprisingly called Loop Quantum Gravity. This one differs from the string versions by not needing any extra dimensions and working in our normal space-time. All three theories, string, M and loop have very passionate disciples as well as unbelievers, but so far nothing concrete's come out of them altho' they have made some very interesting suggestions.

Alec – I can see that it would be very useful if they could unite gravity and quantum, but why is it so important?

Bob – It all goes back to Max Planck and his constant from which he worked out the smallest dimension that anything could have and came up with the ridiculous answer of 1.6×10^{-35} which is ten million billion billion times smaller than an atom.

Alec – That's interesting, but why is knowing that useful?

Bob – The crucial importance is that it's turned out that at this scale gravity has the exact same force as the strong, weak and electromagnetism forces. Down at this point all the four forces are united as one and to get all four forces there they need to come up with a quantum theory of gravity which'll work down at this super miniscule level.

Alec – That would be assuming that gravity's a quantum force, but wouldn't it require an enormous amount of energy to probe things down at that level?

Bob – It would and they've worked out that all that's needed is to build a collider the size of our galaxy. That's the reason why string theorists are currently only able to come up with theories rather than the experiments which will prove or disprove them.

Alec – I remember hearing that the people at CERN were hunting for something called supersymmetry that would prove, or disprove some, if not all of these theories.

Bob – That's all to do with the standard model of physics having some glaring holes in it where particles should be and the string theorists coming up with particles to fill them. The main idea, as you said, is supersymmetry and string theory has proposed that each known particle is balanced by having a partner particle which is identical to it except that if it's a force-carrying one its partner will be a matter particle and vice versa. Over the years billions of collisions at CERN have been searched at higher and higher energies, but so far no trace of any of the super-symmetric partners has been found

Alec – Wouldn't it be better to assume that the starting point for any universe must be a field of energy. If that's the case what type of energy would we be talking about?

Bob – If we include gravity there are only four forces available so it must be one or a combination of them.

Alec – I'd think we could drop gravity as it's the attractive force between particles and they haven't been created yet. Nor for the same reason could it be either of the forces in the nucleus so that leaves us with electromagnetism. Would it make sense for a universe to start out as a field of electromagnetism, but where would that have come from?

Bob – Assuming we're talking Big bang theory it could only have been what's left over from a previous universe. Or maybe energy injected by a universal creator!

Alec – Maybe universes could be serial events. Start with a Big bang, create matter which fades away and we start another cycle.

Bob – It couldn't just fade away to nothing. The First Law says that it would have to fade away to all the energy it started with and that's one of the doomsday questions that the current expansion highlights. Will the Universe go on expanding forever and all solid matter will fade away as it gets colder and colder? Or will it stop expanding and contract back to a singularity? Or maybe even to an inflation field? It's been calculated that if this were to be correct it'll take our present universe two to three hundred billion years 'til it happens. That would make it extremely unlikely that we'll ever know as we've only got a five billion year lease left on our wee bit. That is if we have even that!

Alec – Now there's a happy thought. Here, help yourself to this last tot of Glengoyne, it'll cheer you up.

Bob – Cheers. Maybe we could explain the residual energy as a field of electromagnetism. Or maybe just as a field of electricity, as Faraday proved that it's the movement of one which creates the other.

Alec – Would this idea of a field also apply to dark energy?

Bob – Must do. If it's anywhere dark energy must be everywhere. Throughout space, inside galaxies and even inside us!

Alec – Even inside atoms?

Bob – I'd think so, especially inside atoms!

Alec – Doesn't science now say that space isn't just the empty distance that separates planets and galaxies, but that it contains something called vacuum energy!

Bob - What they actually mean is that they're considering space without any matter present and it can then be looked on as a vacuum. That doesn't mean that it's completely empty as it allows for a field, or fields, of energy to be there. It's now looking more than likely that space will turn out to be our superhighway between suns and galaxies.

Alec – I think that makes more sense if you look at space as a field of energy, or maybe several fields of energy. Is it possible to get an idea of the amount that could be there?

Bob – When the First Law's applied to the whole universe it's been worked out that to balance the conservation of energy, every cubic metre of space will have to contain the energy of one hydrogen atom. That's not to say that there's an actual hydrogen atom there, it's the energy a cubic metre would contain if they were. According to these calculations it's important that it's at this particular level as any other value would give us a completely different universe!

Alec – The energy of one hydrogen atom doesn't seem a lot. Especially when they're compared to a cube with the volume of a metre!

Bob – Scientists are talking in terms of the amount of energy that's present in all the cubic metres and I couldn't even begin to think of how many of them there are in just our wee solar system. It must add up to a sizeable energy field throughout the Universe.

Thirteenth Hole   430 yards par 4 - Burncrook.

From the thirteenth tee the ground drops down then levels out before rising to a green that slopes toward you and is guarded by bunkers on either side. The fairway has an out of bounds wall running down the left-hand side and it narrows down to about 40 yards before slowly widening as it rises up to the green. As their golf cart approached the tee a golfer from the game ahead stepped onto it and hit what they assumed must be his third shot.

Alec – I'm fascinated by the idea of space being counted in cubic metres of force. Would quantum theory also be at work in space?

Bob – If we're to have a joined-up universe quantum theory must work everywhere. The theory also predicts that there'll be fluctuations in spaces' energy field and that'll be constantly creating pairs of particles and 'anti-particles' that instantly annihilate and cancel each other out.

Alec - Do you mean that space might be like the froth on a pint of beer?

Bob – That's one way of looking at it, but the theory also predicts that there'll be other actions taking place called quantum tunnelling and jumping.

Alec – That's a new one to me. What does this involve?

Bob – It's one of the stranger bits of quantum theory and although it's interacting waves that are causing it, it's almost impossible to describe the action as anything other than as particles. It's a weak force interaction that allows for a particle that's being hemmed in by an energy wall to borrow enough energy from the vacuum that'll enable it to tunnel thru', or jump over, the energy wall and as this happens instantly we're not sure whether it burrows thru' or jumps over! The only condition is that it has to pay back the borrowed energy immediately it reaches the other side.

Alec – Does this happen in no time as a result of the Uncertainty Principle?

Bob – It's happening at light speed so it'll be no time in the particles reference frame and the tiniest bit of time in ours. It's not directly caused by uncertainty, but, like neutrons in an atom, probability plays a very large part in it. It allows for one particle to turn up on the far side of the wall while all the other particles remain trapped and this strange action plays an essential part in nuclear fusion. If it didn't happen our Sun, or any other, wouldn't shine!

Alec – That would be pretty inconvenient, but does that mean that there are some suns that shine while others can't?

Bob – All suns shine and they only do so because they're large enough for this effect to be possible and it's all to do with the very low probability of the tunnelling event happening at all. A sun's effectively a factory where gravity's squeezing two hydrogen atoms together to make a helium atom. The process starts with the hydrogen atoms being compressed as gravity pulls them closer and closer to the centre. However, even when they reach there the Sun's gravity is just a wee bit short of the force that's needed to fuse them together and that's where the quantum effects come in. Although the probability's very low, the weak interaction makes it possible for enough particles to tunnel thru' and overcome the last bit of repulsive force between the two positive hydrogen protons and bingo, our Sun's the proud owner of a new helium atom.

Alec – So no quantum tunnelling, no sunshine and probably no us! What if gravity had enough force on its own and didn't need quantum tunnelling's help?

Bob – That would make the difference between you holding a gently fizzing sparkler in your hand, or a very large lit stick of dynamite!

Alec – Do all the suns shine at the same brightness?

Bob – It depends on the size and what the particular sun's made of. In general, the larger the Sun, the greater its gravity will be and the brighter it'll shine. A star with a mass like our Sun can fuse hydrogen for about 10 billion years whereas the most massive stars can burn theirs up and explode in a supernova after only a few million years. It's the explosion of these stars that makes most of the elements, including gold and uranium, without which any form of complex life would be impossible

Alec – I guess that means tunnelling or jumping must be essential, but what else does it do?

Bob – It's useful in the quantum world and transistors couldn't work without it. Nor would memory sticks and it's the main player in the new quantum computers that are being developed. Bill Gates, Microsoft's head honcho, put it in perspective when he said, "If General Motors had achieved what the computer industry has done we'd all be driving around in twenty-five dollar cars that run for a thousand miles on a gallon of petrol.

Alec – I think he's slightly biased, but it looks like the internal combustion engine which has served us well all these years will soon have to give way to electric, or more likely, hydrogen powered vehicles.

Bob – Science is no longer regarded as solely man's work, but ninety years ago a very determined German lady called Emmy Noether pushed her way in with a formula that describes the link between two very important concepts and it's still among the most powerful formula's in physics today. She explained that if you have a law in which things are conserved, there will always be actions or events called symmetries that'll match one thing up with another. For example, the First Law of Thermodynamics is a symmetrical law which insists that no matter how much you shuffle energy around, the total amount in a system will always remain constant. Symmetries have helped physicists to solve problems from the speed of balls rolling down and off the edge of tables to understanding the Sun's nuclear fusion.

Alec – When you say symmetries, what do you mean?

Bob – Symmetry describes the changes that you can make to an object without altering how it looks.

Alec – Is this just a quantum effect or do we see it all around us?

Bob – Symmetries can be found almost anywhere and the simplest one to describe is a table tennis ball as, unlike the golf ball you're holding in your hand, it's completely symmetric. You can turn it whichever way you want and it'll still look the same. If you do that with a rugby ball or American Football you'll find it's only symmetric when you rotate it one way and rotating it in any other direction it will give you a different view of it. The Ancient Greeks believed that the totally symmetric circle represented the perfect object and therefore it must be the work of The Gods.

Alec – Why is symmetry important?

Bob – The genius of Emmy Noether was to prove that if you have a conservation law there will always be a symmetry associated with it. Symmetries have shown us that there are pattern's behind many properties in the Universe that weren't at all obvious in any other way. This led to the search for new patterns and out of them science has built the Standard Model of particle Physics which is the best model we have to describe the basic building blocks of the Universe.

Alec – How did she manage to force her way in?

Bob – Although Emmy had a Ph.D, she had to work as an assistant lecturer without payment for four years before becoming recognised. With the rise of National Socialism she was forced out of Germany and died in America in 1935, just two years after arriving there.

Alec – So the standard model's our blueprint for the Universe.

Bob – Since its early days, symmetries have predicted that there must be particles out there that haven't yet been discovered along with how and where they'd fit into the Standard Model when they're found. The recent proof of the Higgs boson and field are prime examples of the power of symmetries, but as the standard model is a string theory construction which only works in a static universe without time, it can't be considered as the complete story. Also physicists were only able to develop it by ignoring gravity so there's still a long way to go before it can be recognised as the complete blueprint of the Universe.

Alec – Was it the Standard Model that lead on to the various string theories?

Bob – No it was the other way around, but strangely enough there was a sort-of string theory which dates back to the war years with our old friend Werner Heisenberg developing a theory that he called S-matrix which was his early attempt to restore a measure of time to the timeless quantum world. S-matrix was picked up in the 1960s and converted into a theory that describes all the particles in the sub-atomic world as tiny vibrating strings of energy.

The game in front was walking up the rise toward the green so Bob took out his driver and told it he'd give it one more chance 'or else'. He hit a peach of a shot, long and straight down the middle, before kissing it and putting its head cover back on.

Alec - How many years have you been threatening that poor driver with - or else?'

Bob - I've had that driver so long that Alice says it's going in beside me in my coffin when I go. Stupidly it caused me a problem when a few years ago we were having a friendly disagreement and Alice suggested that I loved that driver more than her. I tried to lighten the conversation by saying that wasn't strictly true, I loved all my clubs more than I loved her.

Alec – Ohh dear, that was a bad move. How did you get out of it alive?

Bob – She looked at me very coolly and addressed me as Robert for the next few days. That stupid attempt at a joke cost me an expensive dinner and a fancy pair of running shoes.

Alec laughing – That'll be the last time you'll try that one

He was still smiling when he hit his drive, but stopped as he watched his ball hook wildly out of bounds and said, "That's what comes of me not concentrating, I'll play three off the tee." Bob was feeling confident at two-up so he said, "As this is the first match of the season and I don't need it, I'll give you my joker.

Alec - You can't do that, it's not in the rules.

Bob – Exactly, and because it's not in the rules there's nothing to stop me giving it to you. Even old Henry Longhurst couldn't argue against that.

Alec – OK, I'll accept it in the spirit that it's given, but I'm going to make you regret it.

After hitting his gifted drive Alec continued - Going back to dark energy, could it be hiding in another part of the Universe?

Bob – All things are possible but if we want to make any sense of the Universe we'd have to insist that the laws of nature we live by are the same laws as everywhere else in the Universe. If dark energy's available in some parts but not others, our universal laws would become local laws and life on the borders would be absolute hell. Surprisingly there actually was a particle called The Hell particle. It was proposed by Paul Dirac as part of his theory of Quantum Fields of Energy and he chose the name 'Positron' for it. The proposed particle was an exact copy of an electron except for having the opposite charge and, if they meet, each would annihilate the other so the press quickly dubbed it the Hell particle.

Alec – I thought antimatter was the stuff of science fiction. Like on Saturday mornings at the kid's cinema club when we used to watch Flash Gordon fighting off the dastardly Ming the Merciless. And didn't Dan Dare also use it to power his rocket in the Eagle comics?

Bob - You've usually got a much better memory for that sort of thing that than I have, but I'm fairly certain it was Dan Dare who took on Ming the Merciless to stop him dominating the Universe and Flash Gordon was the one who saved us from the Mekon. Didn't you have a crush on Flash Gordon's side-kick.

Alec – Ahh, Dale Arden, my first pin-up! So antimatter's a fact of life.

Bob – In the early nineteen thirties Paul Dirac, the greatest English scientist since Newton, and probably the second greatest scientist of the last century, was trying to unite quantum mechanics with Einstein's special relativity when he came up with an equation which explained how electrons behave when they're travelling near the speed of light. Like Planck before him he recognised that there was a problem with his equation because it worked equally well for positively charged electrons as it did with negatively charged ones. When he expanded it to include protons and neutrons the equation predicted there must be an anti-particle to every known particle and we might possibly have anti-atoms and anti-molecules. Even up to an anti-universe which might contain anti-dark matter!

Alec – Was this a wild conjecture or has it been proved?

Bob – Not long after he proposed them positrons were proved to be a fact of life by experiments in early cloud chambers.

Alec – Does that not lead to a question for the Big Bang, why does the Universe consist entirely of matter?

Bob – The Big Bang theory skips neatly round that problem by suggesting that in the early Universe there was an extra matter particle created for every billion anti-matter 'particles'. Both billions immediately annihilated each other leaving gazillions of photons and one particle of real matter behind.

Alec – You've mentioned Paul Dirac as `the most famous English scientist since Newton'. Why haven't I heard of him?

Bob –It could be because he seldom used two words when one would do?

Alec – You're joking, there must be more to him than that?

Bob – Of course there was, but there's some truth behind it. He was a peculiar man in several ways and there are many stories about his famous reticence. For example, the first time he met Niels Bohr in Copenhagen they had a long conversation where Dirac's responses were almost exclusively 'yes' or 'no' with the very occasional 'I don't mind' thrown in. Then, during one of his lectures a colleague said to him, "Paul, I don't understand that formula" and Dirac carried on with the lecture. At the end of it the colleague asked if he wouldn't mind answering his question to which Dirac looked astonished and replied, "Question, what question? That was an assertion you made, not a question." On another occasion he sailed from America to Japan in the company of Werner Heisenberg who spent his evenings dancing in the ballroom while Dirac looked on puzzled. Eventually he asked Heisenberg why he danced and was told "Well, when there are nice girls it's a pleasure to dance." Next time Heisenberg sat down he was asked "How do you know beforehand that they're nice girls?"

Alec – It sounds as if he was on the spectrum

Bob – Strange man or not he was the one who took quantum mechanics from being a mish-mash of misty descriptions and equations that worked well but were inexplicable and moulded them into one simple, beautiful whole. Dirac provided the equation that describes the exact nature of the proposed quantum particles but he quickly realised that his equations would apply equally to quantum fields and using quantum fields would make the theory consistent with Einstein's special relativity. Faraday had proved that the Universe consists of lines of energy moving thru fields like electromagnetism. Dirac's proof showed that these lines of energy can only take certain values and therefore they must be the discrete quanta of energy that Plank and Einstein had proposed. He completes the circle. Electromagnetic waves are vibrations of Faraday's lines but looked at on the quantum scale they're swarms of Planck's quanta, or as we know them now, photons. Dirac's equation describes a world that's not made of things and it explains how particles can appear and how they interact with each other. In his explanation of what happens to particles between one interaction and the next is that they cease to exist and he shows that the path taken by any particle is totally unpredictable! With this equation quantum field theory was born and the sharp distinction between fields and particles introduced by Faraday vanishes. Dirac proved that reality consists solely of bursts of energy moving thru' quantum fields.

As a bonus, Quantum Field Theory also accounts for the creation and annihilation of particles, something that ordinary quantum mechanics can't do. Dirac was so far ahead of his compatriots that they said his theories were so astounding that it's hard to see how any human could have imagined them. The standard model that was completed in the 1970's suggests that there are approximately fifteen of Dirac's quantum fields that make up the Universe.

Alec – You lost me there when you mentioned creation and annihilation of particles. What exactly does that mean?

Bob – The easiest way to describe it is when an electron emits a photon and drops down to a lower level. In quantum field theory that's described by two fields, the electromagnetic and electron fields, interacting. They meet and a pulse of energy that we call a photon appears in the electromagnetic field and at the same the time the electron field loses a bit of its energy and momentum.

Alec – OK, but was the Copenhagen Interpretation a consensus between Dirac and the founding fathers?

Bob – At the time there was never a full consensus, but it was Paul Dirac who pulled quantum into a coherent story

Alec – I read that one of the sticking points with quantum theory was whether the wave function should be considered to be real, or was it just a convenient way to explain a point?

Bob –Although everything in the quantum world is waves waving their way thru' fields of energy, matrix mechanics treats them as waves and particles combined. It calls each combined wave and particle its wave function and provides a calculation of the probabilities where you'llfind the particle when you look in the wave. While the wave's moving, the particles said to be in a 'superposition' and it provides a calculation of the probabilities where you'll find the particle when you look in the wave. While the wave's moving the particles are said to be in a 'superposition' of states and that's what created the key problem for quantum non-believers as it allows for particles to be in many different places at once, and as they're travelling at the speed of light, they're all doing it at the same time. The question that non-believers came up with was, 'In that case why are we and our measuring instruments which are made of the same particles never found in a superposition?

Alec – What did Einstein and Schrodinger make of this?

Bob – Schrodinger pointed out that his problem was not with particles being in many different places at the same time, but when you take a measurement you're applying two quite different laws of the Universe. His main problem was with quantum mechanics describing the sub-classical world purely in terms of possibilities and where quantum laws are different from Newton's classical laws in which particles evolve smoothly thru' time and are always in definite positions. Unfortunately he and Einstein were out of step as they kept looking for a classical world description of quantum events.

Alec – And Bohr's description didn't please either of them.

Bob – It certainly didn't please Schrodinger who came up with his famous thought experiment.

Alec – I've heard of that, it's Schrodinger's cat and it got him into trouble with animal lovers who thought he was suggesting that the experiment should be carried out. In the original suggestion Schrodinger asked people to imagine putting a hypothetical cat into a sealed box with a good supply of food and oxygen. Inside the box there's a small lump of uranium, a Geiger counter, a hammer and a jar of cyanide. The first uranium atom to decay will be detected by the Geiger counter which releases the hammer and smashes the jar of cyanide. Recently some more humane scientists have substituted a sleeping gas for the cyanide but kept the point that Schrodinger wanted to make. He said that according to quantum theory. until you open the box the uranium's in a superposition of two states, it's either decayed or it hasn't. This in turn puts the cat into the superposition of being asleep and awake at the same time which he said was impossible as cats can't be in both states at the same time! How did Bohr cope with this line of reasoning?

Bob – Bohr's answer was that as we can never experience the quantum world using Newton's Laws it's pointless to start thinking this way. He insisted that all quantum theory is able to do is to let you know the potential outcomes of events that are taking place within the sub-atomic world. By this time it was the mid 1930's and quantum mechanics had grown into the goose that was starting to lay golden eggs. At the same time a respected mathematician, John von Neumann, wrote a book which mathematically 'proved' that Bohr's theory was the only possible theory in town. Einstein and Schrodinger had been shunted off the main QM line and parked in a siding.

Alec – So there's two quite different laws of physics, one that rules only inside the atom while the other gets to describe the rest of the Universe. Have there been any proposals that would resolve this?

Bob – There hasn't been any yet, but there was a hiccup in 'Bohr's way' in the early 1950's when an American physicist called David Bohm unknowingly re-invented the 1924 idea of Louis de-Broglie that particles and waves are both present at the same time. He'd written a textbook on quantum physics which supported Bohr's interpretation and had received a call from Einstein telling him that he'd succeeded in explaining the theory as well as anyone could, but he was still not satisfied that it was adequate. He told Bohm that his main objection was that the wave function couldn't be a description as it was always having to be referred to an observer. This started Bohm thinking that perhaps Einstein was correct and after running it around in his head he rewrote Schrodinger's equation in a form that gave exactly the same predictions as Bohr and Co. without the need for an observer to collapse the waveform. His proposal was that particles are particles all the time, not just when they're being observed in a certain way.

Back on the fairway Bob hit his rescue club and the ball rolled up to the back of the green. Alec, ten yards nearer, followed this with a long iron but it spun back off the green and ended up on the apron. Alec chipped and putted and Bob matched him with two putts for a half. They moved across to the next tee and weren't surprised when they saw the four in front were waiting beside their golf balls while the game in front of them putted out once again.

Fourteenth Hole 387 yards Par 4 - Drumclog.

The fourteenth hole runs parallel and is similar to the eleventh hole except it doesn't have a fairway bunker. The first part of the hole is level and then it rises up steeply to the green which is the third one perched on top of Mount Zion.

Alec – How was David Bohm's new interpretation received?

Bob – Unfortunately it was a disaster, the timing was all wrong. Not his personal timing, it was the way public opinion in America was unfolding at the time.

Alec – Ahh, was he the one who got caught up in Senator McCarthy's witch hunt? I remember reading of a scientist being hounded out of America for being a communist with a rotten theory.

Bob – That's him. He was Jewish and during the early part of the war he became convinced that it was the Russians who were doing most of the fighting against the Nazis. He got a post as an assistant professor at Princeton University and became an active trade union member. For a short time he joined the university communist party, but was quickly disillusioned and quit. In 1949, he was summoned to appear before The House Committee on Un-American Activities where he plead the First Amendment to the Constitution and walked away thinking that he would hear no more about it. During the Christmas break a year later a US Marshall walked into his office at the university, arrested and took him down to a local court where he was charged with Contempt of Congress to which he pled not guilty. Hearing that he was being held in jail two of his friends bailed him out, but when he returned to the university he was told that the Dean had banned him from the campus and suspended him from teaching. He quickly found out that he was on a blacklist.

Alec – Somebody must've fingered him!

Bob – You've been reading too many American crime novels, but you're probably right. Eighteen months after his arrest he appeared in a Federal Court in Washington and was cleared of all the charges against him. But by then the damage had already been done.

Alec – Had he been chased out of America?

Bob – He wasn't chased out as such, but he found it impossible to get a post at any American university so Einstein stepped in and helped him to get a teaching job in Brazil where he was a great success, but wasn't particularly happy. Apart from being uncomfortable with the climate and disliking most of the local food, his major concern came when he was ordered to the US Consulate and had his passport stamped 'only valid for return to USA'. When Einstein heard of this he arranged a lectureship for Bohm in Israel, but with the restricted passport he couldn't travel to take it up. Einstein suggested he should apply for a Brazilian passport, which he did and eventually left Brazil for Tel-Aviv.

Alec – It's a bit strange that for just being a trade unionist with a brief flirt with communism could get him treated like public enemy number one! What happened to his theory while he was in Brazil?

Bob – He submitted and had it published in a couple of scientific journals, but it didn't get the widespread attention he'd hoped for. Some of his students persuaded Max Dresden, a physicist at the University of Kansas, to give a lecture on Bohm's theory while he was on a visit to Princeton which was Bohm's old university. At the end of the lecture Max was expecting some tough questions, but what he got was a room that erupted in vitriol. Bohm was described as 'a public nuisance' and a 'traitor and a Trotskyite'. Worst of all Robert Oppenheimer, the Institute Director and one of the most influential physicists in the USA, stood up and said 'If we cannot disprove Bohm then we must all agree to ignore him.' This was strange because Oppenheimer had been head of the team building The Bomb and had personally requested that Bohm be transferred to him at Los Alamos. The request was denied by Army Security who lied to him saying that Bohm was a risk to the project as he still had family in Europe. At the time it put Bohm in the ridiculous position of having his Ph.D thesis classified as being beyond his security clearance and he was forbidden to do any more work on it. It was Oppenheimer who stood up for him and assured the awarding committee that Bohm fully deserved his doctorate.

Alec – Getting such reports back from his former colleagues was bad enough, but the kick in the goolies from the man who'd been his mentor must've really hurt. You said a very similar theory by de Broglie had been around for nearly thirty years, why was the reception so different this time?

Bob – I think the difference is probably in the thirty years. In 1924 Prince Louis de-Broglie's doctoral thesis proposed that particles could have both wave and matter properties at the same time. Someone sent a copy of it to Einstein who agreed with it and stressed the importance of de Broglie's work. Erwin Schrödinger also agreed with it and the end result was Wave Mechanics. In 1927 two different experiments by Clinton Davisson and Lester Germer in the United States and George Thomson in Scotland found the first experimental evidence that electrons moved in waves. At that time quantum mechanics was still in its infancy, but within six or seven years it revolutionised science and Bohr's early students had become the hiring professors at major universities. It's natural that if you're part of a revolution you tend to hire like-minded people, so by the early 1950s it was hard to get any job in physics if you didn't subscribe to Bohr's interpretation. McCarthy was still busy investigating academics and, by Oppenheimer showing his opposition to Bohm and keeping him at a safe distance might have helped him to prove that he was a loyal citizen

Alec – So the Copenhagen Interpretation is still gospel.

Bob - There never was a unified interpretation as all the major players believed in slightly different versions. Bohr himself didn't fully agree with most of the others and wrote that no explicit reference should be made to any individual observer whose role is simply to confirm that the measurement's been taken and delivered the particles actual position and properties.

Alec – I'm getting confused by the similarity of their names!

Bob – If you want to get really confused there's a third important chap in the story called Max Born whose subject was maths and he helped Heisenberg to complete his matrix theory. Later he showed that Schrodinger wasn't correct to say that it's the wave function which gives you the probabilities of where you'll find the particle He proved that it's actually the wave function squared which gives you probabilities. Later when the whole thing was cobbled together he took exception to it being called the Copenhagen Interpretation as he was German and had never worked in Copenhagen!

By this time the game in front had played their second shots to the green so Alec and Bob assumed the tee. Bob's driver had decided to behave so he stroked a gentle slice and his ball finished half-way up the hill on the right-hand side of the fairway. Alec followed with his ball finishing a few yards further on.

Alec – When a star or galaxy emits a photon destined for us does the space between us have an effect on it

Bob – Space came into the picture in the late twenties and early thirties when quantum theory moved on with a book written by Paul Dirac. His aim had been to unite Einstein's relativity with Bohr's quantum theory which he hoped would lead on to a theory where gravity would be united with the three quantum forces. Instead his equations gave a precise description of electrons and how particles move thru' space. Rather than helping to understand gravity, his proposal led to the theory that at the basic level our universe is made up of quantum fields.

Alec – Space, the last frontier. Is it also a quantum field?

Bob – The idea that the quantum world's made up of waves moving thru' fields was a really crucial insight and Bohr was 100% correct when he kept insisting that the sub-atomic world doesn't exist in any way that we would recognise. Dirac took it a step further when he said, 'Nothing in the quantum world exists in any meaningful way until we look in on it.

Alec – Why call them particles then?

Bob – In the classical view of the world particles are tiny bits of things, but when physicists talk of particles they have a slightly different interpretation of the meaning. Their way of thinking is that some simple actions inside atoms can be described as waves, but more complex arrangements are easier to describe as tho' they're being created by particles. They call this way of looking at things as wave-particle duality, but the action they're describing always involves them being described as waves or particles. Never as both at the same time.

Alec – Is a quantum particle a burst of energy which has the potential to become a classical particle?

Bob – Waves in quantum fields of energy are all that there is in the atomic world and it's those waves that make up all the atoms and molecules in our everyday classical world. It's relatively easy to think of electrons as waves circling around the nucleus and moving up and down shells, but there's no way I can get a picture of what's happening inside an atom's nucleus by trying to describe it as waves. Even tho' it is!

Alec – I can see that being a problem and I can 'sort of' picture three quark particles being held in a gluon jail. But trying to work that back to being a collection of waves is 'way beyond my imagination.

Bob – The problem we have is that for two hundred years we've had Newton's classical physics where particles describe actual particles whether they're moving particles like light or standing still particles like grains of sand. Someone asked Newton, 'If light's a moving particle, what's it moving thru'? Newton freely admitted that he didn't know, but said that he would leave it to the imagination of his readers. His gravity was simply the attractive force between two bodies and nothing else came into it. We now know the real duality isn't with particles and waves, but with fields of energy and waves of energy moving thru' them. The waves or particles come in two distinct varieties, ones which carry forces and the others which make up matter. Those that carry forces are called bosons and the matter creating ones are fermions.

Alec – I'm trying to form a picture, but I'm still a bit confused. You said Niels Bohr insisted that quantum mechanics can't represent any form of reality, yet now you're talking of groups of particles as tho' they're real!

Bob – Particles are real only in the sense that they're what we get from the waves of energy that everything in the Universe is made of. In the classical world particles are straight-forward, they're just tiny bits of matter, but in Paul Dirac's description particles only exist as indivisible points located at an infinitesimal location.

Alec – Do you mean they're like ghosts? And what's an infinitesimal location?

Bob – Quantum particles are in an infinitesimal location because they're moving waves, not physical particles, so all the fundamental particles have no physical size. I know it's confusing, but that's life.

Alec – That doesn't make sense to me. How can something as substantial as us be made of particles that don't have any size?

Bob – Over the year's physicists have been able to probe and describe the fundamental particles at higher and higher energies which is the same as looking at them on smaller and smaller scales and so far none of them have revealed that they're composed of something smaller. Any deviation of these elementary particles from point-like behaviour would be a strong indication that the particle isn't fundamental, but is made from even more basic building blocks.

Alec – It might be a touch more intuitive if particles and waves had been given different names in the quantum world. Something like tittles and jots then we would know what's being referred to.

Bob – It might make distinguishing between the quantum and classical worlds a bit clearer, but ultimately its waves that make up particles and that still leave us with two different explanations for a mote of dust which is a particle made up of particles. The fundamental problem with wave/particles is that we have one set of rules that describes how they work in the sub-atomic world and a completely different set to describe the atoms and molecules that make up the particles of dust.

Alec – I can see that, but it's getting all the different names into some kind of perspective. What are you laughing at?

Bob – It's as you said, half the problem's getting a bit of clarity with the names and what they represent and I suddenly remembered that it was you who helped me to sort out the bosons from fermions.

Alec – Glad to be of service, but I'm none the wiser.

Bob – Remember the first time you took me into the

student's bar at the Uni. and I noticed a sign behind the counter saying 'No crefdit given'. I turned to you and said that someone can't spell as there's no f in credit. You and your pals at the bar burst out laughing and it took me a few seconds before the penny dropped.

Alec – Yes, I well remember that sign, but I'm still none the wiser.

Bob – Sorry, it's the weird way my mind works. One time I was trying to remember if bosons were the force carriers or the matter particles when that sign popped up in my head and I suddenly realised that bosons and fermions only have one f.

Alec – You've still got me!

Bob – Made it easier for me to remember. Bosons are forces and fermions are matter 'cos there's only one f in each of them! Weird I know, but it works for me.

Alec – Some people's mind works in very mysterious ways. Have you got memory jogs for any of the other strange names involved?

Bob –I've tried to, but it's only worked for a few.

Alec – I've a memory that someone came up with a Many Worlds proposal. Is that the same as Multiple Universes?

Bob – Many Worlds and Multiple Universes share a lot, but it's how they got there that's different. The Many World's proposal came in 1954 with the thesis of a brilliant student called Hugh Everett the Third. He'd been fascinated by science fiction since childhood and when he was older became interested in the mathematics of game theory where John von Neumann was king. He'd a strange personality and delighted in taking people's theories or beliefs apart and proving to them that they were impossible. His pals at the university said that Hugh was the one who always had to win every argument, however long it took. He attended the Catholic University and on one occasion he persuaded a very devout professor that, mathematically, God was impossible. He did it to such an extent that the poor professor went into a serious state of religious despair. Everett later said that he'd no desire to change the world, he just wanted to have his little bit of fun with it.

Alec – I've met a few people like that, practical jokers who want to convince everyone of their brilliance!

Bob – Everett was slightly more than that, he actually was brilliant and wasn't the usual type of undergraduate. His chief aim in life was self-enjoyment and the last thing he wanted was an academic career. He regarded his Ph.D merely as a stepping stone on the way to getting a position in the War Games Department of the US military. For his thesis he took De Broglie and Bohm's ideas further and proposed that all the wave-functions and particles are real so there's no need to measure them to get a result. The big idea he got from treating things this way was that every time a decision is about to be made anywhere in our universe, it splits into multiple copies.

Alec – You mean into multiple universes that are copies of each other. Does that mean that every time I decide something two or more alternative universes spring into existence? What happens to the one I'm in right now?

Bob – It's the one you're in now that splits with each universe representing a different side of the decision you've just taken and there's no original universe left where you're still pondering. Everett was a very heavy smoker and drinker who died before his thesis got any publicity.

Alec – So I'm just short of the green in two and I'm trying to decide whether to chip or putt the ball. At that point the universe splits into two universes with me in both of them. In universe one I'm chipping the ball and universe two I'm putting. How do I know which one I'm actually in and are you the same you in both universes? Does this mean that there's a god-like figure tuned in to my every thought?

Bob – I assume I'm cloned into both universes just as you are. You're in both the new universes and in one of them your chip's hit the flagstick but stayed out, while, in the other one your putt went straight into the hole. In one of them I'm two up and in the other I'm back to one!

Alec – And this is meant to be a serious proposal?

Bob – It seems so and it's called the Many Worlds Interpretation. It's serious enough that some parts of it are still being taken very seriously.

Alec – I prefer the previous idea of a multiverse where our universe is just a small part. Didn't anyone tell Hugh Everett that his proposal was impossible and he was having a sick joke at our expense?

Bob – He was asked about that and his take was that in ancient times it was very difficult to get anyone to accept that the Earth revolves round the Sun as everyone said that was impossible because they didn't feel any movement. He said that it's similarly so with Many Worlds. You're only conscious of the one you're currently in and have no knowledge about any of the others.

Alec – So in some worlds I'm dead because I stepped out in front of a car, while in others I'm all square with you rather than being two down. How did he manage to get round the First Law and where did all the energy for the splitting universes come from?

Bob – I wouldn't be surprised if Everett didn't take his own theory too seriously. He was relatively young when he died and his last wish was that his ashes be put out in a black bag along with the rest of the household rubbish. His family complied and his theory gathered dust for the next ten years.

By this time the four in front had moved over and were standing on the next tee. Bob had the better line into the hole as Alec had the corner of a greenside bunker to clear. His seven iron shot landed on the front of the green and stopped about twenty feet from the hole. Alec played the same club, but his shot was too long and the ball ran off the back of the green. He chipped back to about eight feet and when his return putt didn't drop he conceded the hole as Bob had a tap-in for his four. Bob was now in the recently unusual position of being three up with only four holes to play.

Fifteenth Hole   460 yards par 4 - Allander.

After a brief stoppage for a drink of water they drove off at the most scenic hole on the golf course. It starts from a high tee and sweeps down to a green guarded by bunkers on either side of the entrance. The first 280 yards is downhill then it flattens out and rises slightly to just short of the green. The main problem on this hole is that the fairway slopes noticeably from left to right and any drive that's right of centre risks ending up in the trees that border that side of the course. A good drive has to be down the left side which will follow the contours and set you up nicely for your second shot to the green. Bob's driver was keeping in his good books and his ball followed the slope leaving him in prime position with a straightforward shot of just over two hundred yards to the green. 'Steady Eddie' had uncharacteristically sliced his drive and the ball ran out of the short stuff and ending up in the trees. As they motored down to look for it they resumed their conversation.

Alec – So Bohr's theory's seen off four main challengers and Johnny von Neumann's defence of it is still being quoted to anyone who dares to challenge it.

Bob – Right up to when he died in 1962 Bohr was still insisting that the quantum world doesn't exist in any meaningful way and quantum theory's merely a tool for calculating the probable outcomes of experiments. But by now some people were asking, 'How can you provide probabilities for things that don't exist!

Alec – Are you saying that if this had been asked earlier physicists mightn't have been so keen to knuckle down and produce all the rabbits out of the quantum hat?

Bob – Bit of a mixed metaphor there, but however it

happened the quantum world had become a good line to be in. Especially so when the Cold War started in earnest and countless billions of dollars poured in from the military and arms manufacturers! The order of the day was 'Don't waste your time questioning the foundations, shut up and calculate.' Most did, but there was someone who didn't and he was a red-haired Northern Irishman who was convinced that von Neumann's equations couldn't be correct and, as a pastime, he was going to prove it.

Alec – I've heard of him, John Bell from Belfast. The man who proved that Johnny von Neumann had been wrong all along!

Bob – That's him. A lad from a down to earth family of carpenters, blacksmiths, farm workers and horse dealers. His father left school at eight and all his brothers and sisters were out earning money by fourteen. Bell was unusually bright and by the time he was sixteen he'd been accepted by Queens, the local university. They had a rule that he couldn't start 'til he was seventeen so he spent the year working at setting up and clearing experiments in the labs. After graduating he joined the British Atomic Energy Agency then went on to the European Accelerator Centre in Switzerland. While he was at university he'd studied a bit of quantum theory and all the puzzles over the wave function intrigued him. He read book after book, but concluded that they were all far too vague about the exact nature of the information contained in the wave function. He kept asking his lecturers, 'If the wave-function contains information, whose information is it? This got him into some very heated discussions.

Alec – I dare say that would be his red-haired personality coming out!

Bob – Could well be and it certainly made him a stubborn cookie. He tried to read von Neumann's proof, but as he couldn't speak German he got a fellow student to read him a translation. He read Bohm's non-collapse of the wave function paper and was shocked at the reception it got. Especially after thirty years of people being assured that anything other than Bohr's theory was impossible. He started on a Ph.D and his advisor asked him to give a talk about his interests. Bell said he could do a talk on particle accelerators or on different interpretations of quantum theory. When the advisor told him that the class would very much prefer to hear about particle accelerators Bell realised that the foundations of quantum theory was a no-go area if you wanted to have a successful career as a physicist.

Alec – Was it as bad as that?

Bob – Probably worse, nobody dared to question Bohr or von Neumann. Bell bumped into Bohr at CERN when he was there to celebrate the opening of the accelerator, but it was only for moments in a lift and he didn't have time to say, 'By the way Neils, I think Johnny von Neumann's defence of your interpretation stinks!' Later on he'd a sabbatical year in the USA and took time out to study the celebrated proof. As he read it, which was now available in English, he realised that von Neumann had started out with several assumptions that he couldn't justify. He later said, "The proof wasn't just wrong, it was foolish." And, "As you read it, it falls apart in your hands." As well as showing where von Neumann had gone wrong Bell left a fresh proof in its place. He proved that that the answer's you'll get from quantum mechanics depends solely on the questions you ask and the order in which you ask them.

Alec – Is that not likely to be the case because Heisenberg's original matrix theory required each equation to be in a particular order to give the correct answers?

Bob – Again it could well be, but much more importantly what Bell had actually done was to clear the way to getting the answer to the problem that had plagued physics for over thirty years, Einstein's EPR paradox. This is the test that was carried out with particles on two Spanish Islands more than a hundred miles apart.

Alec – Makes you wonder what would've happened if anyone had listened to Grete Hermann in 1935. What if physicists back then had demanded that the basics be cleared up before they'll use the theory.

Bob – What John Bell had also proved was that Bohr's quantum theory was a 100% correct predictive theory and the general consensus then was that Einstein had wasted away the second half of his life, butting his head against the Copenhagen wall and getting nowhere. Tho' there are some people out there who have a sneaking suspicion that it could be Einstein and Schrodinger who'll eventually get the last laugh.

Alec – Do you remember when we were idealistic teenagers and the Cuban Missile Crisis was front page news every day? Science and nuclear physics had a bad name and there were massive demonstrations all with the single aim of making nuclear warfare illegal.

Bob – That was when you and some of your university pals talked me into going with you on some of those 'Ban the Bomb' marches.

Alec – I remember people calling us cowards and worse. I could understand them thinking that their generations had suffered so much and we were pacifists who were all for throwing in the towel. Some even tagged us as Russian spies and agents.

Bob - Maybe now's the time for all the World's nations take their lead from science and scientists.

By this time the game in front had completed the hole, moved over to the next tee, hit their shots and were halfway to the green. Alec asked Bob if any research had been carried out as to why golf games always speed up as they get nearer to the clubhouse and Bob replied by asking him if the question should be directed to philosophers, scientists or thirsty golfers. They drove slowly along the treeline and found Alec's ball sitting in the middle of a clearing with a small gap thru' the trees giving him an outside chance of a shot that might end up somewhere near the green. Alec took out his three wood and said to himself, 'you're three down and there's only three to play after this one, so you're due a break.' He made the most of his luck and the shot ran up the slope behind the left-hand bunker and back down onto the middle of the green. Bob, who'd been trying not to think that the match was his for the taking, duffed his shot and then sliced the next one into the right-hand bunker! With a sombre look on his face he joined his pal in the buggy and they rode toward the green.

Alec – Back there when I stood over my ball I realised that this shot's probably for the game. I'm three down, lose this and its goodbye to my ten-bob note. When I hit it I thought that it might give me an outside chance of halving the hole, but you've let me off the hook big time and I've still got a chance to make you pay for it. Back on the tee you said that politicians should take lessons from scientists. Getting politicians to listen to anything other than their own voice or being re-elected is a good idea, but how would that work?

Bob – Sound the fanfare as I present you with exhibit number one, the European Large Hadron Collider. The world's largest and most complicated microscope.

Alec – There can't be many people who haven't heard of it, but what lesson does it offer?

Bob – Europe, where wars have been a way of life for many centuries, finally gets its act together and unites. One of the new European Union's first ventures is a particle physics laboratory sitting astride the border between France and Switzerland. From the beginning its efforts have been concentrated on particle detectors which have gradually got larger and more powerful. The current one's a seventeen mile long tunnel in which particles are accelerated to almost light speed then collided head to head so that scientists can examine what comes out.

Alec – But where does this lead us to? Up the philosophical garden path, or could it be finding the Higgs boson!

Bob - The path I'm leading you up is that there are scientists of 110 nationalities from institutes in over 70 all countries working together and cooperating fully. There are Americans working with Russians, Jews with Arabs, people from four corners of the Earth all working together towards common goals. It's the dream that the United Nations has been aspiring to since the end of the last war and for once it's come out of science and not from good or bad philosophies.

Alec – And here endeth the sermon according to Saint Robert, but I see what you're getting at and wholeheartedly agree with you.

Bob – You mentioned the big idea that part of the current accelerator was setup for, finding the Higgs boson.

Alec – I did, but all I know about it is that it's a particle which gives matter its weight and it's commonly known as The God Particle. But what I don't get is what all the fuss is about. We've known since the beginning of time that matter's got weight. Aristotle described it as the force which moves matter to its natural place. Rocks always fall, smoke rises and now they've found the particle that causes it. So what?

Bob – Well said, if a bit tongue in cheek and completely wrong. If it was that easy the reason why things have weight would've been found yonks ago, but it's not the boson that they're really after. Any new particles obviously vastly important, but it's the field behind the particle that's the pot of gold. Incidentally, I recently read in an article that The God Particle's the name of a book written in 1993 by two respected physicists, Leon Lederman and Dick Teresi. Originally they wanted to call their book, 'That Goddamn Particle', but their publisher convinced them they'd get much better sales if they cut it down to, 'The God Particle'. They did and it upset whole swathes of people including scientists of all shades and churches of all creeds. When the second edition was printed Lederman put in a sort-of apology. 'We're sorry that we managed to upset some people who believed in a God and some who didn't'. 'However', he added 'the people in the middle seemed perfectly happy with it'.

Alec – I remember letters about that in the papers and the more letters they published, the more journalists hyped it up. But if it's not the boson that it's all about, what is it?

Bob – We're back to the 'don't look fields, look particles' and in this scenario it's the first bit that's the primary focus.

Alec – Two fields spring to my mind. Newton's gravity and Faradays electromagnetism and you've mentioned the two forces inside atoms. I presume they're also fields?

Bob – Back in school we were shown the magnetic field by scattering iron filings onto a sheet of paper covering a magnet and then we saw how magnetism makes a compass needle twitch. The two nuclear fields you mentioned aren't as easy as that to detect, but along with electromagnetism they make up the three quantum fields of energy.

Alec – You've only mentioned three of the fields, what about gravity?

Bob – I think most people are aware that gravity's a field in our classical world, but whether it's also a field in the quantum world has still to be argued over. A field of anything is simply an area with a number present at every point in it telling you that there's matter or energy present there and quantum fields are no different.

Alec – How does quantum theory fit all this together?

Bob – The published article on Heisenberg's theory starts with – It's the aim of this work to lay the foundations of quantum mechanics based solely on relations between quantities that are observable.

Alec – Why do you need observers? What's so special about them?

Bob – For nearly a century the basic concept of what quantum theory's all about has been discussed relentlessly without arriving at any agreement and central to most disagreements has been the role of 'the observer'. Born said the job of an observer was to confirm that the results matched the predictions while others like de Broglie and Bohr took observers out of the picture all together.

Alec – What happens if there's no observer?

Bob – Scientists carry out experiments in laboratories to prove, or disprove, theories and altho' they talk of actions and interactions being observed that doesn't imply that there would be a different result if there was no human there to 'observe' it!

Alec – So Bohr's right, you need an observer to check and confirm.

Bob – What the observer is focussing on is the result of actions and interaction that've taken place. In other words he, or she, wants to know is how any physical entity acts on any other physical entity. Large entities like us tend to think of the world in terms of things like the Sun and Moon, a bird chirping away in a bush or a pebble on the beach. The main thing to realise is that these things, along with everything else in The Universe don't exist by themselves. They, and everything else, are all part of the one system that is continuously acting and reacting one item against another. If this wasn't happening The Universe wouldn't exist!

Alec – So you're saying that as the quantum system is part of The Universe you can't stand back and take its actions one at a time.

Alec – So you're saying that as the quantum system is part of The Universe you can't stand back and take its actions one at a time.

Bob – Precisely. The world that we live in is a seething mass of continuous actions. It's not a dog here watching a cat over there eying up a chirping bird in the bushes. Nor is it the rays of sunlight being absorbed by trees and plants to create the oxygen that enables cats, dogs, birds, bushes, us and every other living thing to exist.

Alec – So you're saying that all the actions in The Universe is this result of everything reacting on everything else.

Bob – The advantage of looking at it this way tells us that there's nothing special about Heisenberg's observers. Or to put it another way, any interaction between two items can be seen as 'an observation.' Considered this way what quantum theory's describing is the way in which one part of nature reveals itself to any other single part of nature. This is called the relational interpretation of quantum theory and it seems to be currently the best way to describe something which has always been a bit of a mystery to us.

Alec – Are you now saying that an objects properties are just the result of it interacting with another object?

Bob – If we change the idea that 'objects' are particles in the atomic world to being everything in The Universe and change interactions by measuring things to interactions with anything else in The Universe then you can't separate any object from the interactions that combine to make it an object. Reality as we see it just the universal web of interactions and the properties of any object is just the way it acts on other objects.

Alec – Where does the God, sorry, Higgs particle fit into this?

Bob – Over the years science has had two major revolutions. The first was when Isaac Newton showed us that gravity's a force which works everywhere throughout the Universe. Then Niels Bohr and company let us into the secret of how the Universe works down in the basement. Quantum fields with their waves and particles have been there since the planet formed, but we couldn't see them, touch them, smell them or taste them. Or until relatively recently understand what they were and why they're there.

Alec – Ahh, now we're getting somewhere!

Bob – No, what I was going to say was that in the past it was relatively easy to discover how some things worked. It was like walking thru' an orchard picking the low-lying fruit while leaving the higher ones for the mechanised chappies with their cherry pickers. Now all the scientific low-lying discoveries have been picked and the harder parts of the science tree need scientists in their thousands working in close cooperation to pick the cherries. Sorry, that should have been to unravel the secrets of the cherries at the centre of all the atoms.

Alec – I remember someone saying recently that over ninety percent of the scientists who've ever lived are alive today!

Bob – And in a large part due to Planck's quanta and Einstein's equation which tells us that the energy in a system equals the mass multiplied by what looks like an enormous number.

Alec – I've often wondered why its c squared. Apart from its sheer size, what other relevance has it?

Bob – The first thing to realise is that c squared isn't there just to represent a large number. It also tells us how many light years there are in one of our Earth's years and being a mathematician you'll know that the answer to that's one so the equation becomes $E=mc^2$ where c squared equals 1 times 1. In other words, energy equals mass and when matter's static, as it is on our planet, our mass is equal to all the energy we contain and that's called our rest mass.

Alec - I never thought of it that way before. But why do modern problems need so many scientists to solve them?

Bob – We've known everything about electromagnetism and almost all there is to know about gravity for some time. Trying to get the lowdown on the two forces that operate inside an atoms' nucleus is in a different league altogether.

Alec – You mean the gluons and the weak nuclear force. Are they connected in any way?

Bob – They're both only available for work inside an atom's nucleus and they're connected together, but only indirectly. The strong force, as we said, is carried by gluons and the weak force results from three particles, one Z and two W bosons.

Alec – Is the weak force linked to the gluon's field?

Bob – They both work inside the nucleus but they're involved in two totally separate actions. The Z bosons have no electric charge and the two W's have an equal and opposite electric charge of one unit, so they cancel each other out giving it a force with no electric charge. To get any idea of what's going on inside an atom's nucleus is unintuitive because everything down there at the lowest level works in reverse. There's a simple rule in nuclear physics which takes a lot of the weirdness out of quantum theory. It says that the smaller the particle is that you want to detect, the greater is the amount of energy you have to put in to find it!

Alec – And you say that's reality, not weirdness!

Bob – As Yogi Berra the famous baseball player would've put it, 'Reality ain't what it used to be!'

Alec – Yogi Berra! You mean Yogi Bear, the cartoon character.

Bob – No, Yogi Berra and the bear's probably a caricature of him. He was a real live catcher, then a coach at baseball who came up with some of the sayings we now take for granted.

Alec – Such as?

Bob – Just before he died in 2015 he came out with his own epitaph which was, "I never said most of the things I said." Others earlier in his career were, "You can observe a lot by just watching," and, 'When you come to a fork in the road, take it." Most of his one-liners were to gee-up his teammates with gems like, "Baseball's 90% mental and the other half's physical,"and 'We're making too many wrong mistakes today" and the one everyone knows, "It ain't over 'til it's over."

Alec – Where did the reality quote come in?

Bob – His actual quote was, "The future ain't what it used to be" and a similar one was, "It's hard to make predictions, especially about the future."

Alec – I must look him up on the web, but what makes little sense to me is what you said about the LHC in Geneva needing more power to search out the smaller particles. Are you sure you've got that that the right way around?

Bob – I'm afraid so and that's the way actions in the quantum world work. At one point The LHC was in danger of being dwarfed by a US collider built in Texas to be called The Superconducting Super Collider which was planned to be three times the LHC's size and power.

Alec – I don't remember hearing of that?

Bob – It was first discussed in 1979 and fourteen years later it was cancelled with less than one third of the tunnel dug. One of the main champions of the project was the 'God Particle' man, Leon Lederman who, as well as proposing it, was the chief architect. After it was cancelled US scientists threw in their lot with CERN and the increased funding helped to build what's there today.

Alec – I'm still wondering where the Higgs comes in.

Bob – Scientists had known for a long time that they'd a problem with something that we all took for granted, where does matter get its weight from? Here on Earth your weight's simply the force of gravity acting on your mass, but in space the same mass would have less weight simply because as you move further from the centre of Earth its gravity gets weaker. You could even be in an area where gravities are cancelling each other out and be weightless. So the basic question's always been where does this mass come from? Then in the 1960's some hints began to come together and, working independently, three separate groups proposed very similar solutions. The first to publish, in August 1964 was Robert Brout and François Englert in Brussels. They were followed six weeks later by Peter Higgs in Edinburgh and shortly after that by Dick Hagen, Gerald Guralnik and Tom Kibble working in the USA and UK.

Alec - If he wasn't the first to propose it why is it named after Peter Higgs? Was it because he was a group of one with a short name and that would save a lot of paper over the years?

Bob – Makes sense to an eco-warrior like you and it's a pity for the five others. He was given the honour because his paper was the one that best described the particles actions. The three groups built their theories on a hint by a British scientist called Jeffrey Goldstone who had used an earlier theory by Yoichiro Nambu to prove there are some particles which exist yet they don't have any mass. He called them Nambu-Goldstone bosons and said, 'You can't have a new boson without also having a new field associated with it.' He hinted that the new field should contain at least two new force carriers and one of them is likely to be massive. Peter Higgs was the only one to realise the central importance of this massive particle.

Alec – I've heard of it also being called the Higgs mechanism, what's that all about?

Bob – The three groups proposed that there must be a field which differs from the other fields because it's permanently switched on. Science calls this as 'a field with a non-zero value'.

Alec – A non-zero value of what?

Bob – Energy, it's a field of energy which exists throughout the Universe.

Alec – Could this be the dark energy that fills two-thirds of the Universe.

Bob – That's the first thing you'd think of but if it was scientists wouldn't still be hunting for dark energy.

Alec – In that case could it be the energy field that the

Universe started out from?

Bob – That I don't know, but you'd think that the Universe must've got its power from somewhere.

Alec – But whatever else it does, it's the field that adds weight to matter. Could it eventually be proved to be the field that gives us gravity?

Bob – That's a popular misconception and the best way to look at it is that the Higgs field gives us mass then gravity acts on that mass to give us weight, but it does this in a strange way. Because this field is permanently switched on, everything in the Universe is constantly moving thru' it and are getting split up into individual channels or streams. It's a bit like a river flowing into a delta and splitting up into different rivulets. Goldstone said that the field will totally ignore some particles, but it would slow down others and the more they're slowed down the heavier they'll become. Photons and gluons have no mass because they don't interact with this field and that allows them free passage thru' it at the speed of light. All the other particles interact with it and are slowed down. Some a little, some a lot!

Alec – It's as simple as that!

Bob – That was the position back in the sixties, but the proposal had a long struggle to get to where we are now. Hunting for the boson started in earnest in the early 1990s and scientists from CERN were having trouble convincing governments to stump up the money that would enable them to build it. Here in the UK they gave a presentation to the then Science Minister, William Waldegrave, who was having trouble getting his head around why finding it was so important. After the presentation he admitted he was lost and wouldn't be able to support their case. "However," he said, "If someone can come up with a simple one page explanation that I can clearly understand, I'll recommend acceptance and present them with a bottle of vintage champagne.

Alec - Now that's an inducement after my own heart, who got the bottle of champagne?

Bob – It didn't work out that way 'cos five of them put their heads together and each got a bottle!

Alec – How did they convince him?

Bob – Firstly with a bit of flattery about his boss. The Minister was asked to imagine an area full of partygoers which he and the Prime Minister, Margaret Thatcher, have to walk thru' to get to a room where a meeting's scheduled to take place. When they walk into the party room he's unrecognised and is able to walk straight through. Mrs. Thatcher gets a different reception and is mobbed all the way across the room for chats and photos. As she has to stop and start her way across she's being slowed down and Uses7 up more of her energy to cross the room than he did! As Einstein pointed out, if she's using more energy that means she's got more mass. They took pains to point out that this didn't imply that the Prime Minister was getting heavier as she crossed the room. It simply meant that she needed more energy to do it than he did.

Alec – Wasn't there also something about the energy level that was crucial to finding the Higgs?

Bob – Going back to particles and their rest mass, if you add energy to a particle it doesn't affect its rest mass. Its new total mass becomes its rest mass plus the additional energy mass you've added.

Alec – I thought Einstein said that the faster particles travelled the bigger they got. Is that not the case here?

Bob – The faster they go increases their energy mass, but their rest mass always stays the same. I take no pleasure in bringing this up again, but the golf ball you clobbered me with is a good example. When you hit the ball you gave it movement energy which caused it to fly thru' the air and when it bounced off my skull it transferred this relatively small movement energy to me. Thankfully it didn't transfer any of its much larger rest mass energy to me 'cos if it had I wouldn't be here!. After hitting me it went back to having the same rest mass that it had before you sent it on its way. What causes confusion is when you substitute something like a proton for the golf ball and boost it up to almost light speed you get a massive particle by energy but not by mass. As they move round and round the tunnel at CERN the protons length shortens and, to compensate for this, their width and height increases relative to the static tunnel. A scientist at CERN said that protons in flight are like miniscule flying pancakes and their aim is to smash two pancakes head to head and hopefully create a new heavier particle. Another important point he stressed was that particles smashing together aren't like two cars colliding. Tho' they're called protons they're actually three individual quarks bound together by gluons.

Bob went into the bunker and made a couple of attempts to get his ball on the green. When his second attempt left him with a putt that was longer than his opponents he nodded over to Alec and conceded the hole. Alec retrieved the balls while Bob tried to rake out the damage he'd caused to the bunker

Sixteenth Hole   198 yards par 3 - Hell's Bunker.

Bob – Back there I was trying hard not to think that you're deep in the boondocks and I'm in A1 position so that even a five will probably be good enough for the game. Then, lo-and-behold and out of nothing, Steady Eddy produces the goods and I'm back to two-up with three to play. That was one of those shots that I'm sure will live long in your memory and warm you up on those cold winter nights. That's apart from your Brenda of course.

Alec – If warm's another name for energy, she's got more than enough for both of us.

Bob – First Law of Thermodynamics mate, heat and energy's the same thing.

Alec – So you whirl the particles round the tunnel till they're up to speed then smash them together to see what comes out.

Bob – Yes and no and that's one of the main misconceptions about colliders. Physicists know all there is to know about the vast majority of particles that make up the Universe. It used to be said that particle colliders were like taking a sledge hammer to a grandfather clock in an attempt to see how it worked. A much better comparison with the precision of the LHC is that it's like smashing two cheap watches together in the hope of getting a solid gold Rolex out of it!

Alec – Is it the quarks that they smash together to get a Higgs boson?

Bob – The LHC's Sunday name's the Large Hadron Collider and it's the name in the middle that's the clue.

Alec – Hadrons, what do they do?

Bob – It's the name for the group of particles that interact thru' the strong force and the main ones are protons and neutrons. The LHC uses protons because they've an electric charge which makes the results easier to measure. The LHC's composed of two tubes thru' which the protons are accelerated in opposite directions then smashed into each other at two detector points on opposite sides of the circuit. Not many people know this, but as well as being full of massive energy, the LHC's by far the biggest refrigerator in the world.

Alec – Away wi' you, everybody knows that. The cooling system failed the first time it was switched and it caused a big blow-out! It's all about keeping the magnets so cold that the wires lose their resistance to electricity.

Bob – The massive amount of electric current that's needed to keep the beams whizzing round would melt the wires of uncooled magnets and when the colliders are running flat out there's about 250 trillion protons whizzing round in each direction.

Although the next green had been clear for a few minutes neither felt the need to rush and as there didn't appear to be anyone behind them they stood on the tee and continued their talk.

Alec – How do they know when they've caught a Higgs?
Bob - The detectors are something else. The two that are hunting for the Higgs are called Atlas and CMS and as the protons get heavier with the energy they're carrying, the speed at which they have to be slammed together rises exponentially. The Higgs boson was predicted to be very heavy and it'll decay even quicker than some golfers we know picking up their ball when a putt's been conceded

In fact each boson decays so quickly that it only has time to travel less than a billionth of an inch and even with the very latest advanced detectors they've no hope of catching tracks that small.

Alec – Are they like the tracks you get when particles go thru' a cloud chamber?

Bob – Cloud chambers are old hat. The LHC uses what are effectively huge three-dimensional digital cameras which can take up to 40 million snapshots every second. The detectors are built out in layers with each one becoming denser to search for the tracks of different particles. The Standard Model's enabled scientists to match up all the known matter particles to the three forces that work inside atoms. It's explained almost all the experimental results that have been obtained so far and has helped theoretical physicists to predict a wide range of possibility new particles to look for, including the Higgs boson. Every collision will leave a track that can be recognised and what they're particularly focused on is the trace of an event that the theoretical chaps have mapped out for them.

Alec – How do they know when they've found it?

Bob – As all of this is taking place in the quantum world they have to work on probabilities, not certainties. But before they get to do any detecting they have to arrange for the protons to collide and that's no easy task either. Also it's not just once around the race track, smash and Bob's your uncle! When they're up to speed the protons circle round and round the tubes 40 million times a second for an average run of around nine hours. Every time they approach a detector the protons are grouped into bunches which are squeezed down to about the size and shape of a very small sewing needle. Getting them to collide at the detectors has been described like having these two sewing needles spaced more than eight miles apart, being fired at each other to meet head to head exactly in the middle.

Alec – Does every collision make Higgs bosons?

Bob – Even with compacting them as much as is possible the protons will still be mainly empty space and they only manage about twenty or so collisions from each bunch. They reckon that on average the LHC produces a Higgs boson every second, but finding it is like looking for a needle in 40 million haystacks.

Alec – That's an amazing feat. How do they know when they've caught one?

Bob – Using the Standard Model the theoretic people predicted that each Higgs boson will decay into one of seven different sets of 'particles'. Unfortunately none of the seven sets are fool-proof as they're also produced in many other collisions. Again it's important to remember that this is waves which are combining when they meet and not particles bashing together, so even the Rolex description of the interaction isn't a factual one!

Alec – I watched the announcement that they'd found the Higgs and most of the positive results had been found in the two photon channel, what's that all about?

Bob – Each of the seven different possibilities were set up as a channel so that each type of decay could be examined separately. One of the main possibilities was that the boson would almost immediately decay into two quarks. Then, because quarks can't exist outside atoms, they'll immediately decay into two very high energy photons.

Alec – So go and hunt for two high energy photon. Find them and you've trapped the beast. Game over!

Bob – As always there's a slight problem. The LHC is producing photons by the billions at the same time in other collisions and the particular pair they're looking for haven't got labels on them saying 'Made in Higgsland'. The only other clue from the Standard Model was that they would be very energetic and both would be at the same high energy level so they're looking for two matching energetic photons among gazillions of other less energetic little beggars.

Alec – I'd reckon the only way that could be done is to use my favourite bit of maths, statistics. The best way to find an anomaly is to make a graph of it and look for something that sticks out. Preferably like a sore thumb.

Bob – And that's exactly what they did. As they knew all the existing ways to produce photons they went looking for an excess of paired ones at a particularly high energy level. The best way to spot the seven different possibilities was to graph each one and look for a slight change in the numbers produced at various energy levels. They called this 'bump hunting' tho' the babies they were looking for weren't human ones. It sounds quite simple, but when it comes to carrying it out in practice it's anything but!

Alec – When the discovery announcement was made they showed the results from both detectors and you could see there was a slight bump in the graph of the two-photon channel at the same energy level from both detectors.

Bob – The important thing was that they were able to measure the energy level that contained the bump and as one of the lead spokesperson's said, "This isn't the end of a forty year hunt, it marks the start of a whole new range of physics." The other six channels were also monitored and their results were added, or in one case subtracted, to give the final result.

Alec – I assume this is only possible because everything's computerised up to the hilt?

Bob – That was my very simplistic understanding of the basic outline, but of course it's much more difficult and people-intensive than that. For a start checking for the Higgs boson was a world-wide co-operation whics set up on three levels, or as CERN calls them, tiers.

Alec – Good job it worked out for them or their tiers might have been real tears!

Bob – That's as bad as the joke I heard from one of those TV comedians the other week, "What grade of toilet tissues do mathematicians use?"

Alec – You've got me there buddy-boy.

Bob – Multi-ply, and we're down to scraping the bottom of the joke barrel nowadays. But going back to the Higgs, the first thing they had to do was to sift thru' an enormous mass of data and immediately discard the over 99% of particles they already know everything about. This was carried out by throwing all the data into a magic computer called The Trigger which acts as a waste bin for all the particle interactions that they know everything about. The LHC's detectors then worked as tier 0 and performed an ultra-rapid scan of the remaining 1% for interesting events. Around ten thousand events out of many millions got the LHC's stamp of approval and were moved on to tier1.These are fifteen facilities in Europe and the USA and each of them sifts thru' a part of the data for the really,

really interesting events and discards all but a few hundred. The final ones were then sent to tier 2 facilities located all around the globe.

Alec – That's some operation. It must've involved hundreds of people and a massive computer network.

Bob – The computer network's called The Grid and the results from the two Higgs detectors were split up and sent to five thousand collaborators all around the world for complete analysis. When it was set up in 2010 The Grid was made up of 200,000 computers and 150 million gigabytes of storage space distributed across 34 countries. It's now grown to support over 170 computing facilities across 42 countries and it's the largest computer network in the world.

Alec – That's an amazing endeavour and the sheer size of it just to get the low-down on a single particle is jaw dropping. The cost must have been enormous!

Bob – The LHC took about a decade to build and the total cost was around 4.75 billion US dollars. To put this in perspective one of the scientists compared it to how much it would've cost to make them out of best Swiss chocolate and he showed that, kilogram for kilogram, the costs were just about equal.

Alec – Unfortunately our match isn't equal and this isn't the easiest hole on the course to put your ball on the green.

The sixteenth is a 185 yard par three played back across the road leading to the clubhouse. The road doesn't come into play as the tee and green are almost level and the ground between them dips down before rising up again to a plateau green guarded by bunkers on either side and a deep cross bunker just short of it to catch a slightly under-hit shot. Alec played first and his five iron carried the ball right to the back of the green where he said he'd rather be than anywhere short. Bob hit a similar shot, but his ball flew slightly further and rolled off the back of the green down into some straggly grass.

Alec – That was a bit unlucky. You'd normally expect that wee bit of grass behind the green to stop your ball. I can't think of many other courses where there's as much trouble behind the green as there is in front of it.

Bob – There is and that's something you don't really appreciate till you've played here a few times. When a new player asks me for the yardage to the hole I often find myself cautioning them that it's usually better to be a little short rather than run the risk of going thru' the back of the green.

Alec – Except for this hole where Hell's Bunker's waiting for anything just short of a length!

They climbed onto the golf cart and continued their previous conversation.

Bob - The LHC's a prime example of how on some occasions things can be described as waves and at other times as particles. When I first heard of two protons colliding head to head and producing a shower of new particles I got a picture of a couple of circus clowns' cars colliding and falling apart with bits of them strewn all over the place. Colliding protons aren't 'particles, they're waves of energy and they don't actually smash into each other.

What happens is the very high energy they've accumulated forces two of the opposing waves to get so close to each other that they combine and produce a new wave. Or if they're really lucky, a quark then two new waves of high energy photons!

Alec – So the new particles they got from the collisions weren't hiding inside the quarks all the time.

Bob – That's where the analogy of two cars colliding doesn't fit. When two quarks combine they annihilate and disappear leaving behind two completely new particles. It's more like the two circus cars colliding then disappearing and leaving behind a pair of lions in their place.

Alec – And there's a chance that the lions could be the proof that they started out as a Higgs boson!

Bob – That's the important bit 'cos working back from the debris and doing it often enough allows them to say, 'as far as we know, we've found the Higgs boson.' Even tho' they know that there's no chance that they'll ever being able to isolate a stable one outside the Higgs field. We know that everything inside an atom is composed of waves, but it only makes sense to most of us when we think of actions like this as particles colliding.

Alec – So the Large Hadron Collider should really be called The Large Hadron Combiner. Now we know what happens can't we leave it that the nucleus is a positively charged lump of something that's put there to keep the electrons honest?

Bob – We could, but there are a couple of things that are needed to tie up some loose ends.

Alec – Go on then.

Bob – Remember we said that electrons and protons are stable because they're at their lowest possible energy state?

Alec – Electrons offload energy and fall down to the lowest available orbital consistent with the amount of energy they've offload and, according to the First Law, once they're there there's nowhere left for them to dump their remaining energy. I assume it's the same for both protons and neutrons?

Bob – It's a bit like that, but in reverse. It's probably better that we leave the nucleus at that as it gets a bit hairy when you get right down to the basics!

Alec – Just one thing tho', why can't quarks exist outside the nucleus?

Bob – The main reason is because they come in two varieties, up quarks and down quarks and neither of them is blessed with a unit of electric charge. The up quark is possibly called that because it has a positive electric charge of plus two-thirds of a unit whereas the down quark has a negative charge of minus one third of a unit. As a result of this strange arrangement the only way to get a stable nucleus is for three quarks to combine and make up either a proton with a whole of unit of charge, or a neutron with no charge.

Alec – Sorry for going on but let me get this straight. Protons and neutrons aren't basic particles and they're made up of three quarks bound tightly together by gluons. To be stable they need to have either a one unit positive charge or no charge at all and they can only get this when two of one type combines with one of the other.

Bob – Spotted first time, A pair of two third's up quarks adds up to a one and a third positive charge which is reduced to a unit charge by a down quark joining them with its minus one third of a unit charge to give the proton its one unit positive charge.

Alec – And when they combine the other way you'll get a neutron with the two down quarks one-third negative charge balanced out by the positive two-thirds positive charge of the up quark. That seems quite straight forward so why did you say that it's better that we don't dive too deeply into the nucleus.

Bob – The unintuitive part of saying that a nucleus is made up of three quarks is that even when you add the electrons to them they total only 0.1 percent of an atom's total mass. The other 99.9 percent comes from the strong nuclear forces gluons which keeps' the three quarks bound tightly together. The reason it's such a strong force is because it utilises all its force over the shortest of short distances inside the atom.

Alec - That doesn't make a lot of sense to me!

Bob – I did tell you and the main reason that actions like this seem unintuitive is because of your numbering system and it took me some time to get my head round it. You'll understand it better than me because it's all to do with fractions when they go negative.

Alec – That's an interesting way to look at it. Are you saying that when we go down into the quantum region we're operating below zero and as the number on the bottom line of a fraction gets larger, whatever they're describing gets smaller?

Bob – That's as I understand it.

Alec – That makes a lot more sense to me because that's the way we count. Numbers above zero are positive and when they increase whatever they're describing also increases. The opposite is the case below zero where the larger the number on the bottom line tells us that whatever we're describing is getting smaller. What would you say a nucleus weighs in at?

Bob – As I understand it it's around 99.9% of the total weight of the atom.

Alec – In that case the nucleus should take up only 1/99.9th of the space inside an atom leaving the other 99.9% of space free for electrons whose orbitals probably only take up very small amount of space within it.

Bob – That corresponds to what I've read. Protons are given the mass of one unit and on that scale an electron weighs in at .01 of a unit!

Alec – Let's see if I can get my head round this. Apart from hydrogen the nucleus of all the atoms are made up of protons and neutrons which are composed of three quarks held tightly together by gluons. Is it one gluon per quark or do they share them?

Bob – I warned you that it gets a bit hairy inside the nucleus and I accept that they're not, but referring to quarks as particles lets me to get a fuzzy picture of what's happening down there. Gluons bind the three quarks together, but it's not one gluon for each quark and neither do gluons need to be there all the time. Gluons come and go as they're required and because of that they're referred to as virtual particles!

Alec – Assuming that it was possible to see a quark, have scientists got any idea of what it might look like?

Bob – You're thinking of quarks as particles, but like all sub-atomic particles they're no more tangible than any of the sounds that come off a vibrating guitar or violin string. They're measurable and have energy, but they're not something that you can grab and put in your pocket.

Alec – I can see now why sometimes quantum things are called particles instead of waves as I can't see any way I can get a picture of three waves glued together and being kept in jail by other waves.

Bob – Protons and most neutrons which are at their lowest energy level are stable and they'll last till the end of time if they're left to their own devices. Because both types of quarks have only fractions of a charge they're always unstable and because of that they're unable to exist outside a nucleus. If you remove a single quark from a proton or neutron the other two quarks will instantly disappear. So if you're a proton or a neutron its three quarks or bust!

Alec – That sounds a bit like a camera tripod, or even one of those old milkmaid's three-legged stools. If you remove one of their legs they'll no longer be stable and, if that's the case, is three a magic number in quantum-land?

Bob – I hadn't thought of it that way, but groups of three in quantum physics appears to be the most stable arrangement available. In the Standard Model all the particles that make up matter come in families of three, consisting of one basic particle with two heavier cousins. Nothing I've read about in physics rules out there being more than three members of each family, but all the experimental evidence so far suggests that these families aren't like human ones in that they're all limited to three!

Alec – Going back to $E=mc^2$. If it's the energy of the strong force that's giving atoms most of their mass, where does the Higgs field fit in?

Bob – The Higgs field's different from the other fields because it's part of the fabric of our universe and its energy is permanently switched on.

Alec – I'm still trying to get a handle on how the Higgs field manages to give particles their mass. Are they created with no mass and have to go thru' the field to get it?

Bob – The Higgs field's everywhere. It's a universal field and when particles are created they're already travelling thru' it.

Alec – What form does it take?

Bob - The best way I can get a picture of it is to think of it as a vast expanse of very calm water. I imagine it as a massive swimming pool which has a wind blowing down the length of it at light speed.

Alec – You mean it's a bit like the loch where we learned to sail when we were young. But I don't remember the wind being quite as strong as that!

Bob – That sort of thing, but much, much larger and the water's a perfectly flat calm. Look over there, there's some yachts at the starting line waiting to sail off.

Alec – Is this like a regatta with boats zig-zagging everywhere?

Bob – Sort of, but this regatta's more like a sprint race and they're all sailing straight downwind.

Alec – Sound's fun, are we looking out to see who wins the race?

Bob – It isn't a race, it's a trial to decide which class each of the boats belongs in. The starter's just fired his gun and over there I can see two tiny boats that look as tho' they're flying just above the water and not making any waves.

They're being blown along at the same speed as the wind and in fact they're going so fast that I didn't have time to catch the names written on their sides.

Alec – I caught a glimpse of them. One's called Photon and the other's Gluon and they're going so fast that they're already out of sight.

Bob – There's a couple of boats over there with Quark and Electron on their sides, they seem to be very light as they scud along making very small waves.

Alec – There was a very tiny yacht called Neutrino just beyond them that I almost missed and I couldn't decide whether it was touching the water or not!

Bob – I'm watching the group of boats that are nearest to us and they're all making heavy weather of it. The waves they're creating are much larger and closer together than the ones over on the far side and the slower the boats are moving, the bigger are the waves they're creating.

Alec – So what does all this tell us?

Bob – Shut your eyes, the starter's about to make an announcement. That's it, you can open them again.

Alec – What's happened? I heard the announcer saying that he's switched off the wind and now all the boats have disappeared. But that's really odd, all the waves are continuing to be created as if the boats were still present!

Bob – So they are and through the magic of a bit of mathematics called Quantum Mechanics physicists can use the waves to reconstruct each of the boats that were making them. Even tho' the boats were never there in the first place!

Alec – OK, going back to the boats what's actually happening?

Bob – Photons and gluons are going thru' the field without interacting with it and, as they don't taking any energy from the field, they continued to stream along at light speed. The electrons were interacting slightly with the water and took a little bit of energy from it. This slowed them down slightly and, as energy and mass is the same thing, they've gained a little bit of weight which is shown by the tiny waves they're leaving behind them. The boats that were making heavy weather of it are taking greater and greater amounts of energy from the field and that's making them heavier. Being heavier they're moving slower and producing larger waves.

Alec – I see what you're getting at. The more energy a particle takes from the water, the more mass it gets and the slower it moves.

Bob – Yes, but remember that the Higgs field is a field of energy, not water. The particles are continuously moving thru' it with their mass being decided by the energy they take from the field. Waves are fundamental in the quantum world and the theory says that you're not allowed to have waves and boats, sorry particles, on the water at the same time. However, thanks to QM we can conjure up each particles position, direction of travel, speed, mass and other parameters from their waves. But remember the uncertainty principle. You're only allowed to find out about their inter-related quantities one at a time!

Alec – So the more slowed down the waves are as they move thru' the field, the more energy they've taken from it and gained the weight that Aristotle said, 'seeks to move them to their natural place.' Is this mass, the same as the rest mass you talked about earlier?

Bob – It is. Each particles rest mass is the result of the Higgs field slowing it down and it's this slowing down bit that's vitally important for us. If none of the particles reacted to the field and everything whizzed thru' it at light speed the energy waves wouldn't exist. In fact there wouldn't be anything here as here could never have existed. Mass is slowed down energy and without it our universe would've remained a field of pure energy!

Alec – Where does the great mass of neutrinos come into this? You said that they've got a tiny amount of mass, but they didn't seem to interact with the Higgs field?

Bob – I was half-hoping that you wouldn't spot that because there are hundreds of proposed theories for how neutrinos might get their mass. Maybe there's another source of mass that we don't know about or maybe the neutrino masses are the interplay of the Higgs boson and this new source of mass. Neutrinos act as if they have mass and the question you asked then becomes which one of the hundreds of theories is the right one?

Alec – Does gravity play any part inside atoms?

Bob - Although gravity's the dominant force in the classical world, and is present in the quantum world, it doesn't play an active part in how atoms work. The active force inside an atom's nucleus is the strong force's stickiness which glues the quarks together, along with the proton's unit charge of positive electricity.

Alec – What about the magnetic part of electromagnetism. Does it have any part to play inside a nucleus?

Bob - Michael Faraday proved that it's a moving electric field which creates magnetism and, as the nucleus isn't moving with respect to the atom, there isn't a magnetic field being created. Outside the nucleus the electrons are whirling round and creating their own magnetic fields which are cancelled out by them contra-rotating in each orbital and this leaves the protons electric charge as the dominant force in the atom. That said, it's the dominant force by action but certainly not by power. When it comes to a trial of strength the strong force outranks electromagnetism by a hundred times.

Alec – Why has nature gone to all this trouble to give atoms weight if they don't use it inside an atom?

Bob – The bulk of an atom's mass comes from the motion and the confinement of quarks and gluons in the quark jail. As far as forces go the electrons and quarks supply 1% of it with the other 99% coming from the strange interactions of the quarks and gluons.

Alec – Earlier on you mentioned bosons and fermions, where do they come in?

Bob – Force particles like photons, gluons and the weak nuclear force provided by W and Z particles are bosons, most of the rest are 'matter' particles and they're the fermions. The very important difference between them is that you can pile as many bosons into a fermion as it'll take, but the reverse is strictly prohibited. It's this distinction that's the very basic reason why life such as us exists in The Universe and why there's a universe for any life to exist in. Photons are gregarious and you can pile in as many as it'll take into an electron, but you can't pile any electrons into a photon. It also means that you can only have a single matter particle located at any point in space, so it's a very lonely life if you're a matter particle.

Alec – Where does the quarks strange electric forces come from?

Bob – When they were first discovered scientists thought they'd found a new type of matter as all the existing bits had either a unit of electric charge or no charge. These new ones with fractions of a charge were different and at the time it was thought they couldn't be real, so an eminent scientist called Murray Gel-Mann named them quarks for a joke. The word came from a whacky book he was reading called Finnegan Wake by James Joyce and when they were proved to be real particles the name stuck.

Alec – What's the actual value of the unit electric charge?

Bob – Being electric it must be volts, but it's pretty meaningless to talk about it that way as the value's a lot smaller than miniscule. It's based on the charge on a single electron which is nineteen zeros followed by 1.6 volts, so in order to keep it simple they refer to that voltage as 1e.

Alec – How do you measure something as low as 1e? No don't bother, I'm struggling enough as it is.

Bob – Me too. I can understand someone telling me that something's got a charge as small as that, but I can't comprehend what it actually means and I'm used to working with volts. It's probably best to look at it as the amount of energy that protons and electrons have been given so that each of them can have an equal and opposite electric charges.

Alec – Do the gluons use an electric charge to keep the three quarks in place?

Bob – Gluons don't have any electric charge and they're the oddballs of the nuclear world and again it's probably best if we leave it at that!

Alec – Do you mean that there's something there which does the job of gluons but nobody knows what it is?

Bob – Gluons are real in the sense that there's a force present which performs certain necessary actions. They're considered to be the carriers of the strong nuclear force and part of what they're allowed to do is to stick together and make glueballs. Science considers that they, or something very much like them, are a theoretical necessity. But tehey admit that it's unlikely they'll ever to have an experiment that'll prove conclusively how they do what they're doing!

Alec –This is getting weirder and weirder.

Bob – I did tell you, but since we've got this far it's only fair to say that scientists are convinced that the strong nuclear force must be a gluon type field because it allows gluons to interact with each other as well as gluing quarks together.

Alec - You said that they only operate over the shortest of short distances, is that also something to do with the smaller the particle, the greater the amount of energy you have to put in to find it?

Bob – It appears that the greater the force that a particle carries, the smaller is the area that it's allowed to act over.

Alec – That seems reasonable, but why do they have such a large force?

Bob – That's just one of the currently intractable problems that physicists are working hard on.

Alec – So we don't know exactly what gluons are or how they manage to do it, but we know what the result is!

Bob – It's a bit like gravity where we've know all thru' the ages what it is and what it does, but it took a long time to decipher how it does it.

Alec – We've come this far so it would be silly not to try to get a handle on what's actually happening.

Bob – Inside the nucleus, two of the three quarks will have an equal positive or negative charge and, as like charges repel, they'll always be trying to muscle each other out of the nucleus. The way to think about the gluons reaction to this is to think of the two quarks with the same charge being tied to each other by a piece of slightly elastic string. When they're very close to each other the string's slack and the minimum amount of gluon force is needed to keep it that way. If they start to move away from each other the string tightens and the gluon force increases 'til the errant quark is herded back in to jail. It sounds simple, but it's like Einstein's gravity thought that took ten years to pin down. Masses of scientists are working on this simple thought and they're talking in terms of twice, or even four times, Einstein's timescale to solve it. Nuclear weapons work the opposite way. If you can pile enough external energy into a nucleus the string will stretch and eventually snap when the gluons are at their maximum energy. Snap is the maximum distance that they work over, but how gluons glue and why they snap are some of the current threads of great interest.

Alec – And the Higgs field helps to do all this?

Bob – All this and more that's still waiting to be discovered. The simple way to think of the Higgs field is that that it acts as the filter that gives us the Universe we love.

Alec – So the brilliant people in the sixties and seventies thought this process backward and realised that there must be a universal field like this, but we wouldn't be allowed direct access to it. However, as it's a field it must have a carrier particle, so it's heigh-ho and off we go to hunt for the field's carrier boson.

Bob – That's it in a nutshell and the heigh-ho's have resulted in forty years of very expensive hunting!

Alec – How come protons are stable and neutrons aren't.

Bob – Protons, as we said, are normally at their lowest possible energy level and if they go any lower they'll cease to exist. Electrons are in a similar position and that's why they don't spiral down into the nucleus. Neutrons however can have very slightly more energy than protons which makes them a bit unstable and allows the weak force to nibble away at their quarks. Every so often the force wins and changes a down quark into an up quark plus an electron. This in turn changes the neutron into a proton and the atom becomes a different heavier element.

Alec – Again due to the energy in the Higgs field that you said was non-zero?

Bob – That's right. The Higgs is different from the other fields because it seems to be part of the big-daddy energy field that powers the Universe. The major difference between it and the others is that the Higgs field always contains energy whereas the others have to get theirs from the particles that whiz thru' them. The importance of the Higgs field is that even at its lowest point it still contains energy which it doles out in a certain way to particles. I likened it to a very large swimming pool, but the swimming pool is the Universe and every matter particle is constantly travelling thru' it. That includes our atoms and it's where we get our weight!

Alec – I'm still at a loss trying to picture this. When you

say it's got a non-zero value does that mean that it's an unstable field?

Bob – No it's very stable. It's the field that underlies everything and it's what gives matter its stability. It's quite hard to imagine a field like this, but think of it this way. We've gone back to the year 1630 and we're sitting beside our friend Galileo in a Venice church. He's just asked me "Well, what do you make of that?"

Alec – Do we speak to him in Italian, or does he speak English?

Bob – Because we're visitors I've taken the trouble to learn the language so I'll translate. We'd arranged to meet the great man outside this church because we're hoping to get a franchise on his magic seeing tube which we reckon has a good market back home.

Alec – Yea, getting in on telescopes at the ground floor would be a great idea!

Bob – I started talking to him about it but he's more interested in some high up candle-lanterns swinging on chains and it seems that he values our opinion.

Alec – Do you think he's trying to sell us a candle-lantern franchise as well?

Bob – I don't think so because when we came into the church he pointed up at the lanterns and I could see that they were all hanging at an angle instead of pointing straight down at the floor. I've just answered his question with, "Are you sure this church isn't built on a hillside?" He shook his head and said, "No, I've checked the other churches in the area and all their lanterns are hanging similar to the ones here."

Alec – Maybe they've been installed that way

Bob – I've asked him that and he's told me to look at the one directly in front of us as there's a breeze starting to come in through an open window and the lanterns are starting to swing. He's asked me again what I make of it and now all the lanterns are swinging up and down from their starting positions. I nodded my head to confirm that we were watching and now the breeze has gone down and they've all gone back to their off-centre starting positions. I told him "That's really strange, but it's probably just one of those quirks of nature." He replied "So it's not my eyesight that's gone funny and you say that it's a quirk of nature. I like quirks of nature, so first thing tomorrow morning I'll figure it out and if you chaps meet me here again at 4 o'clock I'll explain exactly what's happening"'

Alec – I take it that we didn't hang around till the next day?

Bob – Galileo had wonderful insights, but even he wouldn't have been able to figure out this quirk of nature in twenty four hours. In fact he'd have to hang around for three hundred years to get the idea that there's an off-centre force whose natural starting position isn't pointing straight down the way that gravity says it should.

Alec – If the field's there all the time, why is it when we drop a rock it falls straight down rather than at an angle like the hanging candle-lanterns?

Bob – The Higgs field is only active in the sub-atomic world and it doesn't play any part in actions in our classical world. Sorry, I should have said, as far as science presently knows it plays no part outside the quantum region!

Alec – Surely, in the fullness of time, we'll find a way to detect and explain all these weird things that happen.

Bob – For a hundred years we've had radios like your dad's that could detect hit records being played all the way from Luxembourg and we now have TVs in glorious technicolour providing us with information from the four corners of the planet. We can talk almost instantly to anyone anywhere in the world on our mobile phones and we benefit from many new medical wonders. Being humans we tend to take it all for granted and seldom stop to think about how all these wonders work.

By this time they'd got out of the cart and Bob, only five yards beyond the flag, was weighing up his shot. He knew that a slightly over-hit chip risked his ball running off the front of the green and into Hells Bunker. Then again a slightly under-hit putt could easily end up back at his feet. He opted for neither and tried to bump a seven iron into the bank with the hope that it would bounce up onto the green and stop. This it did, but by the time it stopped it was the same distance beyond the flag that it had started from. Alec rolled his putt down to within inches of the hole and Bob almost holed a curling fifteen footer that would have secured the half. "You were nearly dormie there my old mate, but I'm back to one down and there's still two holes to play," said Alec.

Seventeenth Hole   428 yards par 4 - Jenny's Linn

The second last hole has a narrow undulating fairway sandwiched between an out-of-bounds wall down the right-hand side and various groups of trees down the left. The tee and green are roughly level, but between them the ground slopes slowly down from the tee then back up to a green that's perched on the top of a knoll. The drive's crucial as the fairway narrows in to around fifteen yards at half distance, but a good straight shot sets you up for an attempt at a green that's guarded by three bunkers. The first one's a cross bunker ten or so yards short of the green while the other two are deeper and skirt along either side of the green. Both players hit reasonable looking drives, but Bob, looking to close out the game, got his slice back and groaned inwardly as his ball dropped over the out-of-bounds wall. He hit a provisional ball in case a miracle might happen and they drove down to where Alec's ball sat in A1 position. Bob walked over and retrieved his ball then got back in beside his pal while they waited for the green to clear.

Alec – You said back there that we take some things for granted without even thinking about them, in what way?

Bob – Take the mobile phone you've just been checking up on while I went for my ball. When you make a call do you have to stand still and make sure that the phone's aerial is always pointing directly at the telephone mast where the signal's coming from?

Alec – You know me, I'm one of those people who move around while I'm talking. Sometimes I even move from room to room.

Bob – And sometimes while you're moving around the

signal from the phone mast will be on the other side of your head from the phone?

Alec – Are you saying that the phone signals are going straight thru' my head and I'm unable to detect them?

Bob – It's not just your head they're going thru', they're streaming thru' rest of your body, brick walls and just about anything that's between you and the phone mast.

Alec – And you're suggesting this might have something to do with the Higgs field?

Bob – Consider what would happen if the Higgs field wasn't there. The signals you've received from the telephone mast are photons that have bypassed the Higgs field and travelled thru' the electromagnetic field, so they would still be present. What would be affected is the mast and transmitter, your mobile phone, you, the ground you're standing on and everything else around you. Everything that's made of matter would cease to exist.

Alec - And that's because the Higgs field is slowing down particles as they go thru' it.

Bob – Scientists now realise that if we want to understand how the Universe works we have to accept that space plays at least as big a part in it as matter. The Higgs is a non-zero field that appears to have the same strength everywhere while the gravitational one's a field which has the potential to give mass to anything that's accelerating thru' it. These two fields, along with electromagnetism and gluons, are static fields and seem to be the fundamental parts of what we call space. Everything we see around us is caused by the interactions of matter waves moving thru' them and by interactions between the fields themselves.

Alec – I thought you said that there wasn't a separate magnetic field, it's just the action of something like photons travelling thru' an electromagnetic field that creates magnetism?

Bob – That's right and the photons are a good example. Any drawing I've seen of one of them travelling shows an electric wave creating a magnetic wave which recreates the electric wave and it looks as tho' it's this electric- magnetic-electric action that's causing the photon to fly thru' space.

Alec – Why does light travelling thru' space never lose energy and slow down?

Bob – That's two separate things. Electromagnetic radiation gets stretched out and loses energy as it travels thru expanding space as per Edwin Hubble's observations, but it can never lose speed as it's travelling thru' space. A photon can't travel at anything other than light speed. If it did it would be a matter particle and would have to contain some mass!

Alec – What about when light's slowed down going thru' something like glass or water?

Bob – Bob – Glass, or any other 'light conducting' material, does this by absorbing the photons and instantly re-transmitting them in different directions so they effectively 'jiggle' about 'til they reach the end of the glass where they resume normal operations.

Alec – Is that why you can get a sort-of ghost image of yourself when you look at a glass window?

Bob – As well as eventually going thru, a small portion of the photons lose their way and are reflected back to you. Einstein was in constant awe at what he called 'light quanta' and later on in his life said, "All these 50 years of conscious brooding have brought me no nearer to the answer to the question, what are light quanta? Nowadays every Tom, Dick and Harry thinks he knows, but he's mistaken."

Alec – If Einstein's unsure what chance have we got!

Bob – He's right in a way because scientists are not yet 100% sure that they have the full story about photons.

Alec - I thought they were the simplest of things. Just energy waves waving their way thru' space and now you're saying there's more to it than that.

Bob – Going back to reference frames, how does it look from the photon's angle?

Alec – It's just as I said, a wave waving its way thru' space.

Bob – What about time and the space it's waving thru', how does the photon perceive that?

Alec – Well, I know that for the photon time doesn't exist, but I'm not too sure what it makes of the space it's moving thru'.

Bob - To a photon the Universe doesn't exist. Wherever it's going it's already there and it didn't take any of our time to get there. In its own reference frame, time and space don't exist and this is true for all the massless particles, so why do only those particles with mass experience time? Then again, are time and mass somehow related and does one give rise to the other?

Alec – Doesn't that imply that we're in need of another Einstein who'll work his, or her, magic and possibly solve some other mysteries as well. But here's a weird thought. I accept that at the basic level all matter's composed of waves moving thru' energy fields, does that also apply to objects like you and me?

Bob – It must do, but it makes me feel strange to think of myself as being nothing other than an assorted collection of waves.

Alec – What came into my mind the films we watched at the Saturday Cinema Club and I remember we used to watch Flash Gordon's spaceship landing on an alien planet with what looked suspiciously like a lit firework fizzing away on its tail.

Bob – And you say that my mind works in strange ways, what brought this on? Was it the thought of Dale Arden coming out the spaceship and rushing into your arms?

Alec – Now that's another thought, but no. What I was thinking was, if our grandkids watched the rubbish we watched they'd laugh and say, 'Beam me up Scotty.' I know that filmmakers back when we were young didn't have the effects where they could make people disappear from their spaceship and instantly reappear on a planets' surface. I'm also aware that Captain Kirk and his merry men did it the 'beam me up' way to save an enormous amount of money that staging a realistic landing would cost, but do you think that's the way we're heading when we accept that we're just a bundle of waves?

Bob – Do you mean that if we're ever able to copy our wave-bundle and send it off to be re-assembled on a distant planet we'd have conquered light speed space travel?

Alec – I wasn't thinking that far ahead, it was more about my knee that's starting to give me trouble. I was wondering if we'll ever get to the point where the waveform of my dodgy knee could be replaced by a new healthy waveform knee as it would save me lots of time and trouble.

Bob – And pain too I'd imagine, but you're talking to the wrong man. I used to replace electronic components, not wonky knees. In any case being a mathematician you're probably in a better position to answer that than I am. It's quite a thought tho' and who knows what wonders the future will bring. But going back to space with its atom's worth of energy, it now looks as if that amount's crucial. Apparently if it was just a little less it would make a slight difference to most particles, but it would be catastrophic for electrons. Any reduction in the field's energy would allow them to take up more space inside every atom which would cause the atom to swell. Some of the smaller atoms would still be able clump together and form molecules so we'd still have simple ones like water. But the larger, more complex molecules like DNA would fall apart long before they're anywhere near to assembling themselves.

Alec – That's a nasty thought. It would make the creation of any form of life impossible.

Bob – Good job for us that it's a fixed parameter and doesn't appear to have changed since the Universe was formed!

Alec – Would that not imply that we live in a closed universe as life on Earth's been going on for nearly four billion years and it doesn't seem that the DNA molecule has changed over time.

Bob – That raises another important question. Was the DNA molecule developed here on Earth or could it have flown in from outer space? Perhaps it's endemic throughout the Universe and flew here as a little bit of organic material piggy-backed on a meteorite!

Alec – I don't suppose we'll find that out till we're able to visit other planets and check.

Bob – I'd imagine that the best way to search for life on another planet would entail looking for some form of DNA-like molecules. When we get to explore Mars I'm sure that'll be a top priority.

Alec – Might it be that at the start of the Big bang when there was no particles about it was the Higgs field that provided the initial energy that got the Universe started?

Bob – Science is still in the early days of the Higgs field and there are some expectations that the boson they've found may be just one of three at higher and higher energies. As well as giving matter weight, the Higgs field's been taken as proof that generations of matter particles only do come in three's. Unlike Philipp von Jolly and his successors, we now know now that we're not just a small step from having a complete knowledge of the Universe. Physicists freely admit that there's a long list of things they only know a little about, that there are some things they know almost nothing about and, if the past is anything to go by, there'll be things that they don't yet know that they don't know anything about!

Alec - Hmm, so you don't think we're anywhere near the stage where professors can advise their students not to bother with physics as all that's needed is a bit of tidying up?

Bob - Who knows, maybe the big breakthrough's lurking out there waiting for someone, or some experiment, to bring it out into the open. But every breakthrough seems to spawn new areas of interest, like the actions that only work at almost zero temperature.

That's zero on the Kelvin scale, or minus 273 point something on our normal centigrade one.

Alec – Will it ever be possible to get something down to, or even below zero?

Bob – I think that going to or below zero's a no-no because to cool anything down you have to have something that's at an even lower temperature to drain the heat from whatever you want to cool.

Alec – Are there any obvious problems that the Higgs might help to clear up?

Bob – There's quite a long list, but possibly one of the most pressing would be with the hadrons and leptons that make up atoms.

Alec – I thought the atom was sorted out. Protons and neutrons are three quarks glued together and they're electrically balanced by the electrons swirling around them.

Bob – That would make perfect sense if each of them didn't have a pair of big cousins. We only need the lowest energy versions of each one to create all the matter in our universe, so where do their overweight cousins fit into the story?

Alec – Leptons and hadrons, you haven't mentioned them before. Are they also part of an atom?

Bob – Hadron's the name given to the particles that react to the strong nuclear force and leptons are the ones that work with electromagnetism. Protons and neutrons are hadrons, electrons and their tiny cousins neutrinos are leptons.

Alec – How did we find out about their heavier cousins?

Bob – Mainly by detecting them in collider experiments and we now know that there are three families of those four matter particles when all we need is just the four lowest energy ones. They don't seem to fit into any obvious patterns either. For example take the electron. If a standard electron is given the mass of one then its first cousin, called a muon electron, is more than 200 times heavier than the standard electron. The second cousins are called tau electrons and they're 175 times more massive than the second cousins, which makes them 35,000 times more massive than our everyday normal electrons.

Alec – Are all these particles being produced by 'boats' in the Higgs field?

Bob –They must be and it's also similar for the families of up and down quarks. Quarks are named differently and the up quark has two higher energy cousins called charm and top, while the down pair answers to strange and bottom. The cousins have the same electric charge as the first family member and again the two families of quarks differ only in their energy or mass.

Alec – So what's the big problem with these heavier cousins?

Bob – To make atoms we only need the basic up and down quarks and electrons. What's the reason for their two heavier cousins that don't seem to play any part in our current universe?

Alec – Have they anything in common that might help science to make sense of them?

Bob – They're all very well defined and even before some of them were discovered it was assumed that they must exist because of the three generations of families they have in common.

Alec – Does their heaviness form a pattern that matches

the boats going thru' the Higgs field?

Bob – You'd think that should be the case, but apart from them being heavier there's no obvious pattern to them. Then there's those tiny neutrinos which are so light that billions of them are passing thru' each of your fingernails every second without you being aware of them. They've also two heavier cousins and once again, what service do they provide? Of these twelve basic particles we've got eight that are redundant and we've had to park them as science hasn't come up with a scenario where any of them might conceivably fit in. As for the other unknowns where do you want to start?

Alec – I assume that proof of whether or not gravity's a quantum force would be near the top?

Bob – It would and so would knowing why protons and electrons have exactly the same, but opposite, electric charges and where the quark's fractional charges come from. If that wasn't enough to be going on with there's the small problem of the 95% of the Universe that we're unable to make contact with!

Alec – I remember hearing something about Einstein's Cosmological Constants being measured in two different ways and there was a very big gap between the two answers. What's that all about?

Bob – I'd forgotten about that and it's all to do with the hunt for dark energy. When it was discovered scientists worked out that the expansion of the Universe must be speeding up so they re-introduced Einstein's Cosmological Constant to account for it. However, when they measured the actual expansion they found that the constant was too small to account for all the energy that the theory said must be there and their calculations settled down to be fifty-two orders of magnitudes too small.

Alec – Hmm, that means the answer was fifty-two zeros followed by the actual number and getting minus fifty-two orders of magnitude is an enormous gap. Ten's one order and a hundred is two, so fifty-two orders below zero is an incredibly small number. What did the other way of measuring it work out as?

Bob – The other team used quantum field theory to calculate the constant and it gave them the opposite answer, plus sixty orders of magnitude. This gives a difference of a hundred and twelve orders and that's the largest discrepancy between theory and experiment that there's ever been! Fortunately it's now recognised that a large part of it comes from the different assumptions that both made. The classical measurement team treated space as being completely empty while the quantum people said that it may be empty of normal matter, but that doesn't stop it from containing the atoms worth of energy which will be causing masses of virtual particles to be constantly popping in and out of existence.

Alec – Virtual particles, does that mean there's even more ghost particles out there?

Bob – Strangely enough, the existence of virtual particles was proved by probably the simplest experiment in modern science. In 1948 a Dutch physicist, Hendrik Casimir, predicted that two metal plates which were separated by a tiny gap would of their own accord move closer and closer together and many experiments since then have confirmed that this is what actually happens.

Alec – As it couldn't have been one of the nuclear forces that was causing this, it could only be gravity or electromagnetism.

Bob – It's actually neither of them. It's a basic quantum effect which says that there will be vastly more virtual particles being created in the space outside the plates than there'll be in the much smaller gap in between them. This means that there's more energy available to push the plates together than there is to keep them apart and the smaller the gap between the plates, the greater is the effect.

Alec – When you say gap, what size are we talking about?

Bob – The gap has to be less than a thousandth of a centimetre and that's an enormous gap in the quantum world. This effect's already being used in nano-size structures and micro-sensors some of which are now everyday objects. There's a type of micro-sensor that controls the pressure of the safety air-bags in your car, so one day the Casimir Effect might help to save your life!

Alec - What about the Big bang. Do you think it'll still hold water fifty years from now?

Bob – It's the most comfortable theory we have and I'm sure it'll remain the number one contender 'til a more acceptable alternative comes along.

Alec – What about time? Are there any new pointers on it, or is it still considered being just a measure of change?

Bob – That depends on what time you want. For a start how would you describe time?

Alec – Didn't one of the Saints 'way back in time say, "What is time, if no one asks me I know. But if I wish to explain it to the one who asketh, I know not.

Bob – That was Saint Augustin seventeen centuries ago and I think his words of wisdom are just as valid today.

Alec – Isn't time a measure of things that repeat, like passing seasons or circuits of the Sun. I know that Isaac Newton had a very firm idea of it. He wrote 'Absolute, true and mathematical time, of itself and from its own nature, flows equably without regard to anything external and is called duration.' His view was that time's a mathematical construction which exists independently of us humans and ticks on and on at the same steady rate throughout the Universe. He conceded that there's another time which he called common, or relative time, where duration can be measured using a clock. Which time do you want, the absolute or the common garden variety of it?

Bob – The problem is that they're both describing time's effects, not what actually constitutes time.

Alec – I remember taking part in a discussion about time at the Uni. and someone said that Dick Feynman had a favourite description of time which he saw written on a college lift's wall. 'Time's what prevents everything from happening at once'.

Bob – When you think about it that's probably as good a description as any, but it seems that our first problem with time is that there's not a universally agreed set of words that can be used to describe it.

Alec – What's the problem with space-time, didn't it prove Einstein's general relativity?

Bob – A lot of Einstein's work at the Bern Patent Office was with time and how to synchronise distant clocks on railway stations. But going back to Newton, his concept of time was that if we could spread clocks around the

Universe they'd all tick the same tick and keep identical time. Einstein's relativity updated this concept and showed that the Universe doesn't work that way and there's no such thing as a standard time. He also explained why moving clocks run slower than stationary ones. That's relative to each other of course.

Alec – Does gravity have any effect on time?

Bob – It certainly influences the clocks we use to measure it. You can now buy a couple of super accurate atomic clocks on the internet and put one on a table and the other on the floor. Synchronise and set them running then when you come back after your lunch break you'll find that the clock on the floor's kept a little bit time less than the one on the table and that's where the problems start.

Alec – I don't see a problem with that, gravity's causing one to run slower than the other.

Bob – That's true, but which one of them is keeping the correct time. Or more to the point, can there be ever be such a thing as the correct time. The only answer that makes sense is that they're keeping time relative to each other and neither can be said to be keeping the correct time. It's not just these two clocks that are keeping different times, all the clocks throughout the Universe are keeping different times. Time's always relative and it doesn't just apply to clocks, it applies to all living things. Plants, animals and people age faster when they live at altitude!

Alec – Hasn't that also got something to do with our car's GPS systems?

Bob – GPS gives us the everyday proof that Einstein's theories are spot on as the entire system depends on the clocks up on the satellites being synchronised with the clocks back here on Earth. He showed that every twenty-four hours the satellites clocks run slower by a small fraction of a second and if a correction wasn't built in your cars indicated location would be out by ten kilometres per day.

Alec – I only use the GPS when we go a distance, but Brenda uses it even for quite short journeys.

Bob – Then there's another problem with time and how it applies to the laws that control the Universe.

Alec – Is that to do with time never being allowed to reverse?

Bob – It is and it's our normal experience that cause always comes before effect, but all the basic laws that describe the Universe, bar one, work equally well no matter what direction time's moving.

Alec – So there's actually a law that stops time travel.

Bob – It's the famous Second Law of Thermodynamics which states that heat flows, but only in one direction. Because of this cause must come before effect and time can only move from the past into the future. In all the elementary equations of the Universe, the arrow of time only appears where there's heat, or to be more exact, energy present.

Alec – Back at the Uni. we did a bit of work with Minkowski's spacetime and I found it quite a neat idea.

Bob – Space-times' always bamboozled me and I tend to think of it being another version of Newton's clock. I can't see how spacetime squares with me being able to move around in all three dimensions of space at any speed I want, but I can only do it in a time that moves forward one second at a time. And why is it possible for me to be at the same place as many times as I want, but I'm never allowed to be in two different places at the same time?

Alec – When I was studying we didn't have video recorders, we had some instructional films and one of them featured Richard Feynman giving a lecture on spacetime and the way he explained it gave me a better idea of the concept. He pointed out that the problem with uniting space and time is that time's counted in seconds and space is in metres, so if you want to get anywhere the first thing you have to do is get them both into the same units.

Bob – Einstein linked the speed of light to time.

Alec – He did, but another thing that Feynman pointed out was that we tend to think of space and time as being two different things. But nature doesn't give a hoot to what we think 'cos it says that every time we're in a certain place it's always at a certain time.

Bob – That's all very well, but what's the advantage of treating space and time this way?

Alec – It puts space and time on the same footing so that time and the three dimensions of space can be treated as a four dimensional concept.

Bob – But they're in totally different units. Space is in distances and times in seconds, how do you unite them?

Alec – That's quite easy when you consider it as, what distance is a second? Or even better, what distance does light travel in a second?

Bob – I know that light travels at almost 300,000 kilometres every second, so if you take off three zeros that'll give you the distance in metres it travels in a second.

Alec – And if you turn that round, you'll get the time that it takes for light to travel one metre which, if I remember what Feynman said, is three and a third billionths of a second. You can then use this figure to convert your time to a distance and, hey presto, you've got all four parts in metres and you can use that to get some interesting results.

Bob – I know that physicists can set up equations to work out things like, what time does a sub-atomic event take and put this result into Schrodinger's quantum theory. It'll then tell you how to derive the mass, speed and direction of the particle you've measured and all this comes from measuring it in spacetime!

Alec – Thinking about time that way's very convenient for some physics theories, but the problem is that there's as many differences between space and time as there are similarities. One obvious difference is that you can travel anywhere in space, but you can only travel in one direction of time. Might the idea of multiple universes have anything to do with how we experience space-time?

Bob – Not that I know of as we're definitely denied any knowledge about them.

Alec – What about the other idea of us being part of a multiverse?

Bob – It looks a less improbable theory to me as it proposes that there was a time before the big bang when a small part of a much larger universe contained a sea of seething dark energy which was being compressed 'til it reached a tipping-point and that caused the space all around it to expand at an exponential rate. This is the part of Big bang that's called inflation and when it ends almost all the compressed energy's been converted into a new matter universe. In this theory the Big Bang and inflation still happens, but it's not a singularity that starts the process. This contributes to the idea that inflations don't end with our universe, but carries on creating disconnected universes in various places at random times and you get successive regions of space separated by areas of expanding dark energy so that all the individual universes are unable to interact with their neighbours.

Alec – That sounds a slightly more plausible idea. Is there any way to test it?

Bob – Cosmologists have noticed that the Cosmic Microwave Background Radiation is slightly skewed to one side. It's still a very speculative idea, but they say that sometime in the past when a new bubble universe was being created, it might have collided with our universe and left our CMBR with a skewed imprint.

Alec – Like two floating soap bubbles touching and going off their separate ways.

Bob – The proposal that a multiverse might exist is built out of two theories that have been verified countless times, quantum physics and inflation. We can't rule out the possibility that ours is just a relatively small bubble among masses of them.

Alec – That scenario also gives a more plausible way to describe the conditions before the Big bang. I like the idea of Big Bangs running round the multiverse setting off bubble universes like firecrackers.

Bob – Quite a thought and that still leaves room for a Creator who lights the blue touch-paper!

Alec – I can almost hear Ernst Mach turning in his grave and screaming 'Bubble universes, have you seen one?' Would the same laws apply in all the other universes?

Bob – Couldn't even start to make a guess at that, but when our Big Bang had finished big banging it's left us at the centre of our visible universe, if not quite at the centre of our solar system.

Alec – It's a pity we didn't know all this when we met Galileo, we might've been able to save him from upsetting the Inquisition. But talking about big banging, I'm sure I heard someone shouting fore! There it is again!

They got out of the golf cart and looking back they could see two golfers standing on the tee and waving their drivers in the air. Bob manoeuvred the golf cart out of their line of fire and signalled the twosome to play thru'.

Alec – How long has that green been clear and here's us sitting in the middle of the fairway blocking the course

Bob – That's two cracking drives they've hit. I think it's our Captain David Blair and his Vice Captain Phil Ward coming thru'. We're deep in the merde now!

Alec – I know David quite well, but I don't think I've met Phil.

As they approached the Captain called out "Ahh, so it's you Bob, I should have guessed." When he got closer he added "Is that your pal Alec with you, I haven't seen him for a while." Then, "Did the pair of you fall asleep for your afternoon nap?" Turning to his partner he said, "You know Bob and the other one's Alec, one of our former members." "Pleased to meet you Alec, I'm Phil" said the Vice-Captain. "We saw the green was clear and thought that something must've happened to you or your golf cart." Alec replied

"Sorry, we were deep in a discussion about multiple universes and we forgot to check that the game in front had moved on." The Captain replied "Well that explains it. You've been out touring the Universe and your space buggy's run out of juice. Will I ask one of the greens staff to come out and tow you back to Mother Earth?" Bob looked inside the buggy and replied "It's OK David, we've just enough anti-matter left in the tank to complete our mission, but thanks for the kind thought." "Must move on and thanks for letting us thru" said The Captain. "We're squeezing in a quick round before the general committee meeting tonight." "Phil, this is the pair I told you about who've been playing for their weird trophy since they got out of nappies." Then to Bob, "How's your match going?" "I'm one up. volunteered Bob, but it's looking more likely that we'll soon be all square." They sat back in the golf cart and watched as they played out the hole.

Alec – Where were we, I've lost the plot?

Bob – We were talking about whether we're just a small part of a multiverse.

Alec – So we were. I recently watched a program on the telly where several people were discussing something called the Hubble sphere and the sound was quite low so for a few minutes I thought that they were talking about bubble spheres. Has this anything to do with multiverses?

Bob – This idea goes back to Hubble's photos of very distant galaxies and the speed of light.

Alec – I gathered that bit and it's to do with the distance we can see all around us being limited by the speed that light travels which, in effect, means that our universal horizon is 13.8 billion light years away in every direction. So that makes our total Universe twice that distance across.

Bob – That figure's based on the distance that light we see now has travelled at light speed for 13.8 billion years which would be fine if we lived in a static universe. We now know that the Universe is expanding at an ever increasing rate and the galaxies we're seeing now have moved further away in the intervening 13.8 billion years so they are now around 45 billion light years away. As it's the same distance in every direction 'our' Universe now measure 90 billion light years side to side and the total area that encompasses is called our Hubblesphere or Hubble Bubble.

Alec – Is that now the total size of our Universe and there's nothing beyond that distance?

Bob – We're back to reference frames and that's the Hubble sphere from our reference frame. If the background radiation looked identical in every direction it would imply that what we see is the total area of the Universe. But observations of the CMBR don't quite agree with this and teams of physicists using the assumption that we live in a closed finite universe have come up with different answers. One team says that there's room for at least 250 of these Hubble volumes in it. Another team, using the same assumptions, have come up with 400 volumes and are quoted as saying 'Given the reality of our current capabilities for observation, to us even a finite universe appears to go on forever'. Then again, if the string theorists are correct, this could mean that we might be living in a big multiverse which is just one of billions and billions of universes!

Alec – The mind boggles, but what about gravity and where do we stand with it?

Bob – Gravity's a bit of an enigma. Is it a universal force as Newton described, or could it be the quantum force that Dirac tried to prove?

Alec – I'd go with Newton and say that gravity's the force of attraction between lumps of matter and all the lumps of matter are part of the classical world. As you said, it appears to be having no effects in the quantum one.

Bob – I'd agree with you that gravity's what causes mass to be attracted to other mass, but photons are massless and gravity bends their path. Doesn't that suggest that it might also be a quantum effect?

Alec – You mean that gravity could be a quantum field like the Higgs or nuclear ones, but to do that wouldn't it need a carrier?

Bob – Gravitons have been proposed as the carrier, but so far we've been unable to detect a single one and if they are there then the Universe should be awash with them. The scientists who propose their existence said that it's because their individual force is too small for us to measure.

Alec –What's wrong with Einstein's description of it being the force that bends space?

Bob – There's nothing wrong with it except he says that gravity's the result of matter constantly accelerating which leaves room for a future explanation of how it manages to do it.

Alec – Couldn't gravity be the ideal job for all those tiny neutrinos?

Bob – Neutrinos are probably the most abundant

particles in the Universe, but they're best described as tiny wisps of nothing. They're produced in massive quantities when a star explodes and they probably played a part in the early universe when it was almost parity between matter and anti-matter. We know they've not got a magnetic attraction because they pass straight thru' both metallic and non-metallic things.

Alec – So we have a force that acts throughout the Universe on all matter. How did Einstein get from there to his great theory?

Bob – By none other than one of his favourite thought experiments, tho' in this one he didn't have to travel by tram.

Alec – I've never heard that Einstein had a gravity thought experiment. Where did you find out about that?

Bob – I read it in a book he wrote in 1920 describing the genesis and birth of General Relativity.

Alec – Is it understandable to normal people like me?

Bob – I can get the gist of it and I'm not the mathematician. Remind me to give it to you when we get back home tonight. It's a wonderful description of his amazing thought processes.

Alec – I look forward to reading it, How did he start thinking about gravity that was so different?

Bob – This thought's the opposite of travelling in light-speed trams as it starts with him being motionless and tied down in a static room!

Alec – Why's he tied down, is he in a jail somewhere?

Bob – He's in a plain room and I assume that it's a rope or something similar that's holding him down. But it's not being unable to move that matters, the important point is where the room is located.

Alec – It's not an interrogation room is it!

Bob – If it is the only person he's interrogating is himself! He's in an enclosed room that's located at an impossible place in the Universe, a place where there's absolutely no gravitational force present. As there's no gravity he's tied down to the floor 'cos the slightest touch on it, or any wall, will make him float away in the opposite direction. There's another rope that's attached to a hook on the roof of the room and an external force starts to pull it upwards at an ever increasing speed. Einstein removes the rope that was holding him down and asks himself what effect is this having on me. He answers himself by saying that he's now being held down to the floor by the room accelerating in the opposite direction and he's experiencing a downward force that must be the equal and opposite of the force that's pulling the room up. Therefore gravity must be the result of the room being constantly accelerated upward.

Alec – And if the acceleration had been in the other direction he'd be stuck to the roof! That seems to be far too simple, there must be more to it than that.

Bob – Thinking it out was simple, proving it was something else!

Alec – Is Einstein saying that gravity's not an actual force, but the result of the room being pulled upward?

Bob – He's saying that gravity's the downward force given to him while the room's being accelerated upward, but he quickly realised that this force would disappear as soon as the room stops accelerating. Einstein's view is that gravity's nothing other than the equal and opposite result of mass being accelerated!

Alec – Doesn't that create a major problem as in, what would happen to him when the acceleration reaches the speed of light?

Bob – The thought experiment is describing the room accelerating in a straight line and getting up to light speed that way's obviously impossible. But there's another type of acceleration which you feel when you change direction while you're moving. It's why motorcyclists lean inward when they corner and Wall of Death riders have to go round in circles rather than in a straight line.

Alec – I assume that's why we get pushed to the opposite side when we corner quickly!

Bob – With this simple thought experiment Einstein also explained why gravity's everywhere. Because every bit of matter in the Universe is moving in circles its constantly bending, or warping, the space around it. Einstein showed, and most scientists now believe, that gravity's being constantly created this way rather than it being a physical field that mass has to travel thru'.

Alec – So gravitons might not come into it!

Bob - In Einstein's concept gravity's a force that every single piece of mass creates for itself by constantly changing direction. His explanation is that circling mass curves the space all around it and bends normally straight lines into curved ones which other masses then have to follow. Photons have energy which is the same as mass, so they also have to follow the warped path around the Sun just as lumps of matter have to.

Alec – Is it certain that it's not the job of those tiny neutrinos?

Bob – They're definitely non-starters, as is any form of magnetism.

Alec – We've our own magnetic field does it play any part?

Bob – Apparently not, but without it most life as we know it would in severe danger. It forms our Earth's magnetic shield which protects us by deflecting almost all the harmful very energetic photons that we're constantly being bombarded with.

Alec – After all that, what would be your description of gravity?

Bob – The message coming out of Loop Quantum Gravity is that gravity and space is the same thing. It proposes that space isn't a continuous bit of nothing, but is a quantum field like all the others and made up of atoms of space that are a billion, billion times smaller than a hydrogen atom nucleus. It also proposes a solution to the 'gravitons' problem. They're just the quanta of gravity and unlike photons and other particles they've no place that they can be in as they're the matter that constitutes space. Space is created by the quanta of gravity. Space in Einstein's General Relativity simplifies the Universe by making it becomes an actual field which curves and flexes, as matter continuously moves thru' it. Planets circle the Sun because its massive mass twists straight lines into curves which they must all follow. Our planet Earth is falling in a straight line around the Sun!

Alec – You said that time was also created in this area.

Bob – In 1906 Hermann Minkowski proposed that space and time are linked. Albert Einstein proved that this was correct, but once they're joined you can't unlink them.

In the proposal of Loop Quantum Gravity, time flows from the actions of the space quanta and in this view time doesn't exist as a physical thing like gravity, but as a consequence of gravity. If that's so then Newton's view of time ticking away eternally is impossible

Alec – What about inertia, does it give us another description of gravity?

Bob – Since Thales of Miletus' time it's been assumed that the natural state of matter is to be at rest and if you want to move something you have to apply a force to it. Newton proved that there can't be such a state as 'at rest' and anything can only be 'at rest' with respect to something else. He said that the natural state of matter is to continue doing whatever it's currently doing and inertia's the internal energy that keeps mass doing that.

Alec – Didn't Galileo have something to say about inertia?

Bob – It was Galileo who originally introduced the idea of inertia, but his law only covered objects sliding along horizontally. He described inertia as the force which creates heat and drains energy from moving objects by friction thereby causing them to slow down 'til they cease to move. Humans have known about friction and heat since our earliest days when they created fire by rubbing two sticks together which reminds me again of your old Auntie Sally and her witticisms. I think it was time we were going off to our first Scout Camp and she gave us some pocket money and a wee bit of advice. 'The best way to start a fire is to rub two Boy Scouts together!"

Alec – No, her actual remark was that we'd to rub two Boy Scouts' legs together, not the Scouts themselves. Even back in those less correct days I'd think that rubbing two Boy Scouts together would've been frowned upon. One time I asked her if we'd get the same effect by rubbing two Girl Guides' leg's together, but she told me that Boy Scouts shouldn't be thinking of Girl Guides that way! I can see Einstein's view of gravity and 'sort of' see where it fits in, but I'm still struggling to get an overall picture of how it all fits together.

Bob - Looking at it from our amateur viewpoint there's two ways of looking at it, yours and mine.

Alec – I'm the one that's confused, how can I have a viewpoint?

Bob – Your mathematical viewpoint is as important as mine.

Alec – In what way?

Bob – When we talked about the strong nuclear force you immediately pointed out the maths reason that explains why it's so strong?

Alec – That's simply the way our fraction's numbering system works. When you go below zero the number on the top stays at one while the one on the bottom gets larger and larger. The main consequence is that if you're using fractions to describe the area that the force works within, then the number on the bottom line tells you the amount of force that will be present in that area. Basically, as the area gets smaller the force inside it increases.

Bob – There you are, you've just described the strong force in a way that I couldn't. If you take the number zero as your starting point, where would you put gravity on the scale?

Alec – As Ian Donaldson said, gravity's always an attractive force which can only act in one direction, so I'd put it down as a plus force.

Bob – Photons are the massless things that carry energy, where would you fit them in?

Alec – As they've no mass and get all their energy from their momentum I'd think they'd be somewhere around zero.

Bob – I'd go along with that which leaves us with the weak force and electromagnetism. What would you make of them?

Alec – You said that electromagnetism's caused by particles moving thru' the electric field and it operates both inside and outside atoms so I'd put electromagnetism as being available on both sides of zero, wouldn't you?

Bob – Spot on again Mr Spock, but now the hard one, where would you put the weak force?

Alec – As it only acts inside an atoms nucleus, that's a short range interaction so I'd suspect that it would be similar to the strong force.

Bob - The weak force is different from the other three forces in that it doesn't have a field to operate in. It's got three bosons, one z and two w's, and it's the interactions of them which causes suns to shine and Ian's C14 atoms to turn into C12 ones. It seems that on very, very rare occasions, the three of them plus gravity combine in a certain way and the explanation of how they do it makes my eyes glaze over and my brain turn to marshmallow.

Alec – We've come this far, try it on me?

Bob – Going back to the very beginning, and assuming that we have a point with near zero size and infinite energy, what would you need to start a universe after it went off with a bang?

Alec – I'd reckon that the first things you'd need would be atoms and to do that you'd only need the strong and electromagnetic forces to make them.

Bob – Because the strong force is so powerful some of the nuclei of simple atoms were actually being formed in the first twenty minutes after the Big bang, Then you'll have a 380,000 years wait for the Universe to cool down and reach the stage where the electrons could join in to make the first complete atoms.

Alec – Then gravity plays its part by clumping large amounts of hydrogen and helium atoms together and the weak force comes in and turns on the nuclear furnace!

Bob – The first stars that formed were apparently ten to twenty times the size of ours so they used up their fuel very quickly and exploded in massive supernovas which created and spread more and more complex atoms all over the universe.

Alec – And eventually some of them formed life on our planet which led to us humans.

Bob – They did, but to get to us, it's reckoned that a cataclysmic action was needed and that took place shortly after the original planet was formed.

Alec – I've read about that, isn't it called The Big Splash?

Bob – The current consensus is that there was a Mars size planet in a similar orbit as ours and they came together in a glancing blow where most of the debris melted and reformed as the Earth we have today. Some of the lighter materials were thrown further away and they became our Moon.

Alec – Yes, and then it acted like a giant gyroscope that prevents the Earth from wobbling about on its axis which has that's given us a relatively stable climate for the 3.8 billion years that's taken for us to evolve. Going back to the films of Richard Feynman lectures, he said in one of them that nobody understands quantum theory. If he was alive today would he still be able to say that?

Bob – Ten years ago at a conference of 33 of the worlds' deepest thinkers a poll was taken where they completed sixteen multi-choice questions on the basics of the theory and no two papers fully agreed. The 'shut-up and calculate' answer seems still to be the main response and as quantum gravity and the 'darks' still have to be factored in, his answer would most likely be the same. One of the most telling questions in the poll was whether there will still be conferences about the meaning of quantum theory in 50 years time. Almost fifty percent said "probably yes", while only fifteen percent said "probably not"

Alec – I still think of the theory as being weird, but maybe it's me that's weird for not being able to fully understand it.

Bob - We've covered some ground today my old friend, and I've enjoyed our conversations as much as the golf. It's made me realise how lucky we are compared to our early ancestors and a major part of that's down to the wonderful band of scientists who've worked tirelessly over all these years on our behalf.

Alec – I one hundred percent agree with you there, but being inquisitive sods has always been deep in the psyche of the human race. The more important point at the moment is that this tiny part of the human race has fought back to being all square with you and it's been ages since we had a last hole shootout!

Eighteenth Hole (295 yards par four)

The previous hole had worked out as Bob forecast. Alec was first away and, reverting to Steady Eddie, laid-up leaving himself with a short pitch straight up the green. Bob went for broke and his ball hit a small mound at the back of the green, bounced once and was swallowed up by the ever-present rough.

Today their last hole's being played from a bounce tee which shortens the hole by around seventy yards and turns it into a long par three. It's played to a wide, generous fairway and the only obstacles are two deep bunkers which narrow the entrance to the green. Alec hit first and watched his ball trickle into the front left bunker. Bob hit his best drive of the round which saw his ball run between the bunkers before finishing up five yards beyond the flagstick. They got into the golf cart and motored up to the hole.

Bob – I don't think I'd change anything major. We were born at a time of rationing and scarcity and now live in a world where shops have become cathedrals stacked to the roof with goodies and kids who'll soon have the opportunity to become the Dan Dares and Flash Gordons like we used to pretend to be when we got out the cinema!

Alec – Dan and Flash limited their travel to our next door planets. Do you think we'll ever be able to travel to our next door stars?

Bob – I assume that you mean the planet's revolving round the stars and altho' we should never say never, that's likely to be the answer for a considerable time to come.

Alec – Are you saying that it's impossible that we'll ever be capable of inter-stellar travel?

Bob – I'd think it's the next thing to impossible using the concepts that are currently available and I'd also think that the same would apply for any distant civilization wanting to visit us. Once you get past Pluto, assuming it's a mini-planet, your next stop is a planet on our nearest star in the Milky Way galaxy called Proxima Centuari.

Alec – How far away is that?

Bob – Given that the Milky Way's 150,000 light years across, our target is only a piddling little four light years away from us. With our current technology and using the fastest thing we've ever created, Apollo 10, it would take us over 100,000 years to reach it and four more years to send back the signal that we've arrived.

Alec – So it looks unlikely that we have to worry about little green men massing on a planter somewhere out there and planning to invade us!

Bob – Doesn't seem likely, but who knows.

After looking at it from all the angles, Bob agreed that he was first to play and hit his putt a bit too firmly so it ended up five feet past the hole. Alec's bunker shot was almost as good as his word. His ball hit the pin but re bounded and left him with a curly ten footer. He carefully lined up the putt and it looked in all the way 'til it swung slightly at the end and gently trickled past the hole. He picked up his ball from the conceded putt and, as Bob was lining up his putt for the game, walked over, picked up Bob's ball and shook his hand saying, "I'm playing my reverse joker here and conceding your putt."

Bob – Your reverse joker, you're kidding. Where did you get that from?

Alec – Simple and quite logical. We both started with one joker, OK?

Bob – OK.

Alec – I used my joker on the third hole, OK?

Bob – OK.

Alec – You gifted me your joker on the thirteenth and I used it, OK?

Bob – OK.

Alec – You then had zero jokers and I was minus one joker, OK?

Bob – Not OK! Nowhere in our rules does it say you're allowed to have minus jokers.

Alec – It does in quantum golf rules and as you said they control everything down at the basic level. Reverse jokers are virtual jokers which are allowed to pop in and out of existence as and when they're required!

Bob – Touché. I'll think about that and let you know the next time we play.

Alec – Anyway my old mate, I'm delighted that you've played your best golf for a long time and in any case it was an almost straight putt that I couldn't see you missing. This'll make me sharpen up my game and next time we meet you'd better look out 'cos I'll be gunning to get my ten-bob straight back. They re-holstered their putters and headed for the clubhouse with Bob handing their cherished trophy to Alec ahead of the official presentation at dinner.

Saturday Evening.

This saw them along with wives, families and loads of friends standing, clapping and cheering as Jean gave a brief speech to thank everyone who'd helped her through her too short, fifty fun-laden years with the Players. The boys had been surprised the previous evening when their wives arrived home earlier than expected from Jean's matinee performance where she'd played the star role when the leading lady was unexpectedly delayed. The girls explained that the party they expected to last till well into the evening had broken up early as everyone was complaining of sore sides from laughing so much at the second half of Jean's performance.

All her friends knew that Jean was the victim of a set-up which started with the Theatre Manager apologising to the audience that the auditorium lighting had blown a fuse which couldn't be replaced till the interval. They were delighted when the lights came on for the second half and Jean, once she got over the surprise at seeing so many familiar faces in the audience, resumed the play which quickly degenerated into a classic farce. Some of Jean's special phrases had become folklore within the company so, along with several well-known old boys and girls, the actors made up the script as they went along bringing in as many of her mannerisms and anecdotes as possible. The audience, along with most of the actors, soon became hysterical and Alice said that half way thru' she and Brenda were holding each other up and laughing so much that she kept saying "Stop it, please tell them to stop it!" Brenda said Jean had been heroic all thru' it. "How she played along with a straight face was little short of miraculous." "She's been fifty years of miraculous" Alice replied. When the performance finished they'd staggered over to The Griffin where Jean told them she'd really enjoyed the performance, but would rather have been with them in the audience. Alice told her that if she'd been in the audience with them they'd have missed the performance of a lifetime. Brenda assured her that a full recording of the afternoon had been made and she was looking forward to the many evenings when the three of them and a bottle of wine would get together to watch it again and again. Jean said that would be wonderful, but pleaded with them not to put it on social media. She said that she wanted a quiet retirement, not people pointing at her when she went shopping and nudging each other with 'That's yon stupid woman on Facebook.' Alec said "That's Jean, loves the theatre, but hates the limelight."

Now she was reaching the end of her speech and emotion was starting to overtake her. She mumbled a last "Thank you everybody" and held up the beautiful rosewood and glass case the youngest member of the cast had presented her with. Brenda and Alice turned and gave each other a knowing wink as they'd been part of the organising team. Brenda convinced Jean that her most precious possession, a program from her first production signed by all the cast members, would be safe with one of her nieces who was doing a presentation on Theatre thru' the Ages. Alice went quietly around getting this year's program signed by all the members and as many old boys and girls as she could locate. When she gave it to Alice she quipped, "Most of the old boys have been outlived by the old girls." The case displayed both programs with Jean's latest catchphrase, 'Fifty Years of Fun with The Players' emblazoned in gold above them.

The Director patted Jean on the back, stepped up to the microphone and asked if she would do them the great honour of consenting to becoming their first Honorary President. Bob turned to his wife who was in tears and stealing a line from her favourite group, whispered in her ear "Sod ABBA. The real Super Trouper's standing up there on the stage."

xxx.

Printed in Great Britain
by Amazon